Informed Choices

Informed Choices

A Guide for Teachers of College Writing

Tara Lockhart
San Francisco State University

Mark Roberge
San Francisco State University

Bedford/St. Martin's

Boston • New York

For Bedford/St. Martin's

Vice President, Editorial, Macmillan Higher Education Humanities: Edwin Hill
Editorial Director for English and Music: Karen S. Henry
Publisher for Composition: Leasa Burton
Executive Editor: Karita France dos Santos
Developmental Editor: Rachel C. Childs
Assistant Production Editor: Lidia MacDonald-Carr
Production Manager: Joe Ford
Marketing Manager: Christina Shea
Project Management: Books By Design, Inc.
Director of Rights and Permissions: Hilary Newman
Senior Art Director: Anna Palchik
Text Design: Books By Design, Inc.
Cover Design: Billy Boardman
Composition: Books By Design, Inc.
Printing and Binding: RR Donnelley and Sons

0   9   8   7   6   5
f   e   d   c   b   a

For information, write: Bedford/St. Martin's, 75 Arlington Street, Boston, MA 02116 (617-399-4000)

ISBN 978-1-4576-5273-8

Preface

Whether you have just been assigned a new class a week before the semester begins, you are teaching a different section or level for the first time, or you are hoping to learn more about effective writing pedagogy, *Informed Choices* can help you. Combining sound theory about writing instruction and learning with proven pedagogical techniques and suggestions, this book presents the teaching of writing as a complex and situation-specific set of choices that you, the teacher, must make. As you know, making an informed choice is always better than making a haphazard decision or adopting a practice simply because you have seen another teacher do it (or because you are unsure of what to do in class on Monday morning). This book is designed to help you think through these choices. Guided by your beliefs about writing—your own expertise, experiences, and strengths—and in dialogue with best practices in the field and the expectations of your particular institution, *Informed Choices* will help you clarify your goals and translate them into a cohesive curriculum that will work for your students.

What is novel about this approach is that you will tailor it to your course, your student population, and even your own carefully considered beliefs about writing, writing instruction, and learning. This book is unique in the way that it combines theory and practice, guiding you toward reflecting more deeply about your assignments, your lessons, your assessment methodology, and the connections between all parts of your course. It is also unique, however, in that we do not suggest one right way to teach. Successful teaching requires you to respond to and reflect on the paradoxes, controversies, and trade-offs that the teaching of writing inevitably involves. This book helps you preemptively think through many of these paradoxes, controversies, and trade-offs you will encounter when teaching so that you can both plan ahead and change course when necessary. You will notice that throughout the book we often ask you to identify and work with both the practices or beliefs that resonate with you and those that cause dissonance or tension. We believe it is crucial to be attuned to both of these reactions, as well as to reflect on how these reactions shape your teaching. This book thus embraces the idea that the best teaching comes out of conscious reflection and informed decisions, rather than a cookie-cutter list of "best practices" or a rigid adherence to a single ideological orientation.

As you work through this book, you will explore your own ideas about teaching writing and will integrate those ideas with knowledge from the field.

From our combined thirty-plus years of teaching undergraduate writing, as well as our decades of training college-level writing teachers, we know that a successful writing course depends on having solid answers to three central questions. Richard Fulkerson, in his article "Composition at the Turn of the Twenty-First Century," sums up these questions nicely:

- What is good writing? (We believe teachers need to explore and solidify their beliefs about "good writing" in order to make effective decisions about how to help students become good writers.)
- By what processes does one create good writing? (We believe teachers need to clarify their notions about writing processes and integrate those notions with knowledge from the field in order to create a classroom that fosters effective writing processes.)
- How do we teach students to create good writing? (We believe that teachers need to clarify and articulate their beliefs about teaching and learning, integrating those beliefs with knowledge from the field and knowledge about their own teaching personae, in order to make effective decisions about pedagogy.)

These questions are useful for helping you articulate your core philosophies about writing, teaching, and learning. We deal with the theoretical dimension of the first three questions specifically in Part 1 of the book; we then ask you to apply your understanding as you construct a pedagogically sound curriculum in Part 2 and refine your choices in Parts 3 and 4. Fulkerson also asks a fourth question, which we have adapted as follows:

- How can we be sure that our answers to questions 1 through 3 are correct? How do our answers fit together coherently, driven by our beliefs about knowledge and learning?

The fourth question ultimately describes the method of the book as a whole. There is not one "correct" theory of composition, and there is not one "correct" way to teach composition; instead, teaching composition should be a process of negotiation and reflection. In fact, we argue that the best teachers are reflective practitioners who consistently attempt to answer (and re-answer) Fulkerson's fourth question. Reflective practitioners are teachers who do the following in recursive, reflective, and ongoing ways:

- They have theories about how things work in the writing classroom.
- They test out their ideas through their teaching.
- They carefully observe what happens, noting how student writers react, grow, and develop.
- They modify their theories and continue testing those theories.

As you grow and develop as a teacher, you will constantly need to rethink your ideas. That is to say, even the advice we offer here should be treated as open suggestions you will need to critically examine in light of your beliefs, your students, and the context. In fact, the activities in this book are part of that rethinking process, as we will ask you to rethink and even question "best practices" and familiar teaching advice.

Overview of parts and chapters

Each chapter of *Informed Choices* contains many avenues for grappling with the challenges that teaching writing presents, as well as many activities that will guide you in designing a college-level writing course that will work for you and your students. Part 1 includes several chapters designed to help you articulate your core beliefs about writing, writing processes, and the teaching of writing in conversation with the major theoretical orientations that shape the field. Even if you feel you have a strong background in composition theory, we still strongly encourage you to begin at the beginning of the book and work through these early chapters, since they will help you fully articulate your views of writing, teaching, and learning and perhaps even prompt you to reevaluate some of your beliefs. We will ask you to return to (and revise when necessary) the initial philosophy of writing you craft in these chapters, using it both as a foundation for later chapters and as a touchstone in the creation of your course.

Part 2 asks you to articulate your course goals, put these goals in dialogue with institutional expectations, and then begin creating major writing and reading assignments. These chapters offer you the space to figure out institutional requirements and adapt your course design based on the context of your course. For example, if you teach at the high school level or work primarily with pre-transfer-level (or developmental) students, these chapters will give you a snapshot of the level of work expected at the transfer level; you can thus work backward to design appropriate assignments for your specific student population. Chapter 8 and Chapter 9 will come in handy, as they ask you to work with planning: from big-picture planning all the way down to lessons and individual classes. The final chapter in Part 2 addresses the issue of how to use textbooks effectively in your course. Throughout these chapters, and for the rest of the book, we will ask you to apply your work to a real course that you are designing (rather than to abstract teaching scenarios). Thus, even if you have never taught before, you will create a tangible course design to work on as you think through difficult pedagogical choices.

Part 3 helps you explore and refine essential aspects of composition pedagogy: opportunities for writing and writing instruction, peer support and collaboration, feedback and revision, and assessment. These chapters are useful for (1) teachers-in-training who want to begin thinking more deeply about the nuts and bolts of specific pedagogical practices, (2) new teachers who are looking to strengthen their writing pedagogy on a day-to-day basis, and (3) more experienced teachers who want to re-theorize and refine their practices. Regardless of your level of experience, you may find it helpful to move back and forth among these chapters since they discuss many interrelated issues.

Part 4 focuses on the landscape of twenty-first-century teaching, helping you think about the ever-increasing diversity of our classrooms and the ever-increasing opportunities to use technology. Although approaches to capitalizing on diversity and working with technology are woven through many of the chapters of the book, we address these specific issues more fully in Chapter 15 and Chapter 16. Finally, we look forward and consider your ongoing development as a teacher, including your continued growth as a reflective practitioner and your role within the larger discipline and profession, in Chapter 17.

Features of *Informed Choices*

We have included a variety of useful features in each chapter to help you explore your own ideas and beliefs, develop an informed and cohesive teaching approach, situate your approach within the field of composition, and create courses that are both coherent and theoretically sound.

A rich array of hands-on activities

To help you position yourself among the choices, arguments, and controversies that shape the teaching of writing, we ask you to do several kinds of hands-on activities.

 Brainstorming. In these activities, we ask you to draw on your own experiences and beliefs as a student, as a writer, and as a tutor or teacher.

 Exploring Beliefs and Tensions. In these activities, we ask you to examine contradictory assertions about teaching, clusters of terms related to the teaching of writing, and descriptions of teaching philosophies from various pedagogical orientations, so that you can identify ideas that resonate with your own teaching beliefs and examine tensions within your beliefs. In doing so, we ask you to explore the contexts that shape your teaching directly—seeking out specific information about your institution, program, classes, or students and applying that information to your thinking about teaching.

 Applying Ideas. In these activities, we ask you to apply the thinking that you have done so far in the book in order to create something tangible— a writing prompt, a reading list, a lesson outline, or a plan of action for future teaching scenarios.

Articulating an Evolving Philosophy. At many points throughout the book, we ask you to crystallize the thinking you have done so far and articulate where you now stand by answering discussion questions in a teaching journal. Through the process of journaling, you will expand on ideas that you already have, as well as explore, test out, and synthesize new ideas. These prose activities build on one another throughout the book, offering you plenty of opportunities to examine and reexamine your philosophy as it develops.

Reflective callouts

Callouts throughout the book illustrate the central role that teacher self-reflection, experimentation, and decision making play. In these quotes, we model this kind of reflection by offering insights, memories, questions, and suggestions gleaned from over thirty combined years of teaching. Occasionally, we use the callouts to capture or reflect on the statements we have heard countless times from graduate students preparing to teach, first-time teaching assistants, teachers in their first semester, and seasoned teachers alike. The callouts thus represent thought-in-action and teacher self-reflection. Some of the ideas or concerns voiced in the callouts may sound familiar; they may mirror your own process of wrestling with difficult teaching decisions. Other ideas or queries may be unfamiliar, and thus they will challenge you to think about your professional growth in new ways.

"Turning to the Field"

In each chapter, we introduce you to choices, arguments, and controversies in teaching writing. Although we draw on research, theory, current practice, and collective teacher wisdom throughout the book, we explicitly ask you to engage important ideas in the sections entitled "Turning to the Field." Here we draw on important documents authored by professionals in our field, such as the *Framework for Success in Postsecondary Writing*, the *WPA Outcomes Statement for First-Year Composition*, and various position statements authored by the Conference on College Composition and Communication (CCCC), or we present essential or challenging concepts or practices and ask you to explore them. Our goal is to help you synthesize all this material in a coherent whole while also giving you ample space to stake out your own position within this landscape.

"Taking It Further"

Toward the end of each chapter, we challenge you to complicate "neat and tidy" notions about teaching and learning. If you have a fair amount of teaching experience already, these sections will push you to rethink some of your long-held assumptions and beliefs and to wrestle with some of the more thorny and complex questions in our field. If you have not yet taught, these sections will give you a preview of the tough choices we make continually as composition teachers.

"Reflections from Experienced Teachers"

After delving into the more complex paradoxes and controversies of teaching and learning, you might come to the conclusion that our field consists of nothing but unresolvable tensions and questions. To reground you, we wrap up each chapter with reflections from experienced teachers and present pedagogical insights and perspectives that many teachers do in fact agree on. These perspectives are not merely "teacher lore" but rather praxis—the enactment of theoretical and research-based insights within teaching practice. While these time-tested ideas will not present definitive answers to all your pedagogical questions, they do offer valuable guidance for developing your own teaching philosophy and making your own informed choices about pedagogy.

"Putting It Together"

Throughout the book, you will be brainstorming, writing notes, jotting down lists, and annotating. But for your ideas to fully crystallize, you need to explain—for yourself—where you currently stand in the dense thicket of pedagogical choices and paradoxes. These final "Putting It Together" sections invite you both to distill key concepts in a way you could present them to others and to write out, in prose, various aspects of your own evolving pedagogical understanding and commitments. You will notice that the "Putting It Together" activities will build over the course of the book; as your teaching philosophy

> "Official university learning outcomes for writing courses seem to be based on all sorts of different philosophical views about writing. So my own teaching is always an ongoing process of negotiation between my own philosophy, the new things I'm discovering in the classroom each semester, the expectations of the university, scholarship in the field, and even the teaching philosophies that are embedded in the textbooks and materials we use.
>
> —Mark

develops, you will probably want to go back to prior chapters and revisit, rethink, and revise what you have written.

Further reading

We have kept in-text citations to a minimum throughout the book in order to foreground the big-picture issues and push you to wrestle with the necessary pedagogical choices yourself, rather than let particular theorists or researchers define your thinking. Nonetheless, you will probably be curious to learn more about specific perspectives and the wider conversations in our field. Therefore, each chapter concludes with a list of readings that you can use to explore specific topics in more depth.

These readings—whether academic articles, important documents from our field, or Web-based resources—tend to be short and accessible. We have also taken care to present a range of articles, including important historical articles in the field, tried-and-true favorites, and current research-based scholarship. These end-of-chapter readings might readily be used in a graduate pedagogy seminar or training program to supplement the book and to spur discussion. The bibliography at the end of *Informed Choices* includes longer, book-length works that present a particular pedagogical perspective, collections of foundational scholarship in our field (e.g., *Cross-Talk in Comp Theory*), overviews of various pedagogies (e.g., *A Guide to Composition Pedagogies*), and full-length teacher resources and guidebooks.

As we will discuss in Chapter 17, once you have a good sense of your philosophical orientation and teaching approach, we encourage you to continue your intellectual and professional development by exposing yourself to other pedagogical perspectives, especially those that are quite different from your own.

How to use this book

Given the range of material and interactive prompts included in *Informed Choices*, there are many ways you can productively use this book. If you are new to teaching or are designing a brand-new course for the first time, you may find it is best to work through the book over a few weeks, perhaps during the summer or a term break. Since the activities are designed to build on one another, this will give you adequate time to design, reflect on, and revise your materials without feeling overwhelmed. There is enough material in the book—particularly if combined with the suggested readings and resources—that you may use it over an entire semester as part of a teaching seminar or as support if you are a teaching assistant. *Informed Choices* is especially useful if you are observing a class or teacher, since it will help you pinpoint the philosophical decisions that inform pedagogy. It is also a useful text for writing centers or tutor-training programs to explore with their tutors. Of course, if you are a more experienced teacher or just want to refresh your practice and pedagogy, you might work through those sections or chapters that help you address a more targeted issue in your teaching. And lastly, *Informed Choices* is a wonderful resource to return to while you are teaching, as well as at the end of the semester: Check in with your philosophy, your assignments, and other specific chapters that will help you fine-tune and reflect at the end of your class.

As you read *Informed Choices*, you will notice that we are speaking to you as fellow colleagues, asking you to articulate your thinking, build on your experiences, and stretch yourself by innovating your course materials. To keep you focused and engaged, we will often ask you to write on the spot: to jot ideas down in this book in the spaces provided or on your computer. Although we welcome you to make notes or design materials elsewhere, there is sometimes no better way to get your ideas down and crystallized than to just start writing. (Does this advice sound familiar?) So we invite you to record your thoughts as you work through this book, using it as a "thinking place" to record a history of your impressions, thoughts, and questions.

As you work through the book, we encourage you to keep a running list of ideas or practices you like, as well as ideas or practices that you need to continue grappling with. We suggest that you begin a teaching journal where you can capture these ideas and questions, as well as write longer responses to prompts. Please also feel free to write in the spaces provided in each chapter, in the margins, or in the blank pages at the end of the book. For larger chunks of writing, or those pieces of writing you know you will be returning to and revising over time (writing prompts, your teaching philosophy, your course description), feel free to compose in your teaching journal or on a computer so that you can easily save and change drafts of your work.

If you follow this path, by the end of *Informed Choices* you will have a much richer understanding of the ways that writing, teaching, and learning fit together. You will also know a lot more about how your views fit within the larger conversations in the field of composition. This knowledge will guide you in making informed choices—choices that can make your teaching practices less stressful, more coherent, more effective, and more rewarding.

Acknowledgments

We are especially grateful to our M.A. students at San Francisco State University who have worked with earlier versions of much of the content of this book over the last several years. Their good will and commitment to teaching diverse student populations were essential in helping us revise and refine the materials that follow. We owe many thanks to the reviewers who offered their expertise on an early draft of the book: Erin Campion, Martha Rusk, and Nantanella Wolfson, San Francisco State University; Ellen Cushman, Michigan State University; Christopher Diller, Berry College; Heidi Estrem, Boise State University; Letizia Guglielmo, Kennesaw State University; Alex Reid, University at Buffalo; E. Shelley Reid, George Mason University; Michelle Sidler, Auburn University; Brent Simoneaux, North Carolina State University; and Christian Smith, University of South Carolina. Their generous and thoughtful feedback proved invaluable.

The editorial and production teams at Bedford/St. Martin's expertly shepherded this project from its earliest conception through the final product. We thank Joan Feinberg, Leasa Burton, Karita France dos Santos, Rachel Childs, John Sullivan (for his expertise in Chapter 10), and Lidia MacDonald-Carr, as well as Nancy Benjamin, Judith Riotto, and Linda McLatchie. As always, our colleagues at San Francisco State provided excellent feedback, encouragement, resources, and ongoing support for this book; we are honored to work every day with Sugie Goen-Salter, Jennifer Trainor, Kory Lawson Ching, Nelson Graff, and Paul Morris. And last, our continuing gratitude to our families and friends who have supported us through the many years of crafting this book: our thanks to Reid Spice; Jack, Linda, and Nicole Lockhart; Albert, Freda, and Michael Roberge; Margi Wald; Anne Whiteside; Ali Borjian; Alex Torrubia; Sam Tucker; Gustavo Caldas; and Lewis Nightingale. Along with those teachers, colleagues, and students who continue to inspire and motivate us, we could not have done it without you.

We hope that this book encourages teachers, new and experienced alike, to both own and thoughtfully revise the informed choices they make every day upon entering the classroom. As learning is an iterative and ongoing practice, so, too, is teaching. We hope that this book provides support for deepening understanding, renewing practice, and invigorating relationships and commitments to those students who find their way to our classes each term, hoping to learn and be more than when they entered. It is to not only the teachers, but also their students, that this book is ultimately dedicated.

Tara Lockhart
Mark Roberge

Contents

List of Activities

Activities by Chapter

CHAPTER 16   Choices about Writing in a Digital Age

CHAPTER 17   Choices about Your Future Growth in the Profession

Activities by Type

💡 Brainstorming

Exploring Beliefs and Tensions

Applying Ideas

✐ Articulating Your Evolving Philosophy

PART 1

Establishing a Foundation for Your Teaching

CHAPTER 1

Choices about Your Philosophy of Writing

New teachers of writing often feel overwhelmed by the practical questions of day-to-day teaching: What texts should my students read? What kinds of essays should I assign? How should I grade essays? What should I do in my class on Monday morning? In the first two chapters of this book, we offer an approach to helping you generate answers to these questions—an approach that asks you to think of the larger picture of your course, your goals, and what good writing and effective teaching actually mean. That is, instead of providing tips or pat answers to the very real questions and concerns new teachers have, we begin this book by asking you to step back a bit and think about theory rather than practice. This is crucial, since it will allow you to build a cohesive course that is theoretically sound and connected to the most up-to-date knowledge and practices in the field. In addition, it will give you confidence that you have a reason for what you are doing on Monday morning, instead of casting about for a grab bag of tips and techniques.

What is your "theory of writing"?

A theory is simply an explanation of how and why something works the way it does. You already have many tacit theories about teaching and learning, many of which come from your own educational experiences. You also have many tacit theories about how the writing process works and what constitutes "good writing"—again from your experiences and from things people have said about writing. This chapter will help you articulate those theories more clearly and weave them together into a coherent philosophy that will guide your teaching.

Why should you spend time articulating your teaching philosophy? As we noted in the introduction, teaching is a process of navigating among paradoxes, controversies, and trade-offs, many of which we will be exploring in this book. And teaching writing effectively involves conscious reflection and informed decisions about these paradoxes, controversies, and trade-offs. Your teaching philosophy (a purposeful amalgamation of theories and your own beliefs) is your map for navigating these complex decisions.

Furthermore, if you articulate your teaching philosophy, you will better be able to see how your own ideas fit into the broader field of composition. For centuries, people have been putting forth "theories" of rhetoric, writing, teaching,

> "I always tell teacher trainees: Even if you're not a "theory person," it's important to have a reason for *why* you're doing what you're doing in the classroom. That "why" is your theory.
>
> —*Mark*

and learning. (Think, for example, of Aristotle's admonitions against trusting the written word.) But composition as an academic field has existed for only several decades, roughly since the founding of the Conference on College Composition and Communication (CCCC) in 1949. Nonetheless, composition theorists, researchers, and teachers have already covered a lot of territory, trying to answer many of the same questions that you may have about your own teaching. In other words, others have done a lot of the groundwork for you. Knowing what questions they have been asking and what answers they have been suggesting can save you time and energy.

Finally, as psychologist Kurt Lewin famously said, "There is nothing so practical as a good theory" (1951). If you have a very clear picture in your head of how the writing process works (i.e., "a theory"), it is a lot easier to make all those little day-to-day decisions about what to do in the classroom to support your students' growth as writers.

Turning to the field: Mapping the terrain of teaching approaches

Over the past several decades, composition teachers and scholars have put forth a bewildering variety of theories, philosophies, approaches, pedagogies, and teaching practices. Scholars have also made numerous attempts to categorize and organize this thicket of scholarship. We believe that one of the most useful ways to think about these theories, philosophies, and pedagogies—especially for new teachers—is to ask what a particular philosophy or teaching approach emphasizes:

- Does it emphasize the features of the written text itself?
- Does it emphasize the role of the writer?
- Does it emphasize the context or culture in which the text is produced (i.e., the "real world")?
- Does it emphasize the role of the reader (i.e., the potential audience for the text)?

In his article "Composition at the Turn of the Twenty-First Century," Richard Fulkerson argues that these four different emphases can be mapped onto specific historical periods in our field. Combining Fulkerson's ideas with our own taxonomy of teaching philosophies and practices, we can describe four general orientations—all of which are alive and well in our field today and all of which manifest themselves in one form or another in current composition pedagogies and current composition classrooms.

Text-focused approaches

Texts (both those produced by students and those produced by professional and literary authors) have always been a focus of composition philosophies and pedagogies. Text-focused approaches became prominent in the early twentieth century as a large influx of students entered secondary and postsecondary schools. Faced with an overwhelming workload, secondary and postsecondary writing teachers resorted to teaching from stylebooks, which emphasized simplistic "rules" about good writing, and merely marking errors on student papers. The student writer, the potential audience of the student writing, and the "real world" in which the writing was produced and consumed took a backseat to textual features that could easily be marked, tallied, and graded.

In the late 1960s, many theorists and teachers began to move away from the strong emphasis on textual features. They disparagingly referred to the prior text-focused teaching approaches as "current-traditional" pedagogy, a term they used to describe English-teaching approaches that focused on formulaic writing, sentence diagramming, "skill and drill" instruction, grammatical correctness, and the errors marked in red pen.

Nonetheless, the text itself—whether a student text or a reading under discussion—still plays a prominent role in most current philosophies and pedagogies. In a society in which texts written in "Standard Written English" are seen as a key to social, political, and economic power, composition teachers feel called on both to enforce those standards and to assist students in gaining access to this language of power.

Contemporary composition pedagogies focus, albeit in different ways and magnitudes, on the text. As we will discuss later in this book, genre-based teaching approaches focus in part on the written textual conventions that are used in different discourse communities. The Writing about Writing approach asks students to use composition scholarship to understand how other writers— from students to professionals—produce texts. And multimodal composition pedagogies emphasize text—albeit an expanded definition of *text* that includes digital writing, hypertext, visual images, and video.

Writer-focused approaches

The creative role of the author has long been emphasized in literary studies— think, for example, of literary Romanticism when the author was seen as a creative genius producing works of inspiration that expressed unique inner truths. However, in the late 1960s, composition researchers began to examine *student* writers and *student* writing processes, and pedagogies began to emphasize students' voices, their personal experiences and narratives, and their ways of making meaning through the writing process. The term *expressivism* was used to signify this pedagogical movement, which composition historians have linked to the antiauthoritarian counterculture movements of the 1960s and the individualism of the 1970s. In the expressivist paradigm, texts are seen as vehicles for experimentation, exploration, and self-expression; meaning is located with the writer, and it is "discovered" during the writing process.

As theorists and teachers in the 1980s began to focus more on the real-world contexts of writing (such as writing within academia) and the real-world issues of power and ideology in writing, the term *expressivism* took on more negative connotations and was sometimes used disparagingly to denote self-indulgent, solipsistic, or overly "touchy-feely" pedagogies.

Nonetheless, composition teachers today still see students' confidence and self-efficacy as central to their development as writers, and thus the student-as-writer is still a prominent focus of most current composition philosophies and pedagogies. Many writing teachers assign some form of the personal narrative— ranging from literacy narratives to auto-ethnographies. The student writer's

"My grad course on teaching composition felt like a merry-go-round: Each week we learned a different "right way" to think about writing and teaching. Eventually I realized I needed to stake out my own position among all these ideas.

—*Tara*

voice is also emphasized in much current pedagogy, particularly the voices of ethnolinguistic minority students, which have traditionally been marginalized or excluded from academic discourse. For example, many teachers allow or encourage hybrid discourse, colloquial voices, and code-switching (particularly in informal writing assignments, such as blogging). Such practices, which can be part of a larger critical pedagogy, aim to honor "students' right to their own language," an idea that was first articulated in the field of composition in the early 1970s.

Context/culture-focused approaches

In the 1980s and 1990s, the field of composition took what some refer to as "the social turn," moving away from a focus on the individual student writer toward a focus on the cultural and ideological contexts in which writing is produced and consumed. In this more sociocultural paradigm, meaning is not located solely within the text, nor is it located in the mind of the writer; rather, it resides in the intersection between writer, reader, and text, in particular social contexts.

Given that sociocultural approaches often drew from the intellectual work of the 1980s and 1990s, including cultural studies, feminism, critical theory, queer theory, and postcolonial theory, sociocultural theorists and teachers have sometimes disparaged writer-focused expressivist pedagogy for its lack of emphasis on social context. Instead, sociocultural pedagogies attempted to get students thinking about the larger systemic structures that shape their experiences of writing, education, language use, and power.

Today, the sociocultural orientation remains a dominant philosophy that informs composition pedagogy, and this can clearly be seen when surveying current textbooks, teachers' reading lists, and the writing assignments that students are asked to do. Whether students are writing about their own socially constructed identities, examining how discourse communities work to shape language use, investigating how specific generic conventions developed for a type of writing, or participating in collaborative, service-learning projects, sociocultural perspectives are often at play in shaping current writing pedagogy.

Reader-focused approaches

Unlike the prior three orientations, reader-focused philosophies and pedagogies do not fall neatly into a single historical period or pedagogical movement. Instead, a focus on the readers or audience can be seen reappearing throughout the history of rhetoric and writing, from classical rhetoric (which focused on a physically present audience) to current-day Writing in the Disciplines pedagogies (which focus on an audience that shares professional knowledge and affiliation). In reader-focused pedagogies, then, the emphasis is on clearly communicating a message that readers will readily understand or on persuading readers to think a particular way.

Each of the approaches we have explored thus far contains dimensions of reader-focused pedagogy. Text-focused pedagogies include audience, but they have tended to construe audience (i.e., readers) as a community that shares a single set of stylistics and grammatical rules that the writer must adhere to; the composition teacher is thus the judge and enforcer of those rules. Writer-focused pedagogies also include audience, but they have tended to construe audience as a sounding board for the author; the composition teacher, as a part of the audience, responds to student writing as an interested reader who can help the writer more clearly find and shape his or her message. Context-driven or sociocultural pedagogies not only have included audience but have in fact tended to turn the focus toward the audience itself—including the audience's ideologies and power relations surrounding audiences, texts, and writers.

We can think about a reader focus from a different angle as well: Regardless of your pedagogical orientation, you must decide how you are going to read student texts. In other words, you must decide what combination of roles you will play: curious reader, fellow writer, academic insider, coach, mentor, critic, gatekeeper, grammar checker, and so on. In addition, almost all composition teachers utilize some sort of peer-response activities that position students in the class as readers of one another's texts; this means you must think carefully about the reader role that students in the class will play during peer response. Newer forms of writing (blogging and Web page authoring, for example) also open up student writing to outsider readers; this again raises questions about audience. Finally, many current pedagogical movements and academic disciplines (Writing across the Curriculum, Writing in the Disciplines, Writing about Writing, workplace writing, technical and professional writing, out-of-school literacy studies) strongly emphasize the role of the reader and the discourse communities to which the reader belongs. Thus an audience orientation is always present, even in the most writer-focused pedagogical approaches. (For an interesting example, see Peter Elbow's seminal article, "Closing My Eyes as I Write: An Argument for Ignoring Audience.")

Using text, writer, context, and reader as a framework for your philosophy

We find these four orientations to be a useful heuristic for thinking about and discussing your own pedagogical philosophies and practices. They can also function as a lens for examining other teaching approaches; for example, you can ask, "How does this particular approach construe the role of text, writer, context, and reader? How does this approach construct a relationship between these elements?"

We would like to offer a few caveats here to be clear. First, the four orientations are not distinct, mutually exclusive entities. In fact, teachers and scholars generally draw on ideas and practices from all four orientations. We must thus be cautious not to put ourselves in a box in terms of our thinking. As a teacher, you probably want your students to produce clear, grammatically correct writing (text focus) and find their own voices as writers (writer focus), while simultaneously being aware of the social context that informs their writing (context/culture focus) and effectively addressing a readership (reader focus). We must also be careful not to put specific teaching techniques (or our own colleagues!) in boxes. For example, a teacher who is concerned about textual correctness is not necessarily an adherent of old-school "current-traditional" teaching.

Another important caveat is that the historical terminology associated with each approach can be highly loaded. (In fact, one must always be cautious about slippery pedagogical terminology.) Few teachers would describe themselves using historical labels such as *current-traditional* or *expressivist*, and even those teachers who focus on more ideological aspects of culture and social context may be hesitant to pigeonhole themselves with a *sociocultural* label.

Finally, while the terms *text-focused*, *writer-focused*, *context/culture-focused*, and *reader-focused* are a useful heuristic for this book, they should not be used as shorthand for talking about one's pedagogy with colleagues—especially not in a job interview. If you describe your teaching philosophy simply as "reader-focused," most colleagues will look at you in confusion. However, if you explain how and why your pedagogy focuses on the role of the reader (e.g., by analyzing audience, rhetorical appeals, and the context in which texts are consumed), your colleagues will certainly perceive you as having made thoughtful, informed choices about your pedagogy.

Now that you have an overview of four major orientations in writing theory and pedagogy, you can begin to articulate your own philosophies and theories, situating them within the landscape of our field.

 Activity 1.1 Defining "good writing"

What is good writing? Brainstorm in the space provided.

You can build your evolving definition of good writing by examining other teachers' perspectives. In Activity 1.2, we present four hypothetical teachers, each with a very different notion of "good writing." As you read, note ideas that resonate with your own beliefs; you will return to those notes later when you flesh out your teaching philosophy in prose. Also note any ideas that are perplexing or seem to be in tension with your own beliefs.

 Activity 1.2 Examining diverse views of "good writing"

Circle any ideas that resonate with you, and mark with an asterisk any ideas that cause tension. Unpack at least one of the tensions in your teaching journal.

A more text-oriented teacher might say:	A more context/culture-oriented teacher might say:
Good writing is clear, concise, and cohesive. It exhibits skillful use of organizational, stylistic, and grammatical conventions to effectively express a point.	Good writing demonstrates insightful and perceptive analysis of the world. In other words, one cannot separate good writing from critical thinking and knowledge making. Good writing is not just form or function; instead, it shows us something important about the world, often something hidden or not immediately apparent.
A more writer-oriented teacher might say:	A more reader-oriented teacher might say:
Good writing expresses strong individual voice and has something unique or important to say. Rather than sounding generic or perfunctory, it expresses conviction. You can sense that a real person is behind the writing.	Good writing is purposeful, effective communication. It addresses a specific audience in a specific context and a specific rhetorical situation. If the writing moves the audience to action, it is by definition "good writing."

YOUR TEACHING JOURNAL: Engaging with tensions

Choose the idea that you feel most uncomfortable with, and brainstorm about it in your teaching journal. Consider the following questions:

- Why does this idea cause tension?

- Which of your beliefs does it clash with?

- Are there situations in which you might feel more comfortable with this conception of good writing (e.g., in other school, professional, or civic contexts; with other student populations; or with other readerships)?

- How would you discuss this tension with colleagues or with a hiring committee?

To flesh out your definition of "good writing" even further, you can examine some common tensions in widely held teacher beliefs. In Activity 1.3, we have listed things that teachers have said about "good writing," and we have arranged them in pairs to highlight tensions. Think about which side of each pair best represents your view. It is okay if you feel torn, because the pairs represent tensions rather than opposites. For example, good writing can both follow and break conventions. We are simply using these pairs as a tool to help you articulate your own beliefs about writing and to raise issues and questions that you will want to ponder further as you work your way through this book.

Activity 1.3   Examining seemingly contradictory notions about student writing

Circle any ideas that resonate with you, and mark with an asterisk any ideas that cause tension. Unpack at least one of the tensions in your teaching journal.

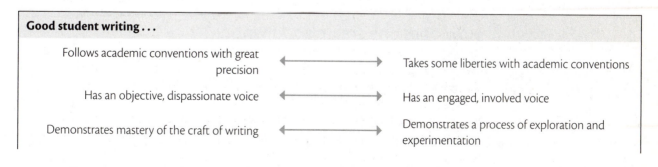

Good student writing . . .

Follows academic conventions with great precision	⟷	Takes some liberties with academic conventions
Has an objective, dispassionate voice	⟷	Has an engaged, involved voice
Demonstrates mastery of the craft of writing	⟷	Demonstrates a process of exploration and experimentation

Can be judged by reading the text alone	⟷	Must be judged in the context of the specific writer
Should have a powerful effect on the reader	⟷	Should have a powerful effect on the writer
Is accessible and reader-friendly	⟷	Is complex and requires "unpacking" by the reader
Confronts the reader	⟷	Informs and convinces the reader
Surprises the reader	⟷	Meets the expectations of the reader
Looks outward to explore and test ideas	⟷	Looks inward to find "truth" and ideas
Is best judged by the reader	⟷	Is best judged by the writer
Can have some grammatical/stylistic errors, as long as it says something important	⟷	Should be relatively error-free, even if it does not necessarily say something important

YOUR TEACHING JOURNAL: Engaging with tensions

Choose a pair of ideas that perplex you — perhaps a pair where you agree equally with both sides — and unpack the tension in your teaching journal. Consider the following questions:

- Are these two statements always mutually contradictory?
- In what types of writing, genres, or contexts does a writer have liberty to move between the two poles, or perhaps even satisfy both statements?
- How would you discuss this tension with colleagues or with a hiring committee?

Now you will turn to your teaching journal and write out — in prose — your evolving definition of "good writing," particularly as it will apply to your own classroom. Draw on your first definition in Activity 1.1, the four hypothetical teachers in Activity 1.2, the pairs of tensions in Activity 1.3, and of course your own experiences as a reader and as a writer. We will ask you to return to this definition, including the tensions and questions it raises, as you work your way through the book.

 Activity 1.4   Creating your own definition of "good writing"

In your teaching journal, discuss the following questions. Be sure to note any questions or issues that you are still wrestling with.

- How would you describe good writing in general?
- How would you describe good student writing?

How does one create good writing?

We now turn to our second question: How does one create good writing? This question is essential for us as teachers because we want to create a classroom atmosphere that fosters writing processes that help students grow as writers. When professional writers talk about their own writing processes, we hear many different "best" ways to create a piece of writing: waiting for a burst of inspiration, jumping in and starting without a clear plan in mind, planning everything in detail, or even laboriously sweating over every word. Every writer appears to have his or her own unique set of processes, sometimes deploying different processes in response to different tasks or situations.

To get started, think about writing projects that have been meaningful to you in school, at work, or in your personal life, and capture your notes in the space provided for Activity 1.5. Here are some questions to consider:

- What are your writing processes?
- Do your processes change, based on the task, the audience, and the amount of time you have?
- How do you go about producing a piece of "good writing"?
- How do you get started?
- How much do you revise?
- Do other people play a role in your writing?
- Do your ideas change significantly as you are drafting?

Activity 1.5   Examining your writing processes

What words and phrases describe your writing processes? Brainstorm in the space provided.

YOUR TEACHING JOURNAL: Engaging with tensions
Review your brainstorming, and respond to the following questions in your teaching journal:

- Do you notice any tensions in your own writing processes?
- Are there differences between your beliefs about how one should write and the ways that you actually write?
- Are there any surprises in your list?
- How might these insights enrich your teaching?
- How would you explain to a hiring committee the relationship between your writing processes and students' writing processes?

To flesh out your definitions of "process" even further, we again turn to things that we have heard teachers say about process. We do this, in part, to show you that *the* writing process is not singular, monolithic, or universal; rather, it can take on many forms based on one's philosophical orientation, the context of the writing, and the task at hand. In Activity 1.6, we have created four hypothetical teachers, each representing a different view of process. Of course, in a real-world classroom, these four versions of process do not play out in such a tidy and distinct way; yet you will find them to be a useful tool for exploring and contextualizing your own beliefs about process.

 Activity 1.6   Examining diverse views of "the writing process"

Circle any ideas that resonate with you, and mark with an asterisk any ideas that cause tension. Unpack at least one of the tensions in your teaching journal.

A more text-focused teacher might say:	**A more context/culture-focused teacher might say:**
The best writing process is a methodical one. Students need to take their time and go through the necessary steps so that they can come up with a final draft that they are proud of. They should likely do brainstorming and prewriting activities first, then drafting. While they are drafting, they can draw on the toolkit of essay templates that I have taught them and put their own ideas into those essay structures. Then they do the final steps: checking paragraphs for cohesion and unity, checking their style, and proofreading. That is what it means to teach the process of writing — you have got to make it somewhat linear for students, whether they are writing an in-class essay, a term paper, or even a blog post. And this is true regardless of whether they are writing something very personal, like a narrative, or something more formal, like an argumentative essay.	The writing process is not a solitary pursuit; it is informed by the social context in which one is writing and the social context one is writing about. Since writing is shaped by power relations, and writing in turn shapes power relations, writers need to think critically about their ideas and how those ideas could have an impact on the world. Students thus need to be looking at and analyzing lots of texts while they are writing — including their own developing texts and one another's texts. The writing process also involves critical reflection on how meaning is constructed, which means that critical lenses such as feminism, Marxism, postcolonial theory, and critical race theory can help students "see" the world and their writing in more situated ways.
A more writer-focused teacher might say:	**A more reader-focused teacher might say:**
The writing process is all about experimentation. I have to give students lots of opportunities to explore, find their own ideas, and figure out what essay form or structure eventually develops out of those ideas. The process is very organic and personal. For example, when I assign a literacy narrative, students have to discover what is important to them in their own individual literacy histories. There is not one single "best way" to do that. For some students, inspiration comes through reading narratives; for some it comes from talking with classmates or doing a multimodal activity; and others just have to write their way into their ideas. Technology makes the students' writing processes even more complex and varied. Think about when students are blogging or putting together a Web site: Some students start with images, others start with a definite writing plan or outline, and some just dive in.	To find out about process, we can look at what "real writers" do in real-world writing situations. They are not just writing for themselves; they always have a real audience that they are addressing and a real purpose or goal in writing. And they are writing under real-world constraints. The writing process is all about trying to figure out how to best accomplish that goal, under those constraints, using whatever stylistic tools are appropriate for that audience and what Aristotle would call "the available means of persuasion." In fact, we are all "real-world writers" — think about the processes we use when we text a friend, write a formal report for work, or post a comment on someone's blog.

YOUR TEACHING JOURNAL: Engaging with tensions

Choose the idea that you feel most uncomfortable with, and brainstorm about it in your teaching journal. Consider the following questions:

- Why does this idea cause tension?
- Which of your beliefs does it clash with?
- Are there situations in which you might feel more comfortable with this conception of process (e.g., in other school, professional, or civic contexts; with other student populations; or with other readerships)?
- How would you discuss this tension with colleagues or with a hiring committee?

As a final exploration of your ideas about process, you will examine other words or terms that might describe the writing process. As you work through the activity, feel free to add additional words that come to mind describing writing processes. After you have completed the top portion of the activity, you will turn to your teaching journal and explore at least one of the tensions that you have found.

Activity 1.7 Examining terms that describe writing processes

Circle any ideas that resonate with you, and mark with an asterisk any ideas that cause tension. Unpack one of the tensions in your teaching journal.

Writing processes are . . .			
idiosyncratic	spontaneous	freeing	well-planned
methodical	laborious	constraining	unintentional
purposeful	solitary	thoughtful	challenging
exploratory	collaborative	messy	fun
goal-directed	frustrating	unpredictable	whimsical
	experimental	disciplined	

Additional terms that come to mind . . .

YOUR TEACHING JOURNAL: Engaging with tensions

Choose the term that you feel most uncomfortable with, and brainstorm about it in your teaching journal. Consider the following questions:

- How does the word clash with your own experience or philosophy?
- Do you think that other writers — professionals or student writers — would feel the same way?
- How might you make space in your classroom for students whose notions about process are different from your own?
- How would you discuss this tension with colleagues or with a hiring committee?

Since writers have multiple and varying writing processes and teachers have varying philosophical orientations to process, you will need to decide how process fits into your personal teaching approach and how you are going to implement process in your class.

 Activity 1.8   Enacting process in your class

We have compiled a list of generalizations about process that come from research on student and professional writing, writers' own narrative accounts, and teachers' accounts of what students do when they write. Think about how you might apply each of these generalizations in your own class—or how you might "test it out" if you are not sure that it resonates with your beliefs about writing, teaching, and learning. Fill in the following chart.

Generalization about writing processes:	How you might apply this idea or "test it out" in your class:
Each student has a different repertoire of writing processes.	
Each student has more than one process. (Think of the student who revises carefully when she can but "cranks out" a single draft when she's pressed for time.)	
Many students and professional writers benefit from hearing about other people's writing processes, approaches, and strategies — and trying them out.	
The process of creating a piece of good writing takes time and often requires multiple drafts and substantial revision.	

To concretize and synthesize your thinking so far, turn to your teaching journal and write out—in prose—your views about fostering and supporting students' writing processes. Draw on your own experiences, things you know about writing, and the activities we have done thus far. We will return to this journal entry and build on it throughout the book.

 Activity 1.9   Fostering effective writing processes in your class

In your teaching journal, discuss the following questions. Be sure to note any questions or issues that you are still wrestling with.

- What kind of environment will you create in your classroom to foster students' writing processes?
- How might you create this environment?

Taking it further:
Unpacking the theories in a teaching approach

As we suggested earlier in this chapter, composition teachers never focus exclusively on text, writer, context, or reader; instead, they draw on and emphasize different aspects of and different relationships between these four elements. These four elements can therefore be useful for analyzing a teaching approach that is new to you (for example, approaches that are used in classes you are observing, that you read about in a teaching methods textbook, or even that are tacitly embodied in first-year composition textbooks that you are perusing).

You will find that it is often difficult to nail down the exact theoretical underpinnings of any particular teaching approach. For example, Wardle and Downs's composition textbook, *Writing about Writing: A College Reader*, offers a pedagogical approach in which students study composition scholarship just as we teachers study it. Students also write about this scholarship, using it to theorize about their own texts, writing processes, and practices. In arguing for this approach, Elizabeth Wardle and Douglas Downs claim that it offers students:

- An increased self-awareness about writing
- Improved reading abilities
- Improved confidence as a student
- Increased awareness of research on writing as an ongoing "conversation"

Activity 1.10   Unpacking philosophies behind a pedagogical approach

To practice unpacking an unfamiliar pedagogy, consider the following course description from a teacher who uses a Writing about Writing (WAW) approach. Then explore how the WAW approach might overlap with and challenge the four orientations we have already explored by answering the questions that follow.

Course description

Welcome to English 101, First-Year Composition. In this course, writing is both what we will do and what we will study; writing will be both our method and our content. We will learn the "what" of writing (what experts in the field of writing studies do and say in order to define, theorize, and teach writing) as well as the "how" of writing (how we can use this expertise to become stronger writers ourselves). Throughout the term, we will read some of the key thinkers who have studied how writing works to see what we can learn from them. You will put their ideas to use in your own writing, using research about writing to help you more deeply understand how writing works and how to produce successful writing for different situations, including different courses and in different disciplines. We will focus quite a bit on developing metacognition — that is, the ability to think about our own thinking and why we think as we do — so that we can assess new writing situations and strategize about how best to meet new writing demands. Hopefully, this will allow you to use what you learn in this class in other writing situations.

---

1. Which philosophical values in WAW might overlap with a text-focused philosophy?

2. Which philosophical values in WAW might overlap with a writer-focused philosophy?

3. Which philosophical values in WAW might overlap with a context/culture-focused philosophy?

4. Which philosophical values in WAW might overlap with an audience-focused philosophy?

5. Finally, what do you see in the WAW approach that seems new or extends beyond the four theoretical orientations we have explored in this chapter?

Reflections from experienced teachers

In this chapter, you have focused on your own definition of good writing and explored the processes writers use to create good writing. You have also begun to articulate not only your beliefs about what makes good writing, but the ways that those beliefs align with larger theoretical positions within the field. Establishing a strong theoretical basis for your teaching is more than just "choosing a camp," however. Effective teachers often pull practices from multiple orientations, crafting them into an individual praxis (theory + practice) that fits both them and their students.

A central way that teachers recursively update their thinking is by engaging with the experiences of other teachers, their colleagues. In the following list, we offer a few pieces of wisdom that experienced teachers frequently suggest to newer teachers or wish they had learned sooner. Such lore, wisdom, and reflection can often be useful to help you examine how you are orienting yourself to composition and pedagogy.

> "My teaching philosophy was one of the hardest things I had to write as a graduate student because I was so afraid of setting in stone who I was as a teacher. But it ultimately helped me pare down my numerous — and often conflicting — beliefs about teaching and writing and articulate *why* I held those beliefs.
>
> —*Mark*

- With experience, you will discover that your definition of good writing and your conception of the processes for creating good writing are always context specific, time specific, and task specific. These will change from the beginning of the semester to the end of the semester, from one class to another, and from one institution to another.

- It is often valuable to share your writing processes with students — but it is crucial to not assume that your process will work best for all students.

- Good writing takes time, effort, feedback, and revision, sometimes in different measure for different students or different assignments. Allowing enough time for students to navigate the process can help make writing a more substantive experience for everyone.

- Although articulating and constantly reflecting on your own values about good writing are essential to engaged teaching, as teachers we also have to contend with institutionally imposed definitions of good writing, some of which we may in fact disagree with. Negotiating these tensions is perhaps one of the most challenging parts of teaching. (We will address this tension more directly in Chapter 4.)

Putting it together:
Articulating your evolving philosophy of writing

The activities that you have done thus far have encouraged you to take a closer look at your own evolving teaching philosophy. You have pondered four general orientations (text, writer, context, reader) that play a role in composition theories, you have explored your own beliefs about writing and your own writing processes, you have challenged the notion that a pedagogical approach embodies a single underlying orientation in the "Taking It Further" activity, and you have looked at reflections from experienced teachers. Now we will wrap up the chapter with two final activities that will help you crystallize your developing philosophy of writing.

Activity 1.11   Listing key terms and phrases describing good student writing

Imagine that you are preparing for a job interview. The hiring committee will ask about the qualities you look for in student writing—that is, how you define "good writing" in the context of a college composition course. In the space provided, brainstorm ten terms or phrases that encapsulate your views. Feel free to draw on your experiences as a writer, tutor, or teacher, but also try to incorporate what you have learned through the activities in this chapter.

Now it is time to take the plunge and start drafting your teaching philosophy, again drawing on your experiences and the activities in this chapter. This will be a working draft that you will return to many times as you work through this book, so nothing is set in stone.

It is important that you actually write out your philosophy *in prose* in your teaching journal because the act of writing will help you organize, deepen, and connect your ideas. It will also help you take a stand that you can then reflect on, interrogate, and rethink in future activities.

In addition to your working draft of a teaching philosophy, we also ask you to write a few paragraphs in your teaching journal about the contradictions, tensions, or questions that came up as you worked through the chapter. We will return to those tensions throughout the book; in the last chapter, we will help you create a career development plan in which you will pursue these questions further.

Activity 1.12   Compositing your teaching philosophy

In your teaching journal, discuss the following questions. Be sure to note any questions or issues that you are still wrestling with.

- How do you define good writing, particularly in the context of student writing? How will you "know it when you see it"? How will you articulate this notion to your students? How could you articulate this notion to a hiring committee?

- What writing processes will you foster in your classroom to help students create good writing? And how will you encourage students to draw on, share, and broaden their repertoire of writing processes?

The activities in this chapter have helped you build a solid foundation for your course. You have considered the many complexities and subtleties inherent in the seemingly simple question "What makes good writing?" And you have begun to stake out your own views and values in dialogue with current research and experts in the field. The work you have done in this chapter can thus act as a touchstone as you make your way through the rest of the book. Although you are well on your way to articulating a cohesive philosophy of teaching, you will want to keep your work from this chapter (including any notes, questions, or unresolved tensions you have captured in your teaching journal) close at hand as you progress through the book, tracking and updating your thinking as needed. You will also find it helpful to return to and revise the work from this chapter, particularly as you finish exploring Part 1 (Chapters 2 through 4) on your beliefs about good teaching and your role as a teacher.

Further Reading

- Bartholomae, David. "What Is Composition and (If You Know What That Is) Why Do We Teach It?" *Composition in the Twenty-First Century*. Ed. Lynn Bloom, Donald Daiker, and Edward White. Carbondale: Southern Illinois UP, 1996. 11–28. Print.

- Berlin, James. "Contemporary Composition: The Major Pedagogical Theories." *College English* 44.8 (1982): 765–77. Print.

- ---. "Rhetoric and Ideology in the Writing Class." *College English* 50.5 (1988): 477–94. Print.

- Elbow, Peter. "Closing My Eyes as I Speak: An Argument for Ignoring Audience." *College English* 49.1 (1987): 50–69. Print.

- Fulkerson, Richard. "Composition at the Turn of the Twenty-First Century." *College Composition and Communication* 56.4 (2005): 654–87. Print.

- Gee, James Paul. "Literacy, Discourse, and Linguistics: Introduction" and "What Is Literacy?" *Literacy: A Critical Sourcebook*. Ed. Ellen Cushman et al. Boston: Bedford/St. Martin's, 2001. 537–44. Print.

- Murray, Donald. "Teach Writing as a Process Not a Product." *Cross-Talk in Comp*. 3rd ed. Ed. Victor Villanueva. Urbana: NCTE, 2011. 3–6. Print.

CHAPTER 2

Choices about Your Philosophy of Teaching

In Chapter 1, you began to articulate your theories about "good writing" and the writing processes that can foster good writing. In this chapter, we turn to Richard Fulkerson's third question: How do we teach students to create good writing? Like the first two questions, this one is also deceptively simple. Many of your decisions about what constitutes good teaching will depend on your values and personality as a teacher in combination with the characteristics and needs of your students. We begin this chapter by asking you to explore some of your own experiences as a student and learner; we then invite you to consider how you can become a reflective practitioner, observing and learning from how your students react to different learning experiences.

How will you help students create good writing?

Our beliefs about great teaching tend to be shaped by the great teachers we had in high school and college. They served as role models and gave us ideas about what constitutes effective pedagogy. Some of these ideas are clearly still useful (e.g., "An English teacher should inspire students"). But some of these ideas may require a bit of rethinking in the context of teaching Freshman Composition (e.g., "An English teacher should instill a love of Shakespeare in students").

To begin this chapter, you will consider your experiences as a student in high school and college and jot down some terms or phrases that describe effective and ineffective teaching. You will then build on this list as you proceed through the chapter.

 Activity 2.1   Drawing on your experiences as a student

Based on your experiences as a student, describe what effective teaching looks like. Then describe what ineffective teaching looks like. Brainstorm in the space provided on the next page.

To begin to flesh out your notion of effective teaching, work through the cluster of terms in Activity 2.2. Feel free to expand on any of these terms or to add additional ones. Also note any terms that you find problematic or perplexing, and unpack one of them in your teaching journal.

 Activity 2.2 Homing in on a definition of good teaching

Circle any ideas that resonate with you, and mark with an asterisk any ideas that cause tension. Unpack at least one of the tensions in your teaching journal.

Terms that describe good teaching . . .

strategies   correction   pushing students   peer work   discipline

caring   time to develop   collaboration   lively   well-managed classroom

supportive   professional writers   role model   current   worksheets

rigorous   love of reading   structuring the writing process   focused   writing as skill

writers' workshop   metacognition   grammar rules   media-rich   style guides

guidance   feedback   teacher as expert   writing as craft   inspirational

models   apprenticeship   playfulness with language   multiple genres   freewriting

practice   fun   encouragement   challenging students   discussion

challenge   reassuring   sharing writing   tough love   peer review

Additional terms that come to mind . . .

YOUR TEACHING JOURNAL: Engaging with tensions

Choose the term that you feel most uncomfortable with, and brainstorm about it in your teaching journal. Consider the following questions:

- How does this clash with your own experience or with your philosophy about good writing or good teaching?
- Do you think that students would feel the same way?
- How might you make space in your classroom for students whose notions about good teaching are different from your own?
- How would you discuss this tension with colleagues or with a hiring committee?

In the next activity, we sketch out some ways that writing instructors have defined effective teaching. We have grouped them into the four theoretical orientations discussed in Chapter 1. As you read, note any ideas that resonate or conflict with your beliefs; you will return to them when you write your teaching philosophy.

 Activity 2.3   Examining notions of good teaching

Circle any ideas that resonate with you, and mark with an asterisk any ideas that cause tension. Unpack at least one of the tensions in your teaching journal.

A more text-focused teacher might say:	A more context/culture-focused teacher might say:
Writing is basically a toolbox of skills — everything from outlining, to quoting, to forming a good thesis statement, to proofreading. An effective teacher introduces students to those tools, gives students ample opportunities to practice using them, and provides useful corrective feedback that helps students understand what they are doing right and what they need to work on.	Teaching students the conventions of academic writing is just a starting point. An effective teacher goes beyond that and helps students critically examine those conventions — as well as the social, political, economic, and cultural forces that determine how texts are conceptualized and constructed in the first place — and how texts are received by readers. An effective teacher is someone who pushes students to think critically about how texts, including how the full range of texts that we encounter in the world, like images, ads, and digital texts, are embedded in relationships of language and power.
A more writer-focused teacher might say:	**A more audience-focused teacher might say:**
Writing is a process of discovery; an effective teacher stands back enough to give students space to experiment and grow. I can model the process of discovery for them and share with them my own "journey" as a writer as I rework drafts and discover what I want to say. But there is not a one-size-fits-all way to write. Effective teaching often looks like setting up a workshop with students working on their own individual writing projects and setting their own individual goals.	An effective teacher is someone who treats writing not as a set of skills, but rather as a set of social practices that occur within discourse communities. The teacher can help students understand the norms and conventions of various writing communities (including the academic writing community) and can help students make purposeful choices when writing. Good writing is not about slavishly following conventions; it is about knowing what you want to accomplish with a specific piece of writing, knowing your audience, and making effective rhetorical choices.

YOUR TEACHING JOURNAL: Engaging with tensions

Choose the idea that you feel most uncomfortable with, and brainstorm about it in your teaching journal. Consider the following questions:

- How does the idea you selected clash with your own experience or with your philosophy about good teaching?
- How will you make space in your classroom for student expectations of good teaching that clash with your own?
- What might you say to colleagues or supervisors whose notions about good teaching clash with your own?

As you begin to flesh out a definition of effective teaching, you will certainly discover that your definition contains tensions. For example, you may want to be both encouraging and strict, notions that on the surface may seem mutually exclusive. Drawing on our work with teachers and teachers-in-training, we list some of the common tensions in the next activity and ask you to position yourself among those tensions.

Activity 2.4 Examining conflicting ideas about effective teaching

Circle any ideas that resonate with you, and mark with an asterisk any ideas that cause tension. Unpack at least one of the tensions in your teaching journal.

Effective teaching means . . .		
Giving students lots of structure	⟷	Giving students lots of freedom
Meticulously organized lessons	⟷	Spontaneous, responsive lessons
Lots of group work	⟷	Lots of individual work
Teacher at the center	⟷	Students at the center
Giving students clear answers	⟷	Making students figure out answers
Focusing heavily on writing	⟷	Focusing heavily on reading
Focusing heavily on skills	⟷	Focusing heavily on critical thinking
Treating all students the same	⟷	Being responsive to individual needs
Creativity in writing	⟷	Conventions in writing
Preparing students for real-world writing demands	⟷	Providing a sheltered environment for students to experiment and grow

YOUR TEACHING JOURNAL: Engaging with tensions

Choose the pair of ideas that causes the most tension for you, and brainstorm about it in your teaching journal. Consider the following questions:

- Why do you feel torn between the two goals?
- Do you think other teachers feel this way? Why?
- Do you think your students feel this way? Why?
- How might you structure your class so that you satisfy both goals?

Because there are many facets to good teaching, you should observe a variety of teachers with different styles and approaches and ponder the theories about good teaching that might inform each teacher's approach. In Activity 2.5, we provide vignettes of four hypothetical classrooms—composites based on our many years of teacher observation. Examine each vignette, and compare it to your own beliefs about good teaching.

 Activity 2.5 Analyzing classroom scenarios for underlying philosophies of teaching

Circle any ideas that resonate with you, and mark with an asterisk any ideas that cause tension. Unpack at least one of the tensions in your teaching journal.

Classroom 1	Classroom 2
Desks are arranged in a U-shape facing the teacher. She puts an academic paragraph on the overhead projector and asks students to read and analyze it. She asks them to identify the topic sentence, then the pieces of evidence in the paragraph that support the topic sentence, and finally the explanation or analysis that ties the paragraph together. She repeats this process several times with paragraphs from academic and professional writing. She often refers students to the definition of a good paragraph in the students' course reader.	The students' desks are pushed together in groups of three or four. In some groups, a single student reads a paper aloud. In others, students read quietly, writing comments on one another's papers, or casually discuss their topics. In yet other groups, students work individually, typing on their laptops, occasionally checking the Web. The teacher has written some general suggestions on the board:
	 • Share what you have so far — it is okay if your draft is not complete. • Push your group mates to give feedback about your ideas rather than your grammar. • Tell them what you, as a writer, want feedback on. • When giving feedback, respond as an interested reader; do not respond as a copy editor!

She then puts a template on the overhead:
 	
Topic sentence: _____
 	
Supporting evidence: _____
 	
Supporting evidence: _____
 	
Explanation: _____
 	
Students create their own paragraphs based on this template and share them in small groups.
  The teacher closes the lesson saying, "When you write your first draft for the next class, be sure to underline each topic sentence and put a little check mark beside each piece of supporting evidence."
	The teacher checks in with the groups to see whether the students are getting the kind of feedback they need.
	  He closes the class by saying, "Continue working on your drafts, and we will continue the workshops tomorrow. And start thinking about whether this paper is something you want to polish for your final portfolio, or if you want to shift gears and start working on a different piece of writing."

Classroom 3	Classroom 4
Students are working in groups analyzing short articles, all on the same topic, but from various media outlets. On the board, the teacher has written three questions: • What beliefs and assumptions are shared by the author and the presumed readership? • How does the author's use of language reveal his or her worldview? • What particular words or terms seem to be "ideologically charged"? When finished, each group shares its analysis. The teacher writes various terms on the board that students have found to be "ideologically charged." The teacher then assigns homework: Choose two different news articles on the same topic but from different media outlets, and write a page analyzing and contrasting the language used in the two articles. She mentions that this assignment will help students prepare for a longer assignment later in the semester — a rhetorical analysis of political discourse.	Students are working in groups analyzing pieces of writing from various "discourse communities" — business, science, sports, and entertainment reporting. Each group is trying to identify the rhetorical, stylistic, and linguistic conventions of the piece of writing. Students then give short presentations on the discourse community and genre they looked at, focusing particularly on language and audience expectations. For homework, the teacher asks students to write about the recent tuition increase in e-mails to two different discourse communities. Students can choose to write to legislators, the school administration, the school newspaper, their parents, their friends, or another audience of their choice.

YOUR TEACHING JOURNAL: Engaging with tensions

Choose the vignette that you feel most uncomfortable with, and brainstorm about it in your teaching journal. Consider the following questions:

• Why does this vignette make you feel uncomfortable?

• Would your students feel equally uncomfortable, or might they like this teaching style? Why?

• How might you bridge your own teaching style and the teaching style depicted in this vignette?

• How would you discuss this tension with colleagues or with a hiring committee?

Turning to the field: Teaching as a reflective practice

From Donald Schön's work in the mid-1980s to the 1995 book *Teaching Writing as Reflective Practice* by George Hillocks Jr., teachers have long known that much of what makes teachers (and teaching) effective is learned on the job through a continual loop of observation, reflection, experimentation, and implementation. Louise Weatherbee Phelps describes this movement as practice-theory-practice (PTP), as teachers move from a dissatisfying practice or one with marginal results, through a confrontation of the theoretical elements of that practice, emerging on the other side with a new practice that is more successful or with which the teacher is more comfortable.

Central to other work on reflective practice, such as Hillocks's, is an awareness of how people learn best. Hillocks draws on the work of literacy theorist Lev Vygotsky and his theory of the zone of proximal development (ZPD). The ZPD is defined as "the distance between the actual developmental level as determined by independent problem-solving and the level of potential

> **When I first started teaching, I thought there was some "best" grading method, "best" peer-response method, and so on. I was looking for a "bag of teaching tricks." But it's not that simple. What you see as "best" depends a lot on your own beliefs about writing, learning, and teaching.**
>
> *—Mark*

It took me a few years of teaching to learn to consider a wider range of teaching and learning strategies than those I had encountered myself. Realizing that not everything that worked for me as a learner might work for students became a huge turning point in my development as a teacher.

—Tara

development as determined through problem-solving under adult guidance or in collaboration with more capable peers" (qtd. in Hillocks 55). Vygotsky's understanding is important as we consider the complex social activity system that is learning, since it articulates the way that we can learn more—and even learn best—when we are challenged by working with "more capable peers."

We can think of the ZPD in terms of teacher learning as well. When we as teachers come together—in a graduate seminar, in a faculty development workshop, or even over lunch to share ideas—we often find that we grow immensely, more than we would have on our own. Coming into contact with fresh ideas and different perspectives, we create a consortium of expertise that is greater than the sum of its parts; we challenge one another, contribute our own expertise and strengths, and move the collective knowledge further as we work with others who are in some ways more or differently capable than we are. This is a phenomenon experienced especially by newer teachers when they work alongside and talk about their teaching with their more seasoned colleagues.

If we continue in this frame of mind—recognizing that our development can be similar to that of our students—we quickly arrive at the notion that we, too, should embody the productive academic "habits of mind" that the *Framework for Success in Postsecondary Writing* lays out for our students. More than just serving as models for our students, our embodiment of these habits also helps us continue to learn and develop as teachers. And these habits can keep us in a sort of continuous ZPD where, open to the learning process, we are engaged with and challenged by those around us.

 Activity 2.6 Practicing openness and engagement

To explore this premise, consider two of the habits of mind suggested and defined by the Framework for Success: *openness and engagement. (We have adapted them slightly for teachers instead of student writers to encourage you to reflect on how you might strive for these habits.) Fill in the following chart.*

Characteristics and examples adapted from the *Framework for Success:*	How could you specifically practice this in your classroom or your teaching?

Openness — the willingness to consider new ways of being and thinking in the world
 	
    Teachers demonstrate openness when they:
 	
• Examine their own perspectives to find connections with the perspectives of others
• Practice different ways of gathering, investigating, developing, and presenting information
• Listen to and reflect on the ideas and responses of others — both peers and students
 	
Engagement — a sense of investment and involvement in learning.
 	
    Teachers demonstrate engagement when they:
 	
• Make connections between their own ideas and those of others
• Find meanings new to them or build on existing meanings as a result of new connections
• Act on the new knowledge that they have discovered	

Taking it further:
Popular conceptions about "good teaching"

Educational institutions and teacher-training programs have long struggled to define good teaching. In many ways the notion seems to be based on common sense, while in other ways it is frustratingly elusive, particularly when it comes to evaluating teaching candidates using some sort of checklist or rubric. In the next activity, we ask you to explore both the commonsense and more elusive notions surrounding good teaching.

 Activity 2.7   Examining diverse notions of good teaching

Do a Web search for the term good teaching. *Of course, this will return a wide variety of articles and Web pages from both popular and professional sources. Peruse at least ten of these sources, and take notes. Fill in the following chart.*

What notions of good teaching come up repeatedly?	What notions of good teaching are infrequent, unusual, or controversial?

Now examine the first list—the "commonsense" notions about good teaching that appeared repeatedly in your sources.

 Activity 2.8   Examining the challenges of good teaching

If we generally agree on what constitutes good teaching, why is it so difficult to achieve? Drawing on Activity 2.7, explore this conundrum by answering the following questions.

1. In what ways are the commonsense notions more complex than they first appear?

2. Are these notions universally applicable to the writing classroom? How could you tweak them to apply them to a writing classroom?

3. Do these ideas really represent good teaching for all students in all teaching contexts? For which students might these ideas be ineffective or inappropriate?

Now examine the second list — the less frequent notions of good teaching. Choose a few of these notions and unpack them.

1. Why do you think these ideas appear infrequently?

2. How do they clash with or complicate the commonsense notions?

3. Which students would benefit from this kind of teaching? Which students might be disadvantaged?

Reflections from experienced teachers

As your teaching career progresses, you will refine your notion of good teaching through experimentation, experience, work with colleagues, and your own professional development. However, to give you a head start, we list several pieces of wisdom gathered from many experienced teachers. Remember that these suggestions represent not a single set of best practices, but rather an ongoing process of reflective teaching and professional growth.

- Since even seasoned teachers continue to experiment and grow, it is important to stay flexible and open-minded; one of the joys of teaching is experimentation with new approaches.
- Eclecticism can be very effective if you are making informed choices. Most seasoned teachers draw on a wide variety of teaching approaches and activities while consistently reflecting on these central teaching questions: What am I doing? Why am I doing it? How does this fit into my overall philosophy?
- Rather than strive to find the one "right way" to teach, try to align your beliefs about good writing, your beliefs about the writing process, and your beliefs about effective teaching. This will also help you consistently reflect on how your philosophy and your teaching approach fit together so that you know why you are doing what you are doing.
- Along similar lines, it can often be helpful to approach your cherished models of teaching with some skepticism. Try not to default to a particular way of teaching because that is what you remember enjoying most from your own education. Although your educational experiences can serve as models, be sure to consider whether a given approach is right for your particular situation and your particular students, as well as whether it is a match for teaching writing effectively.
- In your teaching journal, keep track of your pedagogical experiments and their results; this is one of the best ways to chart your progress and continue to grow as a teacher.

Putting it together:
Articulating your evolving philosophy of teaching

In this chapter, you have explored your notions of good teaching as well as the notions of others. And you have looked at tensions inherent in the concept of good teaching. To consolidate your ideas, you will complete two wrap-up activities, similar to those in Chapter 1.

 Activity 2.9   Using key terms to describe your philosophy

Imagine you are preparing for a job interview; the committee will ask you about your notions of what constitutes good teaching. In the space provided, brainstorm ten important terms, concepts, or phrases that define good teaching for you.

Drawing on your brainstorming in Activity 2.9, turn to your teaching journal and write out — in prose — your philosophy of effective teaching, particularly as it applies to the writing classroom and the contexts in which you are (or will be) teaching. Feel free to build on the draft you wrote at the end of the last chapter, tying your notions of good teaching to your notions of good writing.

Activity 2.10   Firming up your definition of "effective teaching"

In your teaching journal, discuss the following questions. Be sure to note any questions or issues that you are still wrestling with.

- What are the characteristics of effective teaching?
- Why are these characteristics important for student learning?

In this chapter, you have dug deeper into the many dimensions that combine to make effective teaching. Specifically, you have explored the ways that your own educational experiences inform your views about teaching, as well as some of the tensions you will surely face as you create your own teaching approach.

Finally, you have made an initial attempt to articulate your own philosophy of teaching—a crucial step in pinpointing your goals as a teacher. You will put this philosophy of teaching to work in upcoming chapters as you explore how you will enact your philosophy via your teaching persona (Chapter 3 and Chapter 4) and how your philosophy translates into specific course goals (Chapter 5), writing assignments (Chapter 6), and reading assignments (Chapter 7). Although it is fine to not yet have answers to the many complicated negotiations that happen in teaching, beginning to puzzle through these tensions is an important first step in laying the groundwork for your entire course design. Remember to return to these first two chapters as you continue to progress through the book, making note of your evolving thinking and even which tensions you can begin to clarify for yourself.

Further Reading

- Brandt, Deborah. "Sponsors of Literacy." *College Composition and Communication* 49.2 (1998): 165–85. Print.

- *Digital Archive of Literacy Narratives*. Ohio State University Libraries. Web. 25 Sept. 2014. <http://daln.osu.edu/>.

- Freire, Paulo. "The Banking Concept of Education." *Pedagogy of the Oppressed*. Ed. Myra Bergman Ramos and Donaldo Macedo. New York: Bloomsbury, 2000. 71–86. Print.

- Phelps, Louise Wetherbee. "Images of Student Writing: The Deep Structure of Teacher Response." *Writing and Response: Theory, Practice, and Research*. Ed. Chris M. Anson. Urbana: NCTE, 1989. 37–67. Print.

- Robertson, Liane, Kara Taczak, and Kathleen Blake Yancey. "Notes toward a Theory of Prior Knowledge and Its Role in College Composers' Transfer of Knowledge and Practice." *Composition Forum* 26 (2012): n. pag. Web. 25 Sept. 2014. <http://compositionforum.com/issue/26/prior-knowledge-transfer.php>.

- Sommers, Nancy, and Laura Saltz. "The Novice as Expert: Writing the Freshman Year." *College Composition and Communication* 56.1 (2004): 124–49. Print.

CHAPTER 3

Choices about Your Teaching Persona

In Chapter 2, you began to explore your philosophy of teaching; you considered what makes for effective teaching and, given your beliefs about writing, what your writing classroom might look like. In this chapter and the next, you will get more specific about your individual teaching persona. As the teacher, you play a key role in shaping the culture of the class and the expectations to which students will hold themselves accountable; moreover, the expertise and energy you bring to the class contributes much to the overall dynamic. And at the same time, you are modeling what it means to be an engaged thinker, an experienced reader, and a strategic, effective writer. In this chapter, you will explore how you see yourself as a teacher, including the various roles you might play, and how you would like to present your professional self to a class of students.

What kind of teacher do you hope to be?

Your own learning experiences have a great influence on your teaching persona. As important as it is to give some thought to these experiences so that you can draw from them, it is equally important to consider how you can diversify beyond those practices to meet the varied needs of your students. Thus this chapter begins with a brainstorming activity.

Activity 3.1   Reflecting on your experience as a student

Brainstorm answers to the questions that follow.

1. Think about the most influential teacher you have had. What qualities did this person have that you found valuable?

2. Describe a specific moment when you witnessed excellent teaching. What role did that teacher take on (e.g., facilitator, tough coach, good listener) to make learning possible?

3. What motivated, energized, or excited you as a student? What teaching methods or styles did you respond to? What qualities — particularly affective (i.e., emotional) qualities — did you respond to? Why?

> **What I remember working for me as a student was feeling that my teacher believed in my abilities as a student. As I've grown more comfortable teaching, I've been able to become less worried about myself in the classroom and more focused on my students, trying to convey to each student that I believe they can succeed.**
>
> —*Mark*

Reading back over your responses to Activity 3.1, you can begin to see some of the qualities you particularly valued in your past teachers. Circle the characteristics or descriptors that reflect who you would like to be as a teacher. Be guided by your own personality; consider the characteristics that others, perhaps even students (if you are currently teaching), note about you or compliment you on. You will most likely not circle every descriptor, and that is perfectly fine. One thing that makes teachers successful is an awareness of the unique strengths and expertise they bring to a teaching situation. Similarly, all of the words you circle might not be purely positive—you have probably had an experience where someone who was "tough" or "challenging" made a positive impact on you by believing in your abilities and encouraging you to achieve more than you thought you could. Many successful teachers balance positive affective characteristics (helpful, understanding, encouraging) with the high expectations that other descriptors (tough, rigorous) suggest.

As you look back at Activity 3.1, you might also notice that tensions exist between what worked for you as a student and what might work for other students who find different methods and styles supportive and motivating. As you progress through this chapter and as you enter the classroom, it is important to remain aware of the teaching methods and styles that support a range of students. Different models or strategies might likewise be more appropriate for different contexts or for students at different levels. And you might even find that certain teaching methods feel more appropriate at different points in your career. You might feel empowered to be more provocative as a teacher later in your career, for example, than you might at the beginning of your career.

> **Although they felt difficult at the time, I really appreciated larger projects and longer writing assignments that asked me to go above and beyond what I had done before. They were challenging, but they helped me build confidence in myself when I could look back and say, "Wow, I accomplished that!" So now this is a key question I ask myself in my course design: What kinds of projects could help my students stretch themselves and build a similar confidence?**
>
> —*Tara*

Another important tension to note is the one that often emerges between our cherished teaching models (perhaps a genius literature teacher who inspired us through the depth of knowledge displayed in his lectures) and our own beliefs about what a successful writing classroom looks like (perhaps the opposite of a teacher lecturing and students passively listening). This is a crucial tension to keep in mind. As you work through the rest of this chapter, you will identify specific roles and teaching styles that are connected to your view of a productive writing classroom. You may find that your beliefs about writing call on you to be quite different from those inspiring teachers who stand out in your memory.

What roles will you take on as a teacher?

As you work to integrate your personality and your classroom persona, it will be helpful to consider the many roles that teachers can play. Good teachers often take on a range of these roles at different times for different purposes, attending closely to what approach might help a particular student or class at particular junctures. As you read through the many teacher roles described in Activity 3.2, pay attention to your response to each role. You will want to return to these descriptions as you develop your teaching philosophy. We will ask you to work with your responses throughout the rest of this chapter.

Activity 3.2   Examining roles that teachers choose

Circle any ideas that resonate with you, and mark with an asterisk any ideas that cause tension. Unpack at least one of the tensions in your teaching journal.

Coach	Model
We can all think of a "coach" in our lives: someone who summoned the best from us and encouraged us to tackle increasingly hard challenges. A coach sets us tasks that will help us improve, encourages us to practice, and boosts our confidence while simultaneously challenging us. Coaching can be particularly successful in introducing new writing concepts or practices, as well as in working one-on-one with students. A coaching role is also amenable to working with diverse students and their different learning styles and needs.	As teachers, we constantly act as models for our students — demonstrating how more experienced writers achieve tasks or how people in academia ask questions, marshal evidence, and so on. We can model how a productive discussion might occur, provide models of successful papers, or even model how we would get started writing or thinking through a problem. Modeling is often most successful when we are explicit about the fact that we are modeling. When we say to students, "Here's one way you might go about doing X; watch and consider if this could help you," we are both giving students useful strategies and honoring their autonomy in deciding which strategies might work for them.
Facilitator	**Mentor**
For many writing teachers, their central goal in the class-room and in working with student writers is to facilitate the kind of environment that will advance students' writing and thinking. Many teachers want to foster a strong sense of community and student-centered classrooms where student expertise and interests are an integral part of the class. When we act as facilitators, we set up meaningful learning experiences and jump in to help when needed, but mostly we step back and let students take the reins. We keep things moving in a positive direction, but we are flexible in terms of where a discussion moves or where an activity ends up. Successful facilitation means striking the right balance between shaping the flow of events, responding to what is happening in the moment, and getting out of the way.	Whether we recognize it or not, we often act as mentors for our students. This is most clear when we work one-on-one with students or when we build special relationships with particular students to help them succeed or pursue their interests. However, we also mentor all our students in small ways, encouraging them to succeed and acknowledging their individual challenges and successes. In these ways, we bring students along, taking an interest in them and helping them find productive places for themselves in our classes or the academy at large. We mentor students when we differentiate our teaching in response to different student needs, when we take an interest in their progress and ongoing success, and when we offer our help and advice to assist them in continued learning.
Confidant	**Advocate**
Whether we desire this role or not, students may call on us to act as a confidant, a trusted adult figure, a counselor or adviser, or a problem solver. This is particularly likely in a composition class. The class is small, students have a lot of contact with the teacher, and the topics or writing can elicit strong personal reactions from students. When students perceive you as a caring, trustworthy, capable person, they might divulge information that can be challenging to hear	The longer you teach, the more you might find yourself in a position where you can effect change for your students beyond the walls of the classroom. You might recommend students for jobs or scholarships, serve on a committee that shapes curricula, or read student essays submitted for a departmental award. You might even talk to your friends and neighbors about who your students are and how larger policy affects their learning. In situations such as these, you can act

and process, such as health issues, psychological problems, abuse or rape, or family problems. Although it is important to remember that you are not a certified counselor and must point students to the appropriate resources, professionals, and health facilities, you should also acknowledge that the student has come to you with this information for a reason: He or she trusts you. The role of confidant involves acknowledging students' troubles and helping however you can, while still maintaining a professional relationship.

as an advocate for individual students, for your institution, and even for higher learning in general.

YOUR TEACHING JOURNAL: Engaging with tensions

Choose one of the roles that you feel somewhat uncomfortable with, and brainstorm about it in your teaching journal. Consider the following questions:

- Why does this role feel uncomfortable?
- To what extent is this discomfort related to your personality and sense of who you are as a person or as a teacher?
- To what extent is this discomfort related to your teaching philosophy?
- How might you become more comfortable with this role?
- How would you discuss these tensions with colleagues or with a hiring committee?

In addition to the roles described in Activity 3.2, you might find yourself forced to adopt particular roles. Sometimes these other roles come along with the institutional authority we carry (such as grader); other times they emerge from the views that students and others have of us as professional educators. Negotiating these roles is no less important and can sometimes be more difficult than occupying the roles that feel more connected to our personalities. In the next activity, you will examine these additional roles and explore how comfortable you would feel in them.

 Activity 3.3 Examining roles that are imposed on teachers

Circle any ideas that resonate with you, and mark with an asterisk any ideas that cause tension. Unpack at least one of the tensions in your teaching journal.

Gatekeeper	Expert
Although perhaps one of the toughest roles to occupy in a responsible way, the role of gatekeeper (a type of institutional authority) is one that we all must negotiate. This role becomes particularly challenging when we balance issues of access against issues of "readiness" or meeting expectations. These decisions often emerge at the end of the semester or in response to grades. Sometimes the decision will be clear-cut: A student, without a compelling reason, missed the number of classes that the department determines warrants a failing grade. Sometimes decisions will be more murky: A student needs a C to pass and has a high C–. Are there any circumstances or reasons that would warrant this student's passing the class and moving on? This role often involves trying to objectively weigh the costs and benefits of decisions.	Whether we think about our expertise in terms of our advanced reading skills, the rhetorical awareness we bring to writing tasks, or the other factual or practical knowledge we possess, we are experts in the eyes of our students. This does not mean that we need to stand at the front of the class expounding on our expertise for our students to absorb; but we can offer our expertise — including a range of ways to effectively tackle a reading or writing task — when it will help students or when they ask for such advice. When we think about it, this makes sense: We most need and appreciate expertise when it helps us accomplish something and when we are not sure how to proceed. Connecting expertise to specific tasks — making it relevant, that is — ensures that our students can forge a meaningful connection between our words and their goals.

YOUR TEACHING JOURNAL: Engaging with tensions

Choose some aspect of the "Gatekeeper" or "Expert" role that you feel uncomfortable with, and brainstorm about it in your teaching journal. Consider the following questions:

- Why does this role make you feel uncomfortable?
- Given that this role might be imposed on you, how might you deal with it and still stay true to your teaching philosophy?
- What kinds of boundaries might you need to set (for students, colleagues, or yourself)?
- How would you discuss this process of negotiation with colleagues or with a hiring committee?

In Activity 3.2 and Activity 3.3, you surely noticed that your own personal philosophy about writing and teaching is deeply intertwined with your choices about teacher roles. For example, if you believe in writing as an ongoing process in which writers are discovering their own voices and material, you will probably find yourself drawing on the roles of coach and facilitator more than that of expert. It will probably be helpful for you to practice switching between these roles and to explore their dimensions, paying attention to how these roles serve different purposes based on your beliefs about writing, the writing process, and effective teaching. You will want to note which roles seem to fit hand in glove with your teaching persona and which roles you might have to work a bit harder to negotiate. Finally, if you can remember to maintain an awareness of the range of roles you can occupy in the classroom and which roles tend to fit certain situations best, you will be well on your way to establishing a teaching presence that works for you and your students. You will find it helpful to return to the notes you have taken as you practice moving between roles and negotiating the tensions that arise.

As you work to craft an effective teaching persona, you will no doubt experience setbacks and doubts that may challenge your view of yourself as a teacher. Do not despair! Not only does this happen to every teacher, but these moments often present the most salient lessons for us, causing us to reflect deeply and, when warranted, to make necessary changes. There is great value in talking through these moments with others who might be experiencing similar challenges—perhaps others new to teaching or more experienced teachers whom you trust. Setbacks may be emotionally challenging, making us ask, "Why did this happen? What did I do wrong? Am I failing my students?" However, do not miss the opportunity to learn from any missteps. Working through problematic situations, dealings with difficult students, or lessons that went awry may well lead to more growth for you as a teacher than all your successes. That being said, you can do some work up front to anticipate how you might respond to difficulties that arise or how you might prevent some difficulties from occurring in the first place.

> I liked when I felt as though my teachers were learning with us students — when it felt as though they didn't have all the answers but still had some questions, too. It made learning feel less robotic to me. That's something I try to be able to do with my own students.
>
> —*Tara*

Activity 3.4   Examining difficult teaching situations

The following questions will help you prepare for challenging moments. Answer the questions in the first column, and identify helpful teacher roles in the second column.

Teaching challenging and reflective questions:	What teacher roles would be helpful in this situation?
Describe a specific moment when you felt silenced or marginalized as a student or when you witnessed a situation that likely made other students feel this way. What happened? How can you use this experience to inform your own teaching?	
Describe a specific moment when a lesson or the classroom dynamic fell flat. What were the teacher and students doing that was not working? Did anything happen to pull things back to a productive direction? If not, what could the teacher have done? (If you cannot think of a specific moment, imagine such a scenario and describe what could be done to rectify the situation.)	
A student speaks with you before class about getting an extension for the day's paper. What reasons might convince you to allow an extension, and what reasons might be insufficient to convince you? Is "I didn't do my best and I know I can do better with a few more days" a sufficient reason for you? Explain.	

Turning to the field:
Affective dimensions of teaching

Recently, scholars have begun to focus more on the affective dimensions of teaching. As in other relationships in our lives, students respond to how we listen, how we engage them, how we move, and how we emote. As scholars have noted, emotions prompt more than feelings; emotions also trigger physical responses and cognitive reflections, both of which range in intensity and vary in terms of their perceived positivity and negativity. The affective dimensions of teaching and learning also extend beyond: Motivation, beliefs, attitudes, insight and intuition, and much about how we perceive the world all have an affective component. Writing scholar Susan McLeod summarizes the effects of emotion and explores how they may play out in the classroom in her book *Notes on the Heart*. How do students perceive the affective components of our actions, and how do we respond affectively to students and our own perceptions of them? How do these dynamics shape the classroom? McLeod suggests we need to attend not only to emotions and feelings, but also to attitudes and beliefs (including beliefs about learning and overall worldviews), motivation, self-efficacy (our faith in whether we can succeed), and even intuition.

To begin to explore this territory, ponder the teaching practices listed in Activity 3.5, and think about whether they might create a positive affective response in students.

Activity 3.5   Creating a positive learning environment

Circle any ideas that resonate with you, and mark with an asterisk any ideas that cause tension. Unpack at least one of the tensions in your teaching journal.

Practices for creating a positive learning environment . . .

engage student ideas   connect class to student and teacher interests   share stories
ask genuine questions   connect with students   read new materials along with students
explore new topics together   connect academia to the larger world   ask students what matters to them
be curious about students   pinpoint what energizes a discussion   capitalize on diversity
teach new material   show that I care for students   listen intently
joke with students   ask about students' lives
discuss shared interests   ask for feedback   use technology creatively

---

Additional practices that come to mind . . .

YOUR TEACHING JOURNAL: Engaging with tensions

Choose the practice that you feel most uncomfortable with, and brainstorm about it in your teaching journal. Consider the following questions:

- How does the practice clash with your own experience or philosophy about "positive learning environments"?

- Do you think that your students would necessarily feel the same way? Why?

- How might you make space in your classroom for students whose notions about a positive learning environment differ from your own?

- How would you discuss this practice with colleagues or with a hiring committee?

Taking it further:
Your affective responses to students

As McLeod explores in depth, and as you began to explore in Activity 3.5, emotion is a complex creature. Our emotions, beliefs, motivations, and even confidence and self-efficacy all play a significant role in shaping who we are as teachers and the teaching personas we display to our students. We can begin to acknowledge the affective component of our classes by practicing how we attend to our own affective responses, as well as how these responses may encourage different roles. If a student hands in a paper late, do we tend to assume the student had a valid reason, or do we chalk it up to procrastination or laziness? Why do we react this way? Asking questions like these can help us become more in tune with and aware of our reactions and the reasons behind them. It can also help us respond to students more appropriately and recognize when our emotional reactions are not warranted, especially when students present us with new information about their behavior.

In Activity 3.6, you will work with a few scenarios to explore how affective forces play out in the classroom for both teachers and students.

Activity 3.6   Getting learning back on track

For each scenario, try to pinpoint your initial emotional or affective reaction. Then try to think affectively from the student's point of view: What might be prompting or influencing the student's behavior? Finally, use your responses in the first two columns to hypothesize how you might respond to the situation to get learning back on track in the last column, making sure to take your philosophy and possible roles into account. Fill in the chart. We have done the first couple of examples to get you started.

Scenario	How might you feel?	Why might the student act this way?	How might you respond or redirect?
A student challenges something you have said in class.	• Thrown off guard • Insecure about the idea I expressed • Worried that this student does not respect me	• The student may be trying to be intellectually engaged. • The student may be trying to pin down expectations. • The student may feel insecure or threatened by the idea being discussed.	• Acknowledge the student's engagement. • Encourage other students to join the dialogue. • Follow up with the student after class to obtain more information.
A student whom you have asked to stay after class bolts out the door without speaking to you.	• Angry or frustrated • Confused • Worried • Exasperated	• The student knows he or she "messed up" and is scared and embarrassed. • The student genuinely forgot to remain behind. • The student hopes he or she can dodge the issue and you will let it drop. • The student believes you do not care.	• Reiterate that you want to speak to the student in order to help. • Reframe the conversation as making a plan with the student. • Reassure the student that you are not mad.

Without explanation, a student exceeds the number of absences allowed.			
A student consistently derails class by expressing frustration or by asking, "Why are we doing this?"			

We might think of the affective component of teaching in more positive ways as well. You might notice how you feel (and how your students respond) when you walk into the classroom smiling or when you nod encouragingly at each student as they speak in class. We can consider the affective component of teaching habits of mind—traits like curiosity or persistence—and how best to model this relationship for students (see Activity 5.7). And we might use our reflections on our own affective responses to find ways to heighten our interest in our students, strengthen our relationships with them, and remain active and interested in our job and field.

Reflections from experienced teachers

Teaching is a dynamic experience, which is part of what makes it so exciting. The challenges that you will face and the changes you will undergo can feel exhausting and destabilizing at times, however. Just as you might tell your students, remember that every challenge you face is your opportunity to reflect, to learn, and to grow. If you stay open to this idea, you will eventually forge a teaching persona that works for you as a teacher and as a person.

As you continue exploring these issues, consider the following insights from experienced teachers:

- Successful teachers explore the different roles they can occupy in the classroom. Balancing nurturing and supportive roles with challenging roles encourages students to stretch themselves, and allows teachers to notice which roles seem to aid different students in different situations.

- As they explore different roles, veteran teachers often find it helpful to consistently circle back to their philosophies of writing and teaching. Ask yourself, "When I occupy this role, are my actions congruent with my beliefs and theories about writing, process, and teaching?"

- Feelings, emotions, beliefs, and self-efficacy all play a role in effective teaching and learning. Experienced teachers have learned to pay attention to the complexities of the affective domain — their own affective responses, their students' responses and behaviors, and the interconnection between the two.

- Experienced teachers remember that a good source of information is students themselves. Ask students about the teaching styles that work for them, offer options in how you present information, and recognize that certain styles may not work for all students.

- Seasoned teachers often find themselves actively working to maintain their own positive self-efficacy. As you enter the classroom, remember that we are only human. Talking about difficulties and the affective dimension of teaching with other teachers — and even with students — can help us continue to grow and stay engaged.

As we have noted in prior chapters, you must test these pieces of wisdom for yourself, seeing how they align with your teaching persona and teaching philosophy. You may decide to integrate some of these ideas into your professional development plan (see Chapter 17), or you may set them aside for further reflection in the future.

Putting it together:
Integrating your persona, philosophy, and approach

Now that you have explored many of the possible teaching roles and have considered how these roles mesh with your philosophies about teaching and writing, it is time to bring the components of this chapter together. After reviewing your notes from this chapter and perhaps looking back at your notes from the first two chapters, think about how you might describe your teaching persona to a hiring committee.

 Activity 3.7   Articulating your evolving philosophy

Use the first column of this chart to list eight to ten terms or concepts that describe your persona. Next to each term, note how it connects to your teaching philosophy.

Key term or concept describing your persona:	How it relates to your teaching philosophy:

Now you will write a paragraph or two in your teaching journal to help you flesh out a description of your developing teaching persona. As you write, try to be as specific as possible about how you will accomplish your goals in the classroom. For example, what might you do to ensure your questions are engaging, or how might you practice caring? As always, be sure to connect your ideas about your teaching persona to your developing teaching philosophy.

Activity 3.8   Synthesizing ideas about your persona, activities, and philosophy

In your teaching journal, discuss the following questions. Be sure to note any questions or issues that you are still wrestling with.

- Who do you hope to be as a teacher?
- How do you want to present yourself and your teaching persona in the classroom?
- How do your ideas about your teaching persona connect to your teaching philosophy?

This chapter has given you a chance to explore in more depth the roles you might occupy as a teacher and to consider how these roles might be enacted in the classroom. Since teaching personas evolve and change, sometimes in response to the needs of different student populations, this might be a useful chapter to return to throughout your career. Keeping this range of roles in mind will also help you further explore one of the most challenging negotiations teachers face: negotiating authority, which is the subject of Chapter 4.

Further Reading

- Gibson, Michelle, Deborah Meem, and Martha Marinara. "Bi, Butch, and Bar Dyke: Pedagogical Performances of Class, Gender, and Sexuality." *College Composition and Communication* 52.1 (2000): 69–95. Print.

- Lindquist, Julie. "Class Affects, Classroom Affectations: Working through the Paradoxes of Strategic Empathy." *College English* 67.2 (2004): 187–209. Print.

- Tobin, Lad. "Reading Students, Reading Ourselves: Revising the Teacher's Role in the Writing Classroom." *College English* 53.3 (1991): 333–48. Print.

- ---. "Self-Disclosure as a Strategic Tool: What I Do and Do Not Tell My Students." *College English* 73.2 (2010): 196–206. Print.

CHAPTER 4

Choices about Your Authority as a Teacher

In Chapter 3, you explored the roles you may adopt as a teacher and were introduced to the roles you may be given by dint of your institutional authority. When we enter the classroom, we are more than just ourselves; we also carry with us the authority and expectations that define us professionally. At best, these institutional valences help us clearly articulate our expectations and rationale to students and allow us to connect the work we do in our individual classrooms to a larger curriculum or to students' progress in their course of study. At worst, the stamp of institutional authority can mask a clear sense of *why* we are teaching in certain ways or asking students to complete particular tasks, resulting in an unproductive "because I said so" mentality. It often takes us many years as teachers to find productive ways to balance and negotiate the authority we possess in the classroom. In this chapter, we will further explore the dimensions of authority that mark teaching, as well as the tensions you might feel between the roles you choose to occupy and the institutional roles imposed on you by others.

> " I vividly remember my first two years teaching: I would stand at the front of the class, give directions, and feel like an imposter. Did I know enough to be leading this class? Would they find out I was a fraud? In retrospect, these insecurities led me to be more authoritative than I wanted or needed to be; I wanted to keep everything under control so that students would respect me, my authority, and the work of the class. I wish I had known then that other new teachers were undoubtedly feeling the same insecurities.
>
> —*Tara*

How will you negotiate your authority in the classroom?

Many issues can complicate our relationship with authority. When first entering the teaching profession, some teachers are close in age to their students or appear young. Some fear that students will test their authority because of their age, gender, race, or ethnicity. If you are new to teaching, you may feel that students perceive you as a novice. Indeed, there are moments when you might perceive yourself that way (or even think of yourself as an imposter who will soon be found out). These factors, or others, may lead to a heightened awareness of your authority in the classroom, sometimes resulting in an overextension of authoritative behavior to "save face" or to "lay down the law" to minimize the risk of being challenged.

Certainly, we want our students to respect us and the class, especially as mutual respect contributes to a positive learning environment. It thus can be helpful to remember the range of roles we can occupy, such as the roles we explored in Chapter 3. Clear, consistent expectations (with exceptions when necessary) can go far in establishing an equitable environment where everyone works together. However, you will need to explore your relationship with authority in the classroom as you begin teaching, as you develop as a teacher, and even as you encounter different groups of students. As you work to draw on your strengths as an individual and as a teacher, experiment a bit with how authoritative you'd like to be in the classroom and, most importantly, why. Articulate your rationale to your students so they know the intellectual reasons for the rules you enforce or the standards you determine. If you want to be firm about attendance because you have a discussion-based classroom, for example, be sure to make that reasoning clear. In Activity 4.1, you will examine pairs of tensions that teachers often negotiate, positioning yourself between these tensions.

 Activity 4.1   Mapping your beliefs about authority

Circle any ideas that resonate with you, and mark with an asterisk any ideas that cause tension. Unpack at least one of the tensions in your teaching journal.

Beliefs about teacher authority . . .	
Deadlines should have some flexibility. ⟷	Deadlines should be firm.
Boundaries and expectations should be developed with students as needed. ⟷	Clear boundaries are necessary and promote success.
Students often have a good reason for not adhering to certain course policies (e.g., attendance, no cell phones). ⟷	There is rarely a good reason for not adhering to course policies.
It is my job to adapt to students. ⟷	It is the student's job to adapt to my class.
If students do not fulfill a component of the class, it means they probably need more targeted support. ⟷	If students do not fulfill a component of the class, it means they have not made the class a priority.
"Extenuating circumstances" are a reality and affect everyone. ⟷	"Extenuating circumstances" are often just excuses.

YOUR TEACHING JOURNAL: Engaging with tensions
You will notice that the beliefs on the left might be described as "accommodating" and the beliefs on the right might be described as "firm." In your teaching journal, consider the following questions:

- Which side resonated more with your teaching philosophy? Why do you think this is so?
- Now think about the other side: In what teaching contexts or in what situations might it be beneficial for you to adopt those less comfortable notions of authority?
- In what ways might those notions enrich or add another dimension to your teaching?
- How would you discuss authority in the classroom with colleagues or a hiring committee?

As you may have noticed, issues about authority can often emerge when you are asked to make an exception for a particular student. New teachers sometimes believe that exceptions are not fair to other students. However, we all know that extenuating circumstances and individual challenges make a "one size fits all" approach unrealistic. This is particularly the case when you are working with a socioeconomically diverse student population; you will have some students who are juggling an almost overwhelming load of responsibilities in the realms of work, home, and school.

For such students, we recommend that you try to strike a balance between being consistent and making exceptions when they are warranted. Ask yourself, "Will saying yes to this particular request help the student in the long run?" Whether you decide to say yes or no to a particular request or make a particular exception, be sure to track the outcome and reflect on whether it was the right choice. Who benefited from your decision? Were there any negative consequences? You can use this information to negotiate and tweak the ways you use your authority in the classroom, eventually finding a productive authority role that you feel comfortable occupying.

You can use a chart such as the one that follows to help you track your decisions and their results. Consider using your teaching journal to note impressions, ideas, successes, and failures and to gather information to guide your future decisions.

Exception or decision	Who benefited, and how?	Any negative consequences?	Takeaway notes for the future
I extended a deadline for Amy, whose dad was in the hospital.	Amy appreciated my flexibility, which allowed her to focus on her family. She was able to complete the assignment without worrying.	Amy did not have her draft for peer workshop, but she worked in a brainstorming group with others.	This felt like the right decision, especially for a usually responsible student who was obviously going through a tough time emotionally.
I made very flexible deadlines for Tim, who was dealing with recurring health issues.	This decision seemed to relieve Tim's stress and insecurity.	Too much leniency may have hindered Tim from feeling like he was making progress. At the end of the semester, Tim had to take a grade of "incomplete."	Perhaps giving all students two "late essay passes" would have encouraged Tim to meet other deadlines and use his "passes" only when necessary, encouraging him to capitalize on those days when he felt good.

Relationships and boundaries with students

In any difficult situation in which you must balance competing roles or negotiate issues of authority, you will need to make a decision that you can stand behind. If you find yourself in a difficult situation, or you are just not sure how to proceed, remember that you can consult with any resources available to you, like the department chair or the director of your writing program. A good rule of thumb before making any hard decision is to try to objectively weigh the costs and benefits of your decision and then sleep on it.

Part of finding a productive and appropriate authoritative role is being mindful of the relationships you build with students while also being attentive to constructing appropriate boundaries. Sometimes students will be the ones to reach out to you as a resource, perhaps asking you to be a confidant as they share personal, sometimes troubling, information (as explored in Chapter 3). This can be a challenging and at times unsettling position to be placed in; you are not a therapist, but you are a trusted adult and a caring human being. When students reach out to you in this way, they do so in part because of your authority: They think you may be able to help. Do your best to acknowledge what the student shares, to listen, and to be empathetic. Help if you can. Depending on the situation, you may find that you need to establish some boundaries or point students to others who are more qualified to help. For example, you might say, "I hear what you are experiencing; that must be incredibly difficult. Let me help you find someone who can better help you than I can."

Although this is an uncommon occurrence, some students might take advantage of their relationship with you, perhaps unknowingly, in ways that make you uncomfortable. If this is the case, calmly and clearly reestablish appropriate boundaries. Remember that you can always reach out to your colleagues, the person in the office next to yours, your chair, or the director of your writing program if you need extra assistance in working with a troubled or difficult student.

A related issue concerns the way you represent your students and your work to others, whether that be your family and friends, your colleagues, segments of the public, or organizations involved in supporting education. In each of these exchanges, try to honor your students, their struggles, and their efforts in your words. Carry this attitude of advocacy back into the classroom. Particularly since you are in a position of authority, it is important that you use that authority to respect and champion students instead of maligning them. This not only improves your self-efficacy as a teacher but when students feel you are on their side, it also improves their motivation, benefiting both sides of the teacher-student relationship. And using your authority as a vehicle for respecting students through your words and actions has the potential to strengthen support for education even more broadly.

Turning to the field:
Negotiating authority as a developmental process

Figuring out how to negotiate authority is often a lengthy process that may change over time. Longtime teacher and preeminent scholar of student writing Mina Shaughnessy puts some of these issues into perspective in her seminal article "Diving In: An Introduction to Basic Writing." Although written in 1976, her article chronicles the struggles and changes many new teachers experience as they seek to uphold the expectations of the academy and develop themselves and their pedagogies.

Shaughnessy describes the process that she went through as a developing teacher by identifying four stages: Guarding the Tower, Converting the Natives, Sounding the Depths, and Diving In. From the obvious metaphors involved, we can see how new teachers often initially feel more allegiance to the rules and practices of the academy than they do to their students. Initially, some teachers feel that they need to uphold the university's standards in such a way that students are kept out, or they feel the need to "convert" students fully into the sacred realm of academia. In both cases, the teacher is not really learning from his or her students or responding to their needs, but rather is choosing to believe in the immutability of the content or practices that students should "just learn."

When teachers move toward the next stage, Sounding the Depths, they begin to reflect on how well the specific choices they are making in the classroom are

> "A key learning moment happened for me the first time a student asked a question and I responded, "I don't know. How could we find out?" Nothing happened: The class didn't implode; students didn't walk out or snicker. In fact, they seemed to respect my acknowledgment that I didn't know it all. Thinking back, I now realize that admitting what I didn't know actually opened up the classroom dynamic, enabling students to bring their knowledge more to the fore.
>
> —Mark

working; they begin to acknowledge both the "sophistication" that students bring with them in terms of prior knowledge and the "complexity" demanded by writing and specific writing tasks. With this level of reflection in place, teachers can "dive in" and study their students, student learning and writing processes, and themselves as teachers who are also learning.

Taking it further:
Your beliefs about developmental writers

As we have just explored, Shaughnessy provides a framework for thinking about your responsibilities as a teacher. Particularly when your subject is composition—a subject that has historically been connected to issues of access and social justice—careful consideration of your attitude toward students and their written work is a large part of discovering how to be an effective teacher. Although you will have to explore much of this terrain on your own when you begin teaching, continual reflection and an understanding of how teachers develop and change over time can give you a head start on developing a cohesive, successful teaching persona that effectively balances issues of authority. Engaging with Shaughnessy's ideas requires critical self-reflection, but her developmental model of teaching saves new teachers much trial and tribulation. In Activity 4.2, you will explore how your beliefs fit with the framework Shaughnessy provides.

 Activity 4.2 Examining your views of students

In the left column, we have matched statements teachers might make to Shaughnessy's four stages of teacher development. Circle any ideas that resonate with you, and mark with an asterisk any ideas that cause tension. Then use the right column to unpack how you would examine or modify your beliefs.

Shaughnessy's stages of teacher development:	How might you examine or modify this belief?
Guarding the Tower • "So many students — or even all! — seem unprepared." • "These students can't do college-level work. They just aren't ready." • "I feel I need to emphasize standards. I might even have to lower those standards so students can get by."	
Converting the Natives • "Some students might be able to learn, but I'm going to have to do a lot of work to bring them around." • "Students need so much, and they want the knowledge I have so they can succeed and gain access to more opportunities. My job is to give students my knowledge." • "There's a lot to cover, especially about correctness, mechanics, and correct forms." • "I sometimes feel frustrated that students can't learn the simple things I'm teaching them."	

Sounding the Depths • "Are the things I'm teaching really as simple as I thought?" • "In my students' work, the nature of error seems to be contextual and changing." • "Sometimes it seems as if there is a logic to the errors students are making." • "I feel myself trying to puzzle through these difficulties, reading more for students' intentions. I find myself reflecting more on teaching writing and my students."	
Diving In • "Instead of trying to 'remediate' students, I think I also need to 'remediate' myself to learn more about writing and teaching writing." • "There are some things that students don't know how to do, but there is a lot they do know how to do." • "I feel I have a different attitude about error and my students, and I'm guided by my desire to nurture their incipient excellence." • "I strive for new knowledge that will help me and my students learn."	

Reflections from experienced teachers

As we have explored in this chapter, it is not uncommon for new teachers to feel like imposters or frauds when they first begin teaching. Although they have much to offer students, the authority they have been granted sometimes feels like a mismatch for their experience and expertise. Students, however, do not know whether a teacher is teaching for the first time (unless, of course, they are told). As a new teacher, you will feel more confident and act with more assurance if you thoroughly and thoughtfully plan your lessons and if you clearly articulate your goals and rationales to students. (Chapter 1 and Chapter 2 might be helpful in this regard.) Although there may be some bumps along the way, you will start to feel comfortable in your teaching role soon enough. Keep learning from and listening to your students, and you will eventually craft an effective teaching persona that feels comfortable yet remains flexible in response to new situations and students.

As you negotiate the different positions you must occupy as a teacher, keep in mind the following ideas from seasoned teachers. They will help you make your own informed choices.

- Experienced teachers try to remember that they are always learning along with their students. Notice where students challenge their assumptions, and think about what students can teach the teacher.

- Intellectual rationales can go further toward promoting learning goals and helping students understand those goals than "just do it" decrees. If you have good learning-based reasons for your policies and explain those reasons to students, they will understand your expectations and why those expectations are important to their success.

- Many teachers find that keeping track of decisions that were difficult and charting their outcomes (perhaps in a teaching journal) gives them more solid data to use to make increasingly better decisions in the future.

- When grading, teachers' authority sometimes seems to collide with other elements of their teaching personas. (We discuss this topic further in the chapter on assessment, Chapter 14.) For now, you might remember that after you grade papers or establish end-of-term grades, it is often helpful to map the spread of grades. Does this tell you anything? Is everything in order? Do the grades feel right? Wait a day before submitting them just to make sure.

- Nothing can substitute for talking through challenging situations with others who understand and can offer you their insight. The best teachers reach out to other teachers, colleagues, and administrators as needed to find support, strategies, and solutions.

Putting it together: Balancing chosen roles and institutionally imposed roles

Negotiating authority in the classroom is tricky because it is so situational. There is rarely a single right way to uphold institutional authority and promote learning. On a moment-by-moment basis teachers must weigh their responsibilities and standards alongside the learning needs, desires, and goals of individual students and make decisions accordingly.

 Activity 4.3 Articulating your key notions of teacher authority

Imagine that you are preparing for a job interview and will be asked for your views about negotiating teacher authority. In the first column of the chart, brainstorm several key words or terms that you would want to include in your discussion. In the second column, provide a real or hypothetical example that illustrates your views. Then, in the third column, explain the connections between your views of authority and your general teaching philosophy.

Key words about authority:	Specific examples illustrating each key word:	How does each example connect to your teaching philosophy?

Now you are ready to describe your views on teacher authority, drawing on all the activities in this chapter.

Activity 4.4 Negotiating your roles as a teacher

In your teaching journal, discuss the following questions. Be sure to note any questions or issues that you are still wrestling with.

- How will you negotiate authority as a teacher, both in your chosen teacher roles and in institutionally imposed teacher roles?
- How does your negotiation strategy connect to your teaching philosophy?

In this chapter, you have explored how you can balance your authority as a teacher with your teaching persona to best achieve learning goals and support your students. Crafting a teaching persona that students respond well to and that they can trust is an ongoing process; however, remaining aware and reflecting on the authority you bring to the classroom can help inform your decision-making process and guide you in developing a teaching persona that works for both you and your students. As you move forward to Part 2 and start designing actual materials, it will help to keep the persona you have begun to construct in mind as a way to animate your decisions. Likewise, as you begin mapping your course goals (Chapter 5) and writing and reading assignments (Chapter 6 and Chapter 7), new issues may arise that complicate your understanding of your teacher roles. If so, you may find it helpful to return to this chapter and the notes you have made in your teaching journal.

Further Reading

- Bloom, Lynn. "Why I Used to Hate Giving Grades." *College Composition and Communication* 48.3 (1997): 360–71. Print.
- Ching, Kory Lawson. "Peer Response in the Composition Classroom: An Alternative Genealogy." *Rhetoric Review* 26.3 (2007): 303–19. Print.
- Danielewicz, Jane, and Peter Elbow. "A Unilateral Grading Contract to Improve Teaching and Learning." *College Composition and Communication* 61.2 (2009): 244–68. Print.
- Shaughnessy, Mina. "Diving In: An Introduction to Basic Writing." *College Composition and Communication* 27.3 (1976): 234–39. Print.

PART 2

Designing Your Course

CHAPTER 5

Choices about Course Goals

No matter what level or type of course you are teaching, clearly articulated course goals can help you get started and stay focused in both your planning and your day-to-day teaching. Even if your department has very specific, predefined learning goals, it is important for you to think about how best to achieve these goals in ways that dovetail with your theories about writing and teaching (see Chapter 1 and Chapter 2). In this chapter, we will focus on articulating your specific course goals for a first-year writing class; however, you can adapt and use many of the strategies in this chapter to design and plan a class at any level. You will continue to build on the material in this chapter as you learn to construct effective writing assignments (Chapter 6) and reading assignments (Chapter 7).

How will you set goals for your course?

In the first two chapters, you explored your writing and teaching philosophies; then you considered your role and persona as a writing teacher. Building on that work and on the ideas and knowledge you already have about what a writing class can or should look like, you will now ponder your course goals. Your goals should be grounded in your philosophy of writing; however, you may find that your goals extend beyond writing per se to class community, reading, critical thinking, use of technology, and more. Your goals might be specific (e.g., "Students will pinpoint writing processes that work for them and practice when to use them") or more broad (e.g., "Students will feel more confident about writing"). And your goals will likely draw on what you already know about your department's values and objectives.

Activity 5.1 Fleshing out course goals

In the following chart, list five potential goals for your course—things that you would like your students to accomplish. Then brainstorm challenges that students may face in meeting these goals. Finally, brainstorm roles that you may need to take on to help students meet those goals. The chart should reflect where you are now with your class goals; these may change as you work through this chapter and continue to reflect on your objectives throughout the book.

Potential course goals:	Potential challenges for students:	Potential roles you will play:
1		
2		
3		
4		
5		

Articulating the values and goals that you will bring to your class as the teacher is an important first step and will help you identify what you believe about writing and what you have to offer your students. However, no one teaches in a vacuum; your department, your institution, your students, and even the wider culture have expectations about education and writing that you must respond to in some way. Now that you have a general sketch of the overriding goals for your course, it is time to do some research. To be a well-informed and responsible teacher, you need to find out what is expected of you at the departmental, institutional, and disciplinary levels. In this chapter you will find excerpts and examples of expectations from multiple institutional levels. Although the expectations will probably be similar for most teachers of composition, you should research the particular requirements of your department and specific university. Even if you are a more experienced teacher, it is a good idea to check in with departmental and university guidelines regularly, as they can change. And of course, whenever you change institutions or are assigned a new class, it is essential to do this research.

For example, many departments or writing programs collaborate internally to establish the overall learning goals for first-year writing courses. Some departments ask that instructors structure their composition courses in a certain fashion or use a particular textbook. Departments often have guidelines for composition that cover both big-picture issues (e.g., the department's "culture" or approach to teaching composition) as well as little-picture issues (e.g., how many classes students can miss before failing the course).

Your department might have a common syllabus or a core assignment that all teachers use, or you might have a good deal of freedom in designing your own course materials. Whatever the case, you may have access to syllabi from other instructors, which can be quite helpful in giving you a feel for what your colleagues are doing. Check with your department chair or writing program director if you have trouble finding the resources you need or pinning down what is expected of you.

In addition to fulfilling departmental goals, most composition classes are also expected to fulfill university writing requirements. You can usually find information about what your school expects from your course in the official university bulletin. If you have any questions about this, the writing program director or department chair is again your best source of information.

How will you navigate writing program and university mandates?

The best way to inform yourself about departmental expectations is to seek out documents that articulate those expectations, including composition syllabi, requirements, and guidelines. As an example, Activity 5.2 presents the course goals for all first-year composition courses at the University of Pittsburgh. As you read, note how this document establishes a particular culture of writing. Also note places where specific beliefs and theories about writing, the writing processes, and the teaching of writing are articulated. This kind of critical reading will help you practice decoding similar documents from your own institution.

Activity 5.2 Analyzing writing program goals

Circle any ideas that resonate with you, and mark with an asterisk any ideas that cause tension. Unpack at least one of the tensions in your teaching journal.

Engage in writing as a creative, disciplined form of critical inquiry:	Write with precision, nuance, and awareness of textual conventions:
In this course, you'll be asked to use writing to generate ideas as well as explain them. You'll form questions, explore problems, and examine your own experiences, thoughts, and observations. Investigating a multifaceted subject, you'll be expected to make productive use of uncertainty as you participate in sustained scrutiny of the issues at hand.	You'll work on crafting clear, precise prose that uses a variety of sentence and paragraph structures. You'll be required to learn the conventions for quoting and paraphrasing responsibly and adeptly, and you'll be assisted with editing and proofreading strategies that reflect attention to the relation between style and meaning. You'll also have opportunities to consider when and how to challenge conventions as well as follow them.
Compose thoughtfully crafted essays that position your ideas among other views:	**Revise your writing by rethinking the assumptions, aims, and effects of prior drafts:**
In response to reading and discussing challenging texts, you'll write essays in which you develop informed positions that engage with the positions of others. You'll analyze as well as summarize the texts you read, and you'll compose essays that pay close attention both to the ideas voiced by other writers and to specific choices they make with language and form.	This course approaches the essay as a flexible genre that takes on different forms in different contexts — not as a thesis-driven argument that adheres to a rigid structure. Much class time will be devoted to considering the purpose, logic, and design of your own writing, and you'll be given opportunities to revise your work in light of response from your teacher and peers, with the aim of making more attentive decisions as you write.

Source: University of Pittsburgh Department of English Composition Program, "Goals for First-Year Composition Courses." Copyright © 2012 by University of Pittsburgh. Reprinted by permission. www.composition.pitt.edu/undergraduate/first-year-composition.

YOUR TEACHING JOURNAL: Engaging with tensions

Choose the goal that you feel most uncomfortable with, and brainstorm about it in your teaching journal. Consider the following questions:

- How does this goal create tension with your teaching philosophy?
- Why do you think teachers and administrators at the University of Pittsburgh may have included this goal?
- Are there ways that you could fulfill this goal and still be true to your philosophy?

Now that you have seen one example of departmental guidelines, research the departmental guidelines at your own institution or at an institution where you would like to teach. Decode the guidelines as you practiced in Activity 5.2. Ask yourself, "What is the culture of writing in this department? What are the theories that underwrite these guidelines?" As you read through the documents from your department, make connections between your goals and those of the larger body. Focus especially on overlaps and similarities. It might help to print out and annotate the departmental guidelines.

Activity 5.3   Examining your departmental guidelines

Fill in the following chart, comparing your department's guidelines with your course goals, philosophies, and persona. Note both similarities and tensions.

What aspects of the departmental guidelines or culture fit your goals, philosophies, and persona? Explain.	What aspects of the departmental guidelines or culture cause tension or raise questions? Explain.

As you work to align your goals with those of your department or writing program, you might also investigate additional goals or guidelines that your university or college has for writing courses. Since writing courses are often required, your school may have additional language about how these courses serve or prepare students for their future coursework. You will want to know if students are required to take additional courses after they leave your course: If so, what are they, and how are the goals and outcomes both different (more advanced, perhaps) and connected (building on what students learn in your course)? Does your university promote a Writing across the Curriculum approach, where writing is emphasized in many classes, or a Writing in the Disciplines approach, where students will at some point have writing-intensive instruction in their major? Understanding the big picture of student trajectories through writing instruction at your university will help you pinpoint where your course fits in. It can also help you plan your course more effectively and discuss with your students how your course connects to other required writing courses.

As you construct the big picture of when and how students are asked to write throughout their college careers, you will often find information and policies about such things as academic integrity and disability resources at the institutional level. (Some of this information may be replicated by your department.) And you will find the official view of what your class should achieve and how it is situated in a student's overall course of study. You will thus want to think about the match between this official view and your course, as well as any dissonances (and the reasons for those dissonances). For example, here is an official course description that fulfills part of the general education writing requirement at the University of Illinois at Urbana-Champaign.

> **When I first looked at the list of outcomes for the first-year course I was assigned, I felt overwhelmed. How was I going to get students to practice analytical and persuasive writing, think about their writing processes and strategies, reflect on themselves as college students, and read diverse genres? It seemed like too much to even wrap my head around. But as I looked at other teachers' assignments and began brainstorming my own assignments, I found that just one assignment could often address many outcomes at the same time.**
>
> —*Mark*

Rhetoric 105: Writing and Research

Rhetoric 105: Writing and Research is instruction in research-based writing and the construction of academic, argumentative essays that use primary and secondary sources as evidence. This course fulfills the campus Composition I general education requirement. Credit is not given for both RHET 105 and any of these other Comp I courses: RHET 101, RHET 102, CMN 111, or CMN 112. Prerequisite: an ACT English score between 20–31.

After completing Rhetoric 105: Writing and Research, students will be able to:

- Identify and explain the role rhetorical appeals and the rhetorical triangle can play in nonfiction print and/or multimodal texts.
- Create and sustain across one or more pieces of writing a focused research question that responds to an exigent issue, problem, or debate.
- Compose cogent, research-based arguments, in print-based and/or multimodal texts, for specialist and/or nonspecialist audiences.
- Locate, accurately cite (through summary, paraphrasing, and quoting), and critically evaluate primary and secondary sources.
- Demonstrate knowledge of writing as a process, including consideration of peer and/or instructor feedback, in one or more pieces of writing from initial draft to final version.

Source: University of Illinois at Urbana-Champaign Department of English Undergraduate Rhetoric Program, "Rhetoric 105: Writing and Research." Copyright © 2008 by University of Illinois Board of Trustees. Reprinted by permission. www.english.illinois.edu/undergraduate/rhetoric/urp/courseofferings.

The course descriptions include information crucial to understanding how the program views these classes. You will notice how the program depicts the content of the classes by giving an official overview of the course, articulating what students will be able to do upon completion, and situating this course in relationship to requirements or other courses. You might notice prerequisites or other requirements or information, such as placement guidelines, that you will need to be familiar with as the teacher. Lastly, it is important to know that other pathways might exist for fulfilling requirements; if you follow the source link, for example, you will see that students can meet the same requirement by taking a different sequence of courses.

 Activity 5.4   Examining your institution's expectations

First, track down and examine the specific goals that your university or college has for its writing courses. Then use the following chart to summarize what you find, noting any other pertinent information about where your class falls in the sequence of requirements, prerequisites, and so on.

Institutional view of your class:	Other required classes (before or after) and their connection to your class:	Pertinent information, such as prerequisite placement methods, and options:

Now you will put all of this information together to get a snapshot view of the goals that will inform your class. Although it can feel like a lot to juggle, you will notice that goals often build in layers; each level, from your individual classroom to the department to the university, has certain expectations about what students should learn. Often these goals overlap or build upon one another.

Activity 5.5   Mapping overlaps and tensions between goals

To see how your class, department, and university goals overlap, map out these different goals and expectations in the following chart. Note any tensions between them.

Your goals, based on your philosophy:	Additional goals and expectations from your department:	Additional goals and expectations from your university:

Turning to the field:
Putting your goals in conversation with the discipline

A last level to keep in mind when shaping your course and its goals is the established scholarship and best practices articulated by the larger fields of composition, rhetoric, and literacy studies. Two documents in particular can help you situate and align your personal goals with those promoted by leading practitioners in the field. The next two activities feature excerpts from two important documents, the *WPA (Writing Program Administrators) Outcomes Statement for First-Year Composition* (updated in 2014) and the *Framework for Success in Postsecondary Writing* (2011), which was collaboratively authored by the Council of Writing Program Administrators (CWPA), the National Council of Teachers of English (NCTE), and the National Writing Project (NWP). We will discuss the term *outcome* in more detail shortly, but for now, consider how orienting yourself to the documents excerpted in Activity 5.6 and Activity 5.7 might help you further articulate and develop your own course goals.

Please follow the URL provided to access the full documents; it is suggested that you print out these documents and jot down notes about how the goals outlined by the larger field intersect with your own goals.

Activity 5.6   Analyzing goals and learning outcomes

Circle any ideas that resonate with you, and mark with an asterisk any ideas that cause tension. Unpack at least one of the tensions in your teaching journal.

Excerpt from WPA *Outcomes Statement for First-Year Composition*

> **Rhetorical knowledge**
>
> By the end of first-year composition, students should
>
> - Learn and use key rhetorical concepts through analyzing and composing a variety of texts.
> - Gain experience reading and composing in several genres to understand how genre conventions shape and are shaped by readers' and writers' practices and purposes.
> - Develop facility in responding to a variety of situations and contexts calling for purposeful shifts in voice, tone, level of formality, design, medium, and/or structure.
> - Understand and use a variety of technologies to address a range of audiences.
> - Match the capacities of different environments (e.g., print and electronic) to varying rhetorical situations.
>
> **Critical thinking, reading, and writing**
>
> By the end of first-year composition, students should
>
> - Use composing and reading for inquiry, learning, critical thinking, and communicating in various rhetorical contexts.
> - Read a diverse range of texts, attending especially to relationships between assertion and evidence, to patterns of organization, to the interplay between verbal and nonverbal elements, and to how these features function for different audiences and situations.
> - Locate and evaluate (for credibility, sufficiency, accuracy, timeliness, bias, and so on) primary and secondary research materials, including journal articles and essays, books, scholarly and professionally established and maintained databases or archives, and informal electronic networks and Internet sources.
> - Use strategies — such as interpretation, synthesis, response, critique, and design/redesign — to compose texts that integrate the writer's ideas with those from appropriate sources.

Source: Council of Writing Program Administrators, "WPA Outcomes Statement for First-Year Composition." Copyright © 2014 by the Council of Writing Program Administrators. Reprinted by permission. http://wpacouncil .org/positions/outcomes.html.

YOUR TEACHING JOURNAL: Engaging with tensions

Choose one of the outcomes that causes tension for you, and brainstorm about it in your teaching journal. Consider the following questions:

- How does this outcome cause tension with your teaching philosophy?
- Why do you think the writers of the document included this outcome and phrased it the way that they did?
- Are there ways that you can fulfill this outcome and still be true to your philosophy?

Similarly, peruse the excerpt in Activity 5.7 from the *Framework for Success in Postsecondary Writing*, circling any habits of mind that will be important to cultivate in your course.

Activity 5.7 Examining the *Framework for Success*

Circle any ideas that resonate with you, and mark with an asterisk any ideas that cause tension. Unpack at least one of the tensions in your teaching journal.

Excerpt from the *Framework for Success in Postsecondary Writing*

This Framework describes the rhetorical and twenty-first-century skills as well as habits of mind and experiences that are critical for college success. Habits of mind refers to ways of approaching learning that are both intellectual and practical and that will support students' success in a variety of fields and disciplines. The Framework identifies eight habits of mind essential for success in college writing:

- **Curiosity** — the desire to know more about the world.
- **Openness** — the willingness to consider new ways of being and thinking in the world.
- **Engagement** — a sense of investment and involvement in learning.
- **Creativity** — the ability to use novel approaches for generating, investigating, and representing ideas.
- **Persistence** — the ability to sustain interest in and attention to short- and long-term projects.
- **Responsibility** — the ability to take ownership of one's actions and understand the consequences of those actions for oneself and others.
- **Flexibility** — the ability to adapt to situations, expectations, or demands.
- **Metacognition** — the ability to reflect on one's own thinking as well as on the individual and cultural processes used to structure knowledge.

The Framework then explains how teachers can foster these habits of mind through writing, reading, and critical analysis experiences.

Source: Council of Writing Program Administrators, National Council of Teachers of English, and the National Writing Project, "Framework for Success in Postsecondary Writing." Copyright © 2011 by CWPA, NCTE, and NWP. Reprinted by permission. http://wpacouncil.org/framework.

YOUR TEACHING JOURNAL: Engaging with tensions
Choose one of the habits of mind that causes tension for you, and brainstorm about it in your teaching journal. Consider the following questions:

- How does this habit of mind cause tension or raise questions given your teaching philosophy?
- Why do you think the writers of the document included this habit of mind and phrased it the way that they did?

Now that you have reviewed some of the many goals that different constituencies have for composition courses and have thought about your philosophy of writing (Chapter 1) and your role as a teacher (Chapters 2 through 4), take some time to gather your thoughts.

Activity 5.8 Parsing the demands of first-year composition

Synthesize your initial impressions of the materials you have reviewed by answering the following questions about the goals for your first-year composition course.

1. What do you want students to learn?

2. What does your department or writing program want students to learn?

3. What does your institution want students to learn?

4. What do you imagine students themselves want to learn?

5. What goals overlap between the four levels above? What tensions or gaps are present that you need to keep thinking about or ask others about?

You have already come a long way in terms of articulating your course goals and beginning to align them with larger institutional responsibilities. The next step is to begin to particularize the more specific learning objectives that will help your students achieve the overall goals for the class. The terms *course goal* and *learning objective* often overlap or are unclear, and they may be used differently at different institutions or in different locations. Typically, *course goals* are overarching (and sometimes abstract) goals you are striving to meet, whereas *learning objectives* are typically more discrete tasks or strategies that help students achieve the overall course goals. One additional term that you may encounter is *learning outcome* (or *student learning outcome, SLO*). This term is often a more measurable manifestation of an objective: Outcomes are benchmarks which can be assessed to demonstrate that students did in fact learn a specific skill, practice, or idea.

The chart that follows demonstrates how course goals can be related to learning objectives and learning outcomes. Notice how each item, although related to the others, focuses on a different level of learning.

Big-picture course goals: What do you want students to achieve? How do you want them to leave your class?	More specific learning objectives: What will you ask students to do to help them achieve these goals? What would practicing these goals look like in a classroom?	Measurable student learning outcomes (SLOs): What could administrators or others pinpoint that would show that students had achieved these goals? (Outcomes are more bureaucratic and action-oriented in tone.)
• Students will become better writers.	• Students will write regularly and copiously, with many opportunities to revise. • Students will read and write in a range of genres. • Students will consistently reflect on their writing, including what they have done well and what they need to continue to practice.	• Students will write effective expository prose. • Students will use mechanics and grammar correctly. • Students will use evidence and analysis successfully.
• Students will be able to use technology productively and critically to achieve their learning and writing goals.	• Students will practice both informal and formal research, learning about a range of sources and how to evaluate those sources. • Students will use Web 2.0 to share writing (blogs), collaborate and consolidate knowledge (class wiki), and connect with the campus community.	• Students will be able to use a range of sources in their writing. • Students will be able to evaluate sources for bias. • Students will use technology effectively to research, revise writing, and share writing.
• Students will learn what it means to be part of an engaged, intellectual community and will be introduced to academic discourses and academic writing.	• Students will regularly participate in peer review and collaborative activities as respectful, constructive group members. • Students will explore challenging texts and ideas and will formulate their own thoughtful and thorough texts in response.	• Students will utilize a research plan to locate, use, and synthesize information from multiple sources. • Students will demonstrate academic integrity in their writing, including correct use and citation of others' work.

To concretize these differences and to begin particularizing the learning objectives for your course in relation to your overall course goals, look back at the writing you have done in this chapter (Activities 5.1, 5.4, and 5.8 especially). Take a minute to reassess your overall course goals: Have they changed or shifted at all? If so, revise them to reflect where you are now in your thinking.

Activity 5.9 Translating course goals into learning objectives

In the following chart, list three broad goals that you want to achieve in your course. Then, break each goal down into smaller learning objectives. Finally, try to phrase those learning objectives as measurable outcomes.

Course goals: What do you want students to achieve? How do you want them to leave your class?	Learning objectives: What will you ask students to do to help them achieve these goals? What would practicing these goals look like in a classroom?	Measurable learning outcomes: What could administrators or others pinpoint that would show that students had achieved these goals?

Taking it further:
Bridging the tensions between conflicting goals

After pondering goals, objectives, and outcomes, you are now familiar with even more of the tensions inherent in a first-year writing class. Use Activity 5.10 to situate your own views among common tensions in the field regarding course goals.

 Activity 5.10   Balancing competing tensions regarding course goals

For each pair, circle any ideas that resonate with you, and mark with an asterisk any ideas that cause tension.

Common tensions in composition . . .		
I want to let students play with language, take risks, and enjoy writing.	←——————→	I have to evaluate their work fairly.
I want to give students freedom to choose how they write.	←——————→	I want to challenge students to write in new ways beyond their comfort zone.
I want to follow what I think is important pedagogically.	←——————→	I have to get students ready for the next class.
I want students to be exposed to a lot of meaningful reading.	←——————→	I do not want the reading to overwhelm the focus on writing.
I want to help students improve their grammar and style.	←——————→	I do not want to focus too narrowly on mechanics at the expense of students' ideas.

YOUR TEACHING JOURNAL: Engaging with tensions

Using one of the tensions in the chart, brainstorm a potential writing assignment that could allow students (and you) to accomplish the goals on both ends of the tension spectrum. In drafting the assignment, consider the following questions:

- What is the concept or name of the assignment?
- What are the key goals of the assignment?
- How would this assignment meet one of the goals on the tension spectrum?
- How would this assignment meet the opposite goal at the other end of the tension spectrum?
- How would you word the assignment so that it does not seem contradictory to students?

Reflections from experienced teachers

Although there are no easy resolutions to the tensions listed in Activity 5.10, it can help to remember that teaching is an ongoing practice: If you stay alert to the decisions you make, noting when you err too far on one side of a particular tension, you will continually strengthen your teaching practice. Reflecting on your teaching, revising your pedagogy, and assessing your teaching again—this is what being a reflective practitioner is all about. Consider how the following reflections from experienced teachers might also assist you in developing your course goals:

- Teachers are excited and motivated when they are aware of and draw on their own central values about writing. Experienced teachers connect these values, though, to larger goals in their program and in the discipline by continuing to read and talking to others about their teaching choices.

- The strongest teachers, then, usually do not accept their values about writing, learning, and teaching as eternal commitments but are instead open to new research, data gained from observing and talking to students, and new practices they learn from other teachers.

- Department-mandated learning outcomes can feel overwhelming at times. Remembering that each assignment often fulfills or works toward multiple outcomes or learning objectives can give some perspective and help teachers meet competing course goals in ways that feel manageable.

- In a similar fashion, university and department expectations and outcomes can often be both very abstract and at times quite ambitious; instead of being frustrated, teachers can productively view these vague directives as expectations that have some built-in flexibility.

- Do not be afraid to share your rationale with your students as you teach, telling them what they are practicing and why. This is a great time to connect what you are actually doing in class to specific learning objectives or course goals, since knowing why we do what we do helps us learn.

- Effective teachers find ways to keep track of how their teaching is or is not meeting specific goals. Many keep a journal in which they note successes, challenges, and impressions; others make additional notes on their daily lesson plans after class ends or students have turned in work. Having these notes can be a useful way to reflect, revise, test new strategies, and then reflect again, as well as a useful way to remember what worked and what should be revised next term.

- Remember that many other teachers have tackled the challenge of creating interesting and engaging assignments that fulfill specific goals. Identifying and drawing on resources and colleagues who can help is a central way that teachers stay up to date and infuse new practices into their teaching.

Putting it together:
Anchoring key course goals in your teaching philosophy

As you can see from the work you have completed in this chapter, teaching a composition class can sometimes feel like a juggling act: Everyone seems to have a stake in what should be valued and what needs to be accomplished. Returning regularly to your key course goals and your philosophy and revising them as needed will help you stay grounded. And checking in with your colleagues and staying abreast of developments and recommendations from the field will allow you to feel confident that your students are working toward the goals and objectives that will promote their success as writers.

This chapter has explored the many facets, expectations, and stakeholders that can shape your course goals for a first-year or other course. Each of these is crucial. However, the goals that came to your mind at the beginning of this chapter will often be the goals that you will cherish most as a teacher. You will want to keep these ideals in the back of your mind, even as you develop and design a range of assignments that will support students in both attaining your course goals and meeting other required expectations. Of all of the chapters in this book, this chapter may be the one you return to most frequently. You will want to revisit the foundational questions of this chapter again and again:

- What goals are most crucial to me for my composition class?

- Why do I value these goals?

- Why are these goals essential, given the population I am going to teach?

- How do these goals reflect the programmatic goals to which I am accountable?

Activity 5.11 Explaining your goals, values, student population, and program

Imagine that you are preparing for a job interview and that you will be asked to discuss a specific course (perhaps the one that you are using this book to design). In the space provided, brainstorm some key words or terms that will help you address the four foundational questions listed earlier. Be sure to connect your answers to your teaching philosophy.

To synthesize everything you have done so far, describe your key goals for a specific writing class (one that you are teaching or one that you hope to teach). Use the brainstorm you have just completed as well as other activities from this chapter, recognizing that your goals may have shifted from the beginning of this chapter. Explain how your goals are anchored in your beliefs about good student writing (Activity 1.11), your beliefs about writing processes (Activity 1.12), your beliefs about effective teaching (Activity 2.9), and of course the needs of your students. Remember that your knowledge of students' needs can be informed by both department and university guidelines (Activity 5.3 and Activity 5.4) as well as your own knowledge of student needs (Activity 5.8).

Activity 5.12 Connecting your goals and rationales

In your teaching journal, discuss the following questions. Be sure to note any questions or issues that you are still wrestling with.

- What are your key course goals?
- What are your rationales for those goals?
- How are your goals anchored in your beliefs about good writing, writing processes, effective teaching, and the needs of your students?

After exploring this chapter, you should have a sense of your key goals for the course, as well as how these goals dovetail with larger expectations held by the field and your institution. You should also have a better sense of how your course goals connect to your philosophies about writing and teaching from Chapter 1 and Chapter 2. As you progress through the following chapters, and especially as you work to create specific assignments and activities in Chapters 6, 7, and 9, it will be important to return to this chapter to check in with your goals. Notice whether your goals remain consistent or whether they shift. Ask yourself why this might be the case. It is perfectly fine to revise your goals as you move forward, but remember that at the end of the day (or the beginning of your class!) you should have a clear, strong sense of where you are headed and why.

Further Reading

- Bartholomae, David. "Inventing the University." *When a Writer Can't Write: Studies in Writer's Block and Other Composing-Process Problems*. Ed. Mike Rose. New York: Guilford, 1985. Rpt. in *Cross-Talk in Comp Theory: A Reader*. 3rd ed. Ed. Victor Villanueva. Urbana: NCTE, 2011. 523–54. Print.

- *Common Core State Standards Initiative*. National Governors Association and the Council of Chief State School Officers. 2014. Web. 29 Sept. 2014. <http://www.corestandards.org>.

- Elbow, Peter. "Embracing Contraries in the Teaching Process." *College English* 45.4 (1983): 327–39. Print.

- Emig, Janet. "Writing as a Mode of Learning." *College Composition and Communication* 28.2 (1977): 122–28. Print.

- *Framework for Success in Postsecondary Writing*. Council of Writing Program Administrators, National Council of Teachers of English, and the National Writing Project. January 2011. Web. 29 Sept. 2014. <http://wpacouncil.org/framework>.

- Shipka, Jody. "Multimodal Task-Based Framework for Composing." *College Composition and Communication* 57.2 (2005): 277–306. Print.

- *WPA Outcomes Statement for First-Year Composition 3.0*. Council of Writing Program Administrators. 17 July 2014. Web. 29 Sept. 2014. <http://wpacouncil.org/positions/outcomes.html>.

CHAPTER 6

Choices about Writing Assignments

Your writing assignments are the backbone of your writing course. Informed by the philosophy of teaching that you drafted in Chapters 1 through 4 and the course goals you pinpointed in Chapter 5, your writing assignments will inform all the work you do daily in your class. Although there is room to make changes throughout the semester, having a clear vision of your writing assignments—including why you are assigning a particular type and amount of writing—and how your writing assignments connect to and build on one another will help you construct a purposeful and cohesive course. Drafting assignments and articulating the connections between them is the work of this chapter.

What kinds of writing will students do in your class?

In this chapter, we will examine how to make informed choices about the number and types of writing assignments you will include in your course, the sequencing of assignments, and the connection between larger writing assignments and the daily work you will do in class. We will begin with an activity aimed at articulating the kinds of writing that are most important for you and your students.

Activity 6.1   Determining the types of writing (genres) you will assign

Answer the following questions as you consider the types of writing you will assign.

1. What types of writing are you planning to assign for the major writing assignments in your class (e.g., argumentative writing, expository writing, narrative/personal writing, research-based writing)?

2. Why have you selected these types of writing? Consider both your class goals and any institutional guidelines.

3. How will each kind of writing serve your students? Why do your students need to practice this kind of writing?

Turning to the field:
Goals and genres for your writing class

Of course, the kinds of writing you assign will need to be in dialogue with goals larger than your own, including the goals of your department, your university, and the larger field (Chapter 5). Consider, for example, the first category of learning goals presented in the *Framework for Success in Postsecondary Writing*: "Developing Rhetorical Knowledge." This category offers a good entryway into thinking about what your writing assignments should encourage in student writing.

 Activity 6.2   Working with the *Framework for Success*

Circle any ideas that resonate with you, and mark with an asterisk any ideas that cause tension. Unpack at least one of the tensions in your teaching journal.

Developing rhetorical knowledge

Rhetorical knowledge is the ability to analyze and act on understandings of audiences, purposes, and contexts in creating and comprehending texts.

Rhetorical knowledge is the basis of good writing. By developing rhetorical knowledge, writers can adapt to different purposes, audiences, and contexts. Study of and practice with basic rhetorical concepts such as purpose, audience, context, and conventions are important as writers learn to compose a variety of texts for different disciplines and purposes. For example, a writer might draft one version of a text with one audience in mind, then revise the text to meet the needs and expectations of a different audience.

Teachers can help writers develop rhetorical knowledge by providing opportunities and guidance for students to

- learn and practice key rhetorical concepts such as audience, purpose, context, and genre through writing and analysis of a variety of types of texts (nonfiction, informational, imaginative, printed, visual, spatial, auditory, and otherwise);

- write and analyze a variety of types of texts to identify
  - the audiences and purposes for which they are intended,
  - the key choices of content, organization, evidence, and language use made by their author(s),
  - the relationships among these key choices and the ways that the text(s) appeal or speak to different audiences;
- write for different audiences, purposes, and contexts;
- write for real audiences and purposes, and analyze a writer's choices in light of those audiences and purposes; and
- contribute, through writing, their own ideas and opinions about a topic to an ongoing conversation.

Source: Council of Writing Program Administrators, National Council of Teachers of English, and the National Writing Project, "Framework for Success in Postsecondary Writing." Copyright © 2011 by CWPA, NCTE, and NWP. Reprinted by permission. http://wpacouncil.org/framework.

YOUR TEACHING JOURNAL: Engaging with tensions

Choose the activity that least resonates with you, and brainstorm about it in your teaching journal. Consider the following questions:

- Why does this activity not resonate with you? Is it in tension with your beliefs about good writing or writing processes, your course goals, or any other elements of your teaching philosophy?
- Is there a way to bridge this idea and your teaching philosophy?

Now take your brainstorming a bit further by putting Activity 6.1 and Activity 6.2 more directly in conversation. For each type or genre of writing you listed in Activity 6.1, try to break out both the purpose of the genre and the specific skills students will need to write successfully in that genre.

Consider argumentative writing as an example. You might determine that the purpose of a piece of argumentative writing is to convince others of a particular point of view and perhaps get them to act on that point of view. Next, by reflecting on what makes argumentative writing effective, you might conclude that the most important features of this genre are a clear, debatable thesis or controlling idea; the use of a range of rhetorical appeals, from logos (logical appeals) to pathos (emotional appeals); and an acknowledgment and refutation of possible counterarguments.

Activity 6.3 Matching genre and purpose

Use the following chart to focus on three or four kinds of writing you will assign for major writing projects throughout the term. If you plan to focus on one type of writing—such as argument—throughout the entire term, feel free to use the boxes to map subgenres (e.g., problem/solution argumentative writing, research-based argumentative writing, and so forth).

Type of writing:	What is the purpose of this type of writing?	What makes a piece of writing in this genre successful?	What rhetorical knowledge is needed to compose successfully in this genre?

In breaking out the purpose and specific elements or components of different types of writing, you have put your tacit knowledge of *genre* to work — you have begun to think about the expectations readers have for different types of writing. This genre awareness is the first step in articulating for yourself, and eventually for your students, what makes a given piece of writing successful or effective.

You have also begun to think about your rationale for assigning certain kinds of writing. As you may have anticipated, this decision is not solely up to you and your individual preferences; rather, it needs to be in line with the expectations of your department and institution. As with every decision you make in your work with this book, you will need to keep your philosophy of writing and an awareness of your student population at the forefront of your mind as you are building the backbone of your course through your writing assignments. If you look back to the initial writing you completed in this chapter, you should have a clear sense of why you are assigning the writing you listed. You might even compare the types of writing you listed in Activity 6.1 and Activity 6.3 to the goals you articulated in Chapter 5 to make sure the writing you assign matches your overall goals for the course.

Activity 6.4   Matching assignments to goals and outcomes

Keeping your philosophy and students in mind, use the following chart to refresh your memory about how the types of writing you will assign connect to both your personal class goals and institutional expectations or outcomes.

What types of writing will you assign?	How will this writing help fulfill your course goals?	How will this writing help fulfill institutional goals or outcomes?

Now think a bit more about what makes assignments effective. As you know, there is no perfect assignment that will work for all students in all situations at all times. Instead, assignments tend to work best when they are written to meet the needs of a particular population of students at a given point in their academic development.

Listed in Activity 6.5 are some of the tensions that teachers often encounter when crafting major writing assignments. Ponder where you lie on the continua.

Activity 6.5   Examining how you will assign writing

Circle any ideas that resonate with you, and mark with an asterisk any ideas that cause tension. Unpack at least one of the tensions in your teaching journal.

Teachers' views on assigning writing . . .

I tend to write fairly short assignments (a short paragraph or so). I do not want to overwhelm students.	⟷	I tend to write long, detailed assignments of several paragraphs. I want to give students a lot to consider, as well as tips and advice.
I want to leave room for creativity in my assignments. Students do not need to answer every question I pose.	⟷	I want to spell out clearly what students need to do in each assignment. I do not want them to flounder or be uncertain.
My students usually write after we have talked about a text or issue in depth for some time.	⟷	My students often write before we have talked about a text or issue in too much depth.

I tend to build revision into each assignment, assigning a first, second, and final draft.	←——→	I tend to use revision after an initial draft is submitted, since I sometimes want students to combine drafts or be able to choose what they would like to revise.
My students seem to understand from the assignment whom they are writing for and what they are trying to achieve.	←——→	My students often seem unsure about who the audience is for their papers (beyond me) and what their purpose is.
Assignments work best when students have some autonomy, or some elements of choice.	←——→	Assignments work best when all students are held to the same clear standard, topic, and format.
I like to include a context section, or something about where we have been, where we are going, and how this assignment connects to the others.	←——→	I like to let each assignment stand alone as its own task or challenge.

YOUR TEACHING JOURNAL: Engaging with tensions

Choose the pair of ideas that causes the most tension for you, and brainstorm about it in your teaching journal. Consider the following questions:

- Why are you torn?
- How do the two sides fit with different aspects of your teaching philosophy?
- How might you find a balance between the two so that you are true to both aspects of your teaching philosophy?

As you can see, different teachers approach their writing assignments differently. Some teachers believe that the assignment should thoroughly lay out tasks, expectations, reminders, and tips so that students have a clear vision of what they are being asked to do. Other teachers want to leave the assignment more open for interpretation or want to make room for student choice or self-direction. In some ways, these general tendencies connect to your expectations and hopes for the stack of papers your assignments will generate. Do you have in mind a vision of a successful paper that you are trying to help students produce? Or would you rather be surprised by the writing students produce, knowing that you will then work from that starting point (whatever it may be)? Pause for a moment to synthesize your approach to assignments.

 Activity 6.6 Synthesizing your approach to assignments

In your teaching journal, discuss the following questions. Be sure to note any questions or issues that you are still wrestling with.

- What is your general approach to assignments?
- How does this approach fit with your philosophy about good writing, the writing process, and effective teaching?

Wherever you come down on the tensions you have explored in Activity 6.5 and Activity 6.6, there are some general strategies that can help you write assignments that are clear and useful for both you and your students. Assignment prompts walk a fine line between giving students the information they need to be successful (and being relatively clear about the task at hand) and challenging students to find their own approach or spin on academic topics or readings. The clearer your sense of the work an assignment asks students to engage in and why this work is important, the better positioned you are to write a clear, interesting assignment.

In our experience, effective assignment prompts usually contain some combination of the following elements, depending on what the assignment is designed to help students achieve, which expectations are well understood and thus do not need to be repeated, and so on:

- A title for the assignment or a question that frames it
- A due date (or a series of due dates if drafts are required)
- The context or rationale for the writing task, including how it connects to earlier or later assignments (e.g., "Building on our practice with summary, paraphrase, and quotation, this essay asks you to use all three to respond to Freire's arguments about educational systems.")
- A clear statement of the writing task, often captured by specifying a genre (e.g., "Write an argumentative essay") or by a "demand verb" (e.g., evaluate, analyze, describe, propose)
- A sense of the audience and purpose associated with the genre or task
- An intellectual dimension, often a set of questions that students must or might consider
- Information about key features the writing should include (such as vivid description for a literacy narrative, or response to a counterargument for an argumentative essay)
- Any useful tips, including how to get started, how to avoid possible pitfalls, and things to consider while writing, as well as encouragement or reminders
- Any information about formatting or presentation that are not already part of the ongoing expectations for the course

Of course, you may not need all of these elements in every assignment, and you may choose to convey this information in class rather than on the prompt sheet. However, if you omit some of this information entirely, you should have a clear reason and purpose for doing so.

> I used to pack too much into each writing assignment. I'd ask students to do ten different things and go in ten different directions in their paper. Now I think more carefully about the purpose of each writing assignment. I ask myself, "What kind of writing and thinking do I want them to do in this assignment — and why?" Then I streamline around this purpose.
>
> —*Tara*

How will you create effective writing assignments?

Many instructors find that to achieve their specific course goals and to create a cohesive, well-structured class they must write their own assignments. Writing your own assignments allows you to be more responsive to your students' needs and to draw on your own expertise and interests as a teacher. It also gives you the opportunity to create a more systematic course of study that proceeds at the right pace for your students, instead of working around a more generic curriculum and trying to make it fit. (See Chapter 10 for more information on how to revise or amend assignments from textbooks.)

Writing your own assignments will take some work—and, of course, some revision!—but you have already gotten started on this task. You will soon build on that work to flesh out the gist of your major assignments. But first we'd like to highlight the approach that we are asking you to take toward your assignments and why that approach makes sense. We often work with teachers who, instead of beginning with the kinds of writing they will require, begin with a topic or perhaps a reading. These teachers will ask, "What is a good literacy narrative assignment?" or "What is a good assignment about problems in the community?" The answer is that it really depends on what you are trying to accomplish (and have students accomplish) with that assignment; there is no magic bullet assignment that will just work for every situation. By beginning with the type of writing you are working toward, you will be better able to clarify how your writing assignments fulfill the overall goals of the course. You can then plan backward to connect the types of writing you are assigning to course themes or course readings (as we will do in Chapter 7). You can also generate different options for assignments, depending on your specific goals for a class, a group of students, or when the assignment will be given during the semester.

We will discuss backward planning in more depth in Chapter 8, which covers big-picture planning, but first we will see how you can be more strategic in thinking through your writing assignments. The following chart shows how a teacher might transform a topic such as "problem in the community" into different options for writing assignments and how some of these options might be more effective for different purposes, different students, or different times in the semester. After reviewing the chart, you will brainstorm different assignments that require different types of writing on the topic of literacy/education (a popular topic with many first-year composition teachers). Then you will try to discern when such assignments might be most useful.

"Problem in the community" assignments	When would be a good time to give this assignment? For whom would it be most effective? Why would it be effective?
Short essay. Define a problem in the community, and analyze the basic causes of the problem. Explain why this problem is important to you.	• An initial assignment beginning the unit • Students unaccustomed to writing longer essays or who need support • Assignment draws on students' interests and knowledge outside of school, increasing engagement to begin the course
Ethnographic project. Identify a problem in your community as well as a place where this problem plays out. Observe how people inside and outside your community experience this problem. Do they take action to address the problem or not? Write up your observations using specific details.	• An early assignment targeted at getting students to pay attention to a problem and its dynamics • Students from diverse communities, especially if this diversity will be engaged as part of the class • Gets students out of the classroom and into the world; suggests that real-life problems can be analyzed in academic ways
Researched problem/solution essay. Use your research into a community problem to summarize the problem, its causes, and whom it affects. Propose a viable solution to this problem. Explain, using research, how your solution would help alleviate the problem. Argue how your solution should be implemented, and by whom.	• Middle or end of the semester or unit, once students have defined, explored, and researched a problem • Asks students to use research and to make specific recommendations • Appeals to students interested in advocacy or policy • Positions students as agents of change and potentially powerful rhetors

Call to action. You have identified an audience that is in a position to do something to help solve your community problem. Choosing the appropriate genre with which to present your message, persuade this population to take specific actions to address the problem.	• Middle or end of the semester or unit • Appeals to students interested in advocacy or public writing • Requires more self-direction, as students choose their own audience and genre • Provides many options for digital writing and gives students a chance to effect change in the world
Blog. Write a series of blog posts that describe the problem, its effects, and the affected populations; offer solutions; and update the community on efforts to solve the problem.	• Creates a semester or half-semester writing project that students can (to varying degrees) self-create and direct • Useful for beginning or advanced writers • Uses Web 2.0 to help students engage audiences beyond the class

Activity 6.7   Unpacking an assignment

Now try your hand at generating different types of writing assignments based on the popular issue of literacy/education or another issue or topic that you plan to explore in your class. Fill in the chart that follows.

What kinds of literacy/education writing might you assign?	When would be a good time to give this assignment? For whom would it be most effective? Why would it be effective?

How will the major assignments in your course fit together?

Many first-year composition teachers are advised to give their students between four and six major writing assignments per semester, and these writing assignments usually average four pages, perhaps with later assignments or revisions requiring a bit more length. If you teach on a quarter system or work with students who need more support or a slower pace, you might need to reduce the number or length of assignments. If you are new to teaching, beginning with the guideline above can help you start generating your own writing assignments; however, at some point you will likely need to question the length and number of your assignments in relation to your students, their needs, and your writing program's goals.

In Chapter 11, we will focus more on the role that revision plays (when and where to include different types of revision in your semester). For now, though, you will sketch out a few major assignments that will get your students writing and practicing the skills, strategies, and academic habits of mind that your first-year composition course is teaching.

 Activity 6.8   Mapping your assignments

Look back at your work in this chapter, particularly Activity 6.1 and Activity 6.3, to create an initial map of your assignments. Drawing on your work in previous chapters—including your view of good writing (Activity 1.11) and your course goals (Activity 5.12)—craft several major writing assignments that will define your course.

Type of writing:	Purpose of this writing:	Content or inquiry question:	Necessary elements (key features of the writing):	Presentation (length, format):

Once you have a sketch of your major assignments, it is time to jump in and try composing the actual prompts. Using the information in Activity 6.8, start fleshing out each prompt. Since effective writing prompts often take several drafts, feel free to do this on a computer where you can save your work and continue to revise your prompts as you work through subsequent activities.

How will you write effective prompts?

Once your prompts are drafted, they will certainly need revision to help both develop and clarify the writing task and the goals of the assignment. One of the most useful ways to revise your assignment prompts is to use a heuristic, such as the one created by Erika Lindemann, which is excerpted below. A heuristic allows you to "check in" to make sure you have considered the various angles and dimensions of a solid writing prompt. Heuristics are thus useful not only in guiding the revision of your own assignments, but also in helping you revise assignments written by others (which you will do in Activity 6.11). The following is an excerpt from one of our favorite heuristics. You will customize it for your own use in Activity 6.9.

Lindemann's heuristic for the writer of writing assignments

A. **Task definition, meaning, and sequencing.** What do I want the students to do? Is it worth doing? Why? Is it interesting and appropriate? What will it specifically teach the student? How does it fit my objectives at this point in the course? What can students do before they undertake the assignment, and where do I expect them to be after completing it? What do I anticipate this assignment will tell me? Along those lines, how, when, and what is being assessed in this assignment? Does the task have meaning outside as well as inside the class setting? Have I given enough class time to discuss the assignment, its purpose, and its goals?

B. **Writing processes.** How do I want my students to complete the assignment? Are there opportunities for collaboration? In what ways will they practice prewriting, writing, and revising? Have I given enough class time to discuss (and learn) these procedures? Have I given enough information about what I want so that students can make effective choices about subject, purpose, form, mode, and tone? Have I given them enough information about required length and about the use of sources? Are good examples, or models, appropriate?

C. **Audience.** For whom are the students writing? If the audience is the teacher, do the students really know who the teacher is and what can be assumed? Are there ways and reasons to expand the audience beyond the teacher? Can the audience be productively expanded to those beyond the classroom?

D. **Schedule.** How does the assignment relate to what comes before and after it in the course? Is the assignment sequenced to give enough time for prewriting, writing, revision, and editing? How much time inside and outside of class will students need? To what extent will I guide and grade students' work? Will others, including peers or the students themselves, also assess student work, and at what stage? What deadlines (and penalties) do I want to set for collecting papers or for various stages of the project? Have I given enough class time to discussion (or practice) of writing processes?

E. Assessment. What will I do with the assignment? How will I evaluate the work? What constitutes a successful response to the assignment? Will other students or the writer have a say in evaluating the paper? Does the grading system encourage revision? Have I attempted to write the paper myself; if so, what problems did I encounter? Will I discuss evaluation criteria with the students before they begin work, and will I discuss what I expect again as the due date approaches?

Source: A Rhetoric for Writing Teachers, 4th Edition, by Lindemann and Anderson (2001) from pp. 220–21. © 1995 by Erika Lindemann. By permission of Oxford University Press, USA.

 Activity 6.9   Creating a personalized heuristic

Drawing on Lindemann's work, develop your own heuristic. Which of Lindemann's questions or issues do you especially need to think about when you write or revise assignments? Will you use the same categories to organize your questions, or will you revise Lindemann's classifications? After you have constructed your personalized heuristic, try it out on at least one of your assignment drafts.

Personalized heuristic questions adapted from Lindemann's heuristic:

A. Task definition, meaning, and sequencing:

-
-
-

B. Writing processes:

-
-
-

C. Audience:

-
-
-

D. Schedule:

-
-
-

E. Assessment:

-
-
-

F. Additional categories and questions:

If you take the time to put each of your assignments through the gristmill of a detailed heuristic like Lindemann's, you will feel more confident that you have a clear rationale for your choices and that your instruction, assignments, and assessment are working together cohesively. Use the short checklist you created in Activity 6.9 to analyze your assignments periodically. Eventually, these types of questions will become more automatic; you will find yourself consistently asking, "Why am I doing this?" as you make your pedagogical choices.

Although we will explore how to assess textbooks in Chapter 10, it is worth commenting briefly on how you might revise assignments given to you by either a textbook, another teacher, or a writing program. The best assignments are often connected to the ongoing work and culture of a particular classroom. Thus it is important to learn how to deconstruct someone else's assignment in order to revise it as necessary for your particular context, students, and goals.

Just as a student would, you can read another teacher's prompt to discern the purpose of an assignment. Focusing on the "demand verbs" will help you get started. Does the prompt ask students to "discuss," "analyze," or "argue"? What do you think the intended difference might be in asking students to "examine" versus "critically analyze," for example? Has the teacher stated other goals of the assignment or identified other skills for students to practice?

Once you have a sense of the assignment's purpose, you can try to puzzle out a bit more about the assignment, including what the teacher seems to expect and how the writing will be evaluated. Does the prompt provide specific directions, criteria, or expectations? Given the prompt, what would a successful paper look like? Finally, what do you imagine students will have learned or practiced in preparation for this assignment? If you borrowed the assignment from another teacher, you may, of course, gain additional information by asking some of these questions directly; however, it is useful to be able to deconstruct a prompt on your own, as well, for times when the original author is unavailable.

> When I first began teaching, I gathered assignments that had "gone really well" from other teachers to use in my class. I quickly found that this hodgepodge approach left my students confused. I was confused, too, because I didn't have a clear sense of why I was even assigning these assignments! Once I took a step back and thought about the kinds of writing that were most important for my students to practice, I revised some of these assignments and wrote a few of my own to better practice the specific kinds of writing my students needed to work on. This gave both me and my students a clearer sense of purpose and assignments that actually worked together.
>
> —Mark

Activity 6.10   Analyzing prompts written by others

Deconstructing or unpacking an assignment in order to understand it fully is the first step in modifying it to better fit your goals and your class. Once you understand how an assignment works, you can begin to shape it to your particular context. Obtain an assignment written by another teacher or one available online, and answer the questions in the following chart.

Borrowed prompt name or task:	Stated purpose or goals of assignment:	Unstated criteria (implied values or criteria):	Preceding lessons, stated or inferred (what students will have already worked on or practiced):

Activity 6.11   Adapting borrowed prompts

Think about how you can change or adapt borrowed prompts so that they will better fit your teaching philosophy and course goals. Fill in the following chart using the same prompt as in Activity 6.10.

Summary of borrowed prompt task:	What you need to change, and why:

While it may be tempting to use others' assignments—"They are already made! Why reinvent the wheel? My friend said this assignment worked great in her class!"—it is crucial to remember that there is no magic bullet assignment. An assignment that works well in one context or for one teacher may not work well for you. (Sometimes even your own assignment might be effective in one section of your course but fall flat in another section.) Adapting assignments is the best way to make these mistranslations less frequent (and sometimes less painful). Use your insider knowledge about your class and students, the goals you have articulated for your course, and your expert position as a situated participant in your class to adapt and revise assignments—whether you are revising your own assignments or assignments originally authored by someone else.

The most frequent cause of problems in assignments is a lack of clarity about the purpose, the task required to fulfill that purpose, or the expectations for success (including how the assignment will be evaluated). The next activity will help you troubleshoot your assignments.

Activity 6.12   Troubleshooting assignment features

Once you have a solid draft of an assignment, troubleshoot it by comparing it to the suggestions in the following chart. Note revisions to make in the column on the right. For this activity, you can also use an assignment that did not produce the results you expected.

Troubleshooting suggestions:	Specific revisions to make to your targeted assignment:
Length. Your assignment prompt should provide enough detail and intellectual challenge without going on too long or overwhelming students. Hitting this "sweet spot" is difficult, as it will vary with the assignment's purpose and goals. Check whether your prompt is too brief to help students achieve the assignment's purpose, or whether it is too long, cluttered with unnecessary information and repetition. Consider, too, the length you require for the finished paper, which will depend on your desired outcome. Do you want a quick response to a reading to get students warmed up? Or do you want a longer response that engages and analyzes the text more closely or that brings in additional voices or perspectives to support an argument?	
Demand verbs. Students can be confused about what an assignment actually requires. For students, assignments that instruct them to "analyze" or "argue" might mean nearly the same thing; however, teachers might have something much more specific in mind when they use one word rather than the other. Additionally, many teachers might find that students need to work on something like "analysis" throughout the semester. You will want to discuss both the thinking and the writing that the verbs you use in your assignments demand in order to make your tacit knowledge and your expectations as clear as possible. Think about why you are using the demand verbs you have chosen for your assignments, and what you really mean by those verbs, clarifying your prompt as needed.	
Hidden expectations. Along similar lines, you will want to do all that you can to unearth any expectations that might not be explicit in your prompts. You do not necessarily need a laundry list of expectations, but if you do have set expectations for an assignment, why not communicate them? To identify your hidden expectations, investigate the descriptors you use in your prompt (including adjectives or adverbs). What are you suggesting to students when you instruct them to "write lively prose," "communicate effectively," or "be sure to consider your audience"? Is there something specific that you will be looking for in their essays? If so, see if you can be more explicit.	
Possible outcomes. Think ahead to what your assignment is likely to produce in terms of results. You will want to think about both what a successful performance of the assignment would look like and what range of written work you might get in response to the assignment. Where do you think students will be most successful, and what do you anticipate they might have trouble with? Given what you anticipate, do you want to revise your prompt to point students in the right direction?	

How will your assignments build upon each other?

Once you have written your prompts, you will need to consider the best order, or sequence, for your assignments. Building connections between assignments and establishing a logic to your sequence is the key to ensuring a cohesive course and a productive progression in which students build on earlier skills to progressively complete more complex tasks.

You are probably already familiar with typical progressions from your own teaching or learning. For example, some courses begin with a broad overview of an issue or problem and then continue with more complex examinations, multiple perspectives, or different ways to solve a particular issue. Other courses begin by focusing on the individual students and their personal experiences or histories and then widen the view to consider others or the larger world. In either case, writing courses tend to ask students to write in more depth, with more complexity, in new genres, or in response to a range of sources or ideas toward the conclusion of the semester. Greater student choice about what they would like to focus on or research sometimes accompanies this move. The goal, of course, is to support students in practicing the increasingly complex reading and writing tasks the university demands. Beginning more simply and increasing the challenge and complexity of assignments throughout the term is a common pattern.

This section demonstrates how you might begin to chart a cohesive trajectory, or progression, for the assignments in your course. Although we will discuss this more in Chapter 8, it is useful to begin to get a feel for this technique as you work to craft your major writing assignments.

First, find a logical order to sequence your assignments:

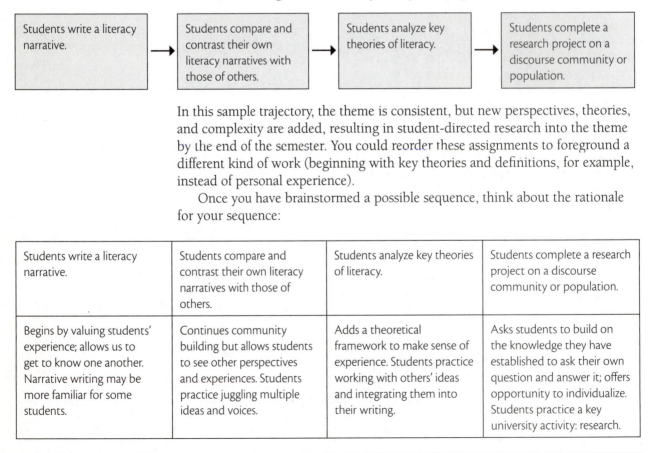

In this sample trajectory, the theme is consistent, but new perspectives, theories, and complexity are added, resulting in student-directed research into the theme by the end of the semester. You could reorder these assignments to foreground a different kind of work (beginning with key theories and definitions, for example, instead of personal experience).

Once you have brainstormed a possible sequence, think about the rationale for your sequence:

Students write a literacy narrative.	Students compare and contrast their own literacy narratives with those of others.	Students analyze key theories of literacy.	Students complete a research project on a discourse community or population.
Begins by valuing students' experience; allows us to get to know one another. Narrative writing may be more familiar for some students.	Continues community building but allows students to see other perspectives and experiences. Students practice juggling multiple ideas and voices.	Adds a theoretical framework to make sense of experience. Students practice working with others' ideas and integrating them into their writing.	Asks students to build on the knowledge they have established to ask their own question and answer it; offers opportunity to individualize. Students practice a key university activity: research.

Then build connections or bridges between assignments to create cohesion and demonstrate connections between assignments:

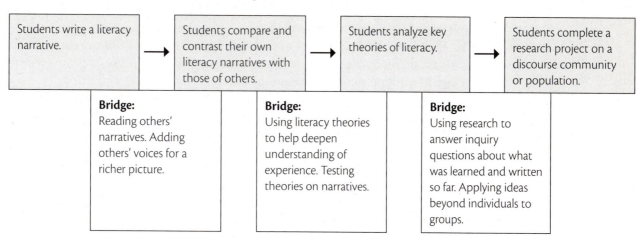

| Students write a literacy narrative. | | Students compare and contrast their own literacy narratives with those of others. | | Students analyze key theories of literacy. | | Students complete a research project on a discourse community or population. |

Bridge:
Reading others' narratives. Adding others' voices for a richer picture.

Bridge:
Using literacy theories to help deepen understanding of experience. Testing theories on narratives.

Bridge:
Using research to answer inquiry questions about what was learned and written so far. Applying ideas beyond individuals to groups.

📁 **Activity 6.13** Building bridges between and across assignments

Use the following graphic to order your writing tasks (assignments) and rationale for their order, as well as to articulate the bridges that will link those assignments.

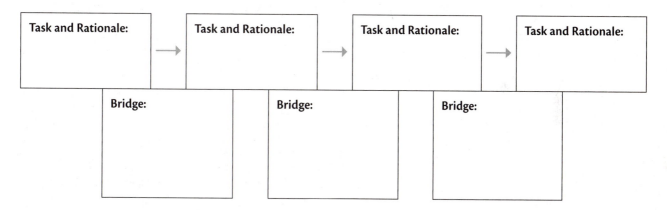

Task and Rationale: **Task and Rationale:** **Task and Rationale:** **Task and Rationale:**

Bridge: **Bridge:** **Bridge:**

Finally, remember that you can always revise or adapt upcoming assignments to address any difficulties that students have with earlier assignments. If students struggle with a particular task, you might revise an upcoming assignment to give them a chance to practice that task again. Use the feedback you are getting from their written work to make small adaptations and to focus class work or writing workshops on elements that most students need to continue practicing. (We will consider feedback and revision more in Chapter 13.)

Taking it further:
Planning by "backward design"

If you can articulate where you would like your students to end up by the end of the semester—what you would like them to be able to accomplish in their written work, for example—you can work backward from that idea to construct a series of smaller tasks. This is called "backward design," a planning approach made popular by Grant Wiggins and Jay McTighe.

For example, if your department requires students to be able to conduct and present independent research by the end of the term, you can sequence the necessary component parts or types of writing that will help support that goal: asking productive questions; learning how to answer those questions with research; learning summary, paraphrase, and quotation skills; and being able to analyze research to identify next steps or what is missing. As demonstrated, you will want to work backward to map writing, reading, and even thinking practices, especially if you will eventually expect a complex performance of all three skills.

In short, keeping in mind the end goals—for a particular unit or even for the final expectations for the semester—can help you more successfully build toward those goals. In many ways, you are also drawing on principles of sequencing (What easier tasks can build to more difficult tasks and in what order?) and scaffolding (What supports do students need to complete complex tasks?).

Although you will practice backward planning more in Chapter 8 and Chapter 9, which are devoted specifically to planning, it is worth practicing this kind of thinking a bit now to see how it might inform your larger course trajectory and sequence.

 Activity 6.14 Using "backward design" to sequence assignments and support informal writing

Use your written assignment prompts and the work you have done in this chapter (especially Activity 6.8) to work backward from the concluding, and likely most complex, assignment in your course. Fill in the following chart.

Describe a possible concluding assignment for the term:	List the reading, writing, and thinking skills this assignment demands:	List the major writing assignments that will lead up to the concluding assignment (and build skills that will be needed for the final assignment):	List some shorter, informal writing assignments that could help scaffold the concluding assignment:

Reflections from experienced teachers

As you continue to work on crafting effective assignments, consider the following wisdom from experienced teachers for further reflection and action:

- Seasoned teachers know that having a topic (or even a question) does not equal having an assignment. They must also work to identify the type of writing students will produce—and know why they are assigning that particular type of writing.

- Effective prompts often go through several revisions (much like the writing you are assigning in the prompts). Consider taking the advice you give students: Put your prompts away for a few days before going back to refine and revise them with fresh eyes.

- Many teachers like to have the first few assignment prompts set, yet they may adapt later prompts to respond to the needs of a particular class, the direction the course has taken, or interesting conversations that have emerged. If this sounds like something you would be interested in, you might consider keeping "rough prompts" but adapting them as the assignment draws closer or after you have seen more student writing.

- Experienced teachers often find that one of the best ways to revise assignment prompts is to try them out with students or even to try to write the assignment themselves. You will often learn where your prompt needs work after you have read the writing students have completed in response to it.

- Along similar lines, veteran teachers often troubleshoot their assignments throughout the semester, making notes about how they would like to revise current assignment prompts for the following semester.

- One way to effectively revise an assignment that does not live up to your expectations is to ask students what would have helped them be more successful with it.

- Lastly, seasoned teachers know that few assignments will produce strong student writing if they are just handed to students on their way out the door. Effective teachers take the time to read and discuss assignments with their students; they teach them how to read assignments, ascertain what is being asked, and brainstorm ways to get started.

Putting it together:
Explaining how you sequence assignments

Creating successful assignments is one of the major balancing acts you will encounter in your teaching. Fortunately, you will have a large stream of "data" in the form of your students' written work that you can use to assess your assignment prompts. Reflecting on what worked and what did not (and trying to figure out why) can help you continually improve and refine your prompts. Continue thinking about the following issues as you strive to craft the most effective assignments and assignment sequence:

- Have I left enough room for real thinking and creativity in my assignments?
- Have I balanced enough information (to help students succeed) with enough choice (to give students some autonomy)?
- Have I ordered my assignments to create a cohesive course that allows students to keep using and extending what they have learned?

 Activity 6.15   Explaining your assignment sequence

Imagine that you are preparing for a job interview. You will be asked to discuss potential writing assignments and articulate your rationale for those assignments. Using the work you have done in this chapter, briefly outline a sequence of assignments that you might create for a specific course. What would the writing prompts emphasize, and what would these assignments show about what you value in terms of writing? As you fill in the following chart, be sure to answer the three questions just listed.

Sequence of assignments:	What would each assignment emphasize and why?

If you have made thoughtful, informed choices about your assignments, the assignments will serve as a window into your teaching philosophy. A colleague who looks at your assignments will get a clear notion of what you value in student writing, what processes you foster in the classroom, and how you promote student success. To wrap up this chapter, think about the sequence of assignments that you sketched out in Activity 6.8 and Activity 6.13, as well as your explanation in Activity 6.15, and discuss that sequence in your teaching journal.

 Activity 6.16   Contextualizing your assignments in your teaching philosophy

In your teaching journal, discuss the following questions. Be sure to note any questions or issues that you are still wrestling with.

- How do your assignments embody your beliefs about good writing, writing processes, and effective teaching?
- How do your assignments create a coherent sequence that moves students toward your course goals?
- What kinds of bridges will you build between assignments?

Now that you have worked through this chapter, you should have a much clearer sense of the kinds of writing you will assign in your course, as well as how you will sequence those assignments. You have done significant work to match your writing assignments to the course goals you intend your assignments to address. In Chapter 7, you will be asked to make an additional set of connections: linking your writing assignments to reading assignments. Then, with the partnership between reading and writing firmly in mind, in Chapter 8 and Chapter 9 you will more fully flesh out how your plans will support students as they work on the assignments you have designed.

Further Reading

- Graff, Nelson. "'An Effective and Agonizing Way to Learn': Backwards Design and New Teachers' Preparation for Planning." *Teacher Education Quarterly* 38.3 (2011): 151–68. Print.

- Johns, Anne M. "Written Argumentation for Real Audiences: Suggestions for Teacher Research and Classroom Practice." *TESOL Quarterly* 27.1 (1993): 75–90. Print.

- Lindblom, Kenneth. "Teaching English in the World: Writing for Real." *English Journal* 94.1 (2004): 104–8. Print.

- Strasma, Kip. "Assignments by Design." *Teaching English in the Two-Year College* 34.3 (2007): 248–63. Print.

CHAPTER 7

Choices about Reading Assignments

Choosing the reading for a course is one of the difficulties that new teachers often mention encountering. Newer teachers often spend much time wrestling with questions about reading, asking: What should students read? Where can I find readings? Should I teach texts that I love or not? This chapter explores how to choose readings in concert with the writing assignments you developed in Chapter 6 and the overall course goals you identified in Chapter 5. Thus you may find it useful to move back and forth between these three chapters as you plan your course readings.

What role will reading play in your class?

Most teachers are voracious readers and readily appreciate the value of reading in terms of developing writing skills. Many students, however, have complex and sometimes negative experiences with reading. Composition scholarship thus capitalizes on what teachers and researchers know about the positive impact reading plays on both writing and thinking, while at the same time acknowledging the range of student experiences and dispositions toward reading. Composition scholarship also considers the relationship between reading and writing both from the less familiar angle of how writing might make someone a stronger reader and from the perspective of an integrated approach (how writing and reading mutually benefit each other).

 Activity 7.1   Thinking about your own reading experiences and your students' reading experiences

As you begin thinking about reading, its value, and the role it will play in your writing course, it may help to reflect on some big-picture questions. Answer the questions that follow.

1. Why do you read? What do you value about reading? What is the benefit of reading different kinds of texts?

2. What do you hope your students will value about reading?

3. Why might your students read? Why might they not read?

4. How will your knowledge about whether and how your students read shape your selection of texts, presentation of texts, class activities, or learning goals?

5. Does writing make one a better reader? If so, how?

As you begin to think about readings for your course, you may notice that often the first readings that come to mind are either texts that you have read recently or cherished texts that have been important to you as a reader. Another common way of thinking about readings is to consider a particular theme that interests you or that you think will interest students. While both of these strategies are good for brainstorming, the activities that follow will help you think about selecting your course reading in more purposeful and concrete ways that will better serve both the goals of your course and the needs of your students.

The first strategy we suggest for filling in your reading list is to identify the key intellectual issues you are asking students to explore. Centering readings on genuine inquiry or on a central intellectual project that will span the term (rather than on a theme, topic, or unit) will both link the readings together and create stronger connections between the acts of reading and writing.

Let us work more with this idea of inquiry questions or an intellectual project in which your class will engage. By "inquiry questions," we mean the big-picture, in many ways unanswerable, questions that you might investigate with your students. With several guiding inquiry questions (or even one substantial question that changes slightly from assignment to assignment), you can conceive of your course as an intellectual project or investigation that you and your students embark on together. Once you have generated some inquiry questions, you can then brainstorm the readings that will provide rich, generative, and perhaps conflicting fodder to help students explore and answer those questions.

In Chapter 6, you worked to pinpoint the types of writing students will produce in your course. Now you can begin searching for readings that make sense and connect to the writing assignments.

> **As an undergrad English major, I never really thought about why teachers assigned specific readings. Of course, there was a debate about the canon and the cultural diversity of the authors, but I didn't really connect the reading I was doing to my own writing. I was never asked to consider how reading helped me write, or how writing might help make me a better, more strategic reader. But once I started paying attention to these connections, it was really helpful. I began reading texts more as models, and that helped my writing develop in new ways.**
>
> —*Mark*

Activity 7.2 Generating inquiry questions and readings

For each major writing assignment you designed in Activity 6.8, brainstorm the key inquiry questions that will shape that unit or writing project. Then note possible readings that will help students pursue those questions. Fill in the following chart. We have provided an example to help you get started.

	Inquiry questions:	**Readings to pursue those questions:**
Sample assignment: Defining community based on observations.	Sample inquiry questions: • What characteristics define a community? • Do members shape the community, or does the community shape members (or both)? • What are the rules and roles for the members of the specific community you are investigating? • What do communities allow individuals to achieve?	Sample readings: • Community mission statements • Poems on tensions between communities and individuals • Article on fan culture • Tony Mirabelli, "Learning to Serve: The Language and Literacy of Food Service Workers" • Excerpt from Étienne Wenger on "communities of practice"
Assignment 1:		
Assignment 2:		
Assignment 3:		
Assignment 4:		
Assignment 5:		

You have now laid the groundwork for the types of readings that might help students read, think, and write in your course. Staying grounded in the writing you will ask students to do, and understanding how reading can help further those specific goals, will help you avoid choosing a set of readings that feel disconnected or random. Once you have completed Activity 7.2, you should begin to see some clear clusters of readings for each assignment, or a progression of texts, for your course.

As we have suggested, your choice of readings might be better guided by a purposeful awareness of the types of writing you want students to practice, instead of simply selecting those readings you connect to as a reader. Choosing texts that will facilitate the kinds of thinking and writing you ask students to do, as well as texts that model the genres or types of writing you assign, is often most effective for students. The next activity thus asks you to brainstorm both "topical" readings—readings that provide content or engage the inquiry questions or themes under investigation—and "model" readings that students can turn to as they produce a particular genre of writing.

📁 **Activity 7.3**   Using topical readings and model readings

Using the same writing assignments as in Activity 7.2, divide the readings into those that serve primarily to generate content or spur thinking and those that serve as models for writing. Some readings may very well serve both functions; feel free to list them under both categories.

	Type of writing:	Topical readings:	Model readings:
Assignment 1:			
Assignment 2:			
Assignment 3:			
Assignment 4:			
Assignment 5:			

Turning to the field:
Reading, critical thinking, and multimodality

For many teachers, reading is strongly connected to critical thinking. We assign challenging reading to students to encourage them to think in new, increasingly academic ways, to engage a range of perspectives, and to reflect deeply on their own lives and actions. As you consider the following excerpt from the *Framework for Success in Postsecondary Writing*, consider how critical reading and critical writing can spur the critical thinking practices we hope to develop in our students.

Activity 7.4   Thinking about critical thinking

Circle any ideas that resonate with you, and mark with an asterisk any ideas that cause tension. Unpack at least one of the tensions in your teaching journal.

Developing critical thinking through writing, reading, and research

Critical thinking is the ability to analyze a situation or text and make thoughtful decisions based on that analysis.

Writers use critical writing and reading to develop and represent the processes and products of their critical thinking. For example, writers may be asked to write about familiar or unfamiliar texts, examining assumptions about the texts held by different audiences. Through critical writing and reading, writers think through ideas, problems, and issues; identify and challenge assumptions; and explore multiple ways of understanding. This is important in college as writers are asked to move past obvious or surface-level interpretations and use writing to make sense of and respond to written, visual, verbal, and other texts that they encounter.

Teachers can help writers develop critical thinking by providing opportunities and guidance for students to

- read texts from multiple points of view (e.g., sympathetic to a writer's position and critical of it) and in ways that are appropriate to the academic discipline or other contexts where the texts are being used;

- write about texts for multiple purposes including (but not limited to) interpretation, synthesis, response, summary, critique, and analysis;

- craft written responses to texts that put the writer's ideas in conversation with those in a text in ways that are appropriate to the academic discipline or context;

- create multiple kinds of texts to extend and synthesize their thinking (e.g., analytic essays, scripts, brochures, short stories, graphic narratives);

- evaluate sources for credibility, bias, quality of evidence, and quality of reasoning;

- conduct primary and secondary research using a variety of print and non-print sources;

- write texts for various audiences and purposes that are informed by research (e.g., to support ideas or positions, to illustrate alternative perspectives, to provide additional contexts); and

- generate questions to guide research.

Source: Council of Writing Program Administrators, National Council of Teachers of English, and the National Writing Project, "Framework for Success in Postsecondary Writing." Copyright © 2011 by CWPA, NCTE, and NWP. Reprinted by permission. http://wpacouncil.org/framework.

YOUR TEACHING JOURNAL: Engaging with tensions
Choose the activity that least resonates with you, and answer the following questions in your teaching journal:

- Why does this activity not resonate with you? Is it in tension with your beliefs about good writing or writing processes, your course goals, or any other elements of your teaching philosophy?

- If you were to try out the activity in your classroom, how might you make it fit with your philosophy?

Now you will engage these ideas a bit more by thinking about how reading and writing could pair to help students begin thinking critically. In the following activity, we use the oft-taught essay by George Orwell, "Politics and the English Language," as an example to chart how reading and writing tasks can combine to help students achieve critical thinking. The second and third columns build on the core text, asking students to think critically by engaging a different point of view and to compose writing that puts their own ideas in conversation with other writers' ideas (writing from summary to analysis to synthesis). The next two columns further extend the recommendations about critical thinking from the *Framework for Success* by considering how students might research the topic further and follow up with "multiple kinds of texts . . . for various audiences and purposes." (The sample texts cited in the activity are listed at the end of this chapter.)

📁 **Activity 7.5**   Pairing reading and writing for critical thinking

In the following chart, we ask you to map a reading of your choice along several of the dimensions of critical thinking bulleted in the Framework for Success *excerpt.*

Core reading:	"New perspective" reading (bullet 1):	Written responses to readings (bullets 2 and 3):	Research tasks for further critical thinking (bullets 5, 6, and 8):	Multiple kinds of texts created in response (bullets 4 and 7):
Orwell's "Politics and the English Language"	Steven Poole's "My Problem with George Orwell" (*The Guardian*, 2013)	• Separate summary of and response to each article • Analysis of current political speech to test Orwell's and Poole's claims • Synthesis and/or argument in response to readings	• Generate questions about "grammar rants" and their motivations • Create a research plan to find and analyze grammar rants (print and nonprint) • Use Lindblom and Dunn model article, "Analyzing Grammar Rants," to analyze rants	• Revision of synthesis and argument • Video/speech response to a "grammar rant" • Updated essay-manifesto of Orwell's claims in student's words • Interpretive guide/brochure to help other students analyze political speech

Today's teachers must consider the role of reading as it pertains not only to the printed page but also to the myriad texts we read and engage with online. While some might bemoan this turn away from "traditional" reading (or alphabetic texts), others celebrate that people are reading more frequently and in new ways. Multimodal texts—or texts that make use of a combination of modes such as words, sounds, performance, or images—are now an integral part of our lived experience and, as such, are winding their way into education (for a good overview, see the multimodal Web resource "Creating Multimodal Texts").

Since our students' reading lives are intimately shaped by a host of readings beyond the printed page, literacy theorists from Glynda Hull to Richard and Cynthia Selfe have convincingly argued that multimodal and new media texts offer extensive learning opportunities, particularly when it comes to learning about how different texts achieve their rhetorical purposes. They ask us to consider what we can learn from reading, engaging, analyzing, and composing such texts beyond the printed page.

Activity 7.6 Gaining rhetorical knowledge through reading multimodal texts

Looking back at the work you completed about rhetorical knowledge in Chapter 6 (the excerpted recommendations from the Framework for Success *and Activities 6.2, 6.3, and 6.8), use this activity to explore what multimodal texts can offer. Map the rhetorical knowledge students might gain by reading and analyzing the following multimodal texts. We have filled in the first column as a model to spur your thinking.*

	Mission statement or strategic plan from a college Web site:	Graphic novel:	Informative brochure (with images):	Video of State of the Union address:
What does this text teach students about audience and purpose?	Succinctly communicates mission to different populations.			
What does this text teach students about organizational choices and design?	Images, font, color, and interactivity all contribute to reader engagement.			
What does this text teach students about tone, voice, or ethos?	Text might create an ethos of service, access, and so on by word choice and images.			
What does this text teach students about the relationships between the key composition choices made in the text?	How to create a broad message to reach multiple audiences using concrete language, buzzwords, and design.			

Activity 7.7 Developing habits of mind

Now you can take your brainstorming about multimodal texts a bit further and examine how different types of reading can help stretch and develop students' habits of mind. For example, how might reading, engaging, and analyzing these texts help your readers develop the following "habits of mind" from the Framework for Success?

Habit of mind:	Graphic novel:	Informative brochure (with images):	Video of State of the Union address:
Curiosity — the desire to know more about the world			
Creativity (tied to purpose) — the ability to use novel approaches for generating, investigating, and representing ideas			
Flexibility — the ability to adapt to situations, expectations, or demands			

How will you select readings?

New teachers often feel logistically overwhelmed by locating readings, particularly when time is tight in designing a class. Remember that you can wait to select readings that will be used later in the semester or even have students search out the readings that will help them complete a particular writing assignment or answer particular inquiry questions (best left until later in the term). If you are pressed for time, try to finalize your first month of readings and continue your search as the semester progresses.

Activity 7.8 Examining conflicting notions about reading

Circle any ideas that resonate with you, and mark with an asterisk any ideas that cause tension. Unpack at least one of the tensions in your teaching journal.

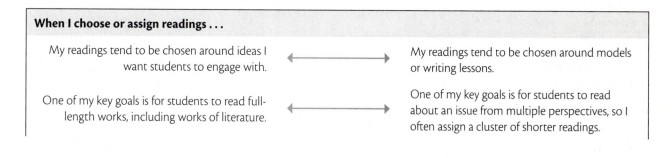

When I choose or assign readings . . .

| My readings tend to be chosen around ideas I want students to engage with. | ⟷ | My readings tend to be chosen around models or writing lessons. |

| One of my key goals is for students to read full-length works, including works of literature. | ⟷ | One of my key goals is for students to read about an issue from multiple perspectives, so I often assign a cluster of shorter readings. |

I tend to assign at least some readings that are also new to me.	←——————→	I tend to assign tried-and-true readings.
I prefer students to have a hard copy of the reading; it helps them annotate.	←——————→	I prefer students to read in whatever medium they are comfortable with (e.g., print, online, e-book reader).
I want students to draw from a range of texts, including works not written by professionals.	←——————→	I want students to draw mainly on published or scholarly texts.
I am comfortable assigning and discussing a range of media: print and digital texts, graphic novels, advertisements, speeches, and more.	←——————→	I am most comfortable assigning print texts so that students can focus on creating the writing that is most frequently assigned in an academic environment.

YOUR TEACHING JOURNAL: Engaging with tensions

Choose the pair of ideas that causes the most tension for you, and brainstorm about it in your teaching journal. Consider the following questions:

- Why did the pair cause tension?
- How does the left side of the pair fit with your teaching philosophy, or why does it not seem to fit?
- How does the right side of the pair fit with your teaching philosophy, or why does it not seem to fit?
- How might you find a middle ground between the two sides?
- How might this balancing act play out as you move between different institutions, writing programs, classes, and student populations?

Now that you have an idea of the range of readings you would like to include in your course, you will find that there are actually many places you can search to locate readings. Here are a few examples:

- Your department may have a wealth of resources, either in a physical binder or perhaps online. If your department collects syllabi from faculty, ask if you might peruse that collection to get ideas for readings.
- Textbooks provide abundant readings, as well as sequences or clusters of readings. Even if your writing program does not require a particular textbook, or if you are not planning on using one, textbooks can be a great resource. Ask if your department has sample textbooks, borrow textbooks from colleagues, or browse publisher Web sites to get ideas and to request sample copies. (The use of textbooks as resources is explored more fully in Chapter 10.)
- Browse your university bookstore to see which books and readings other teachers are assigning.
- Consider the sources you read and enjoy, particularly sources that provide complex treatments of contemporary issues instead of pat answers. *The Atlantic, The New Yorker,* Slate.com, Salon.com, and other current periodicals might have good readings that will help your students consider and write in response to contemporary issues.
- Search teacher-based Web sites (such as ncte.org or chronicle.com) or find syllabi that other teachers have posted online to get a wide selection of possible readings.

"As a high school teacher and literacy program developer, my main question was always "How engaging will this reading be for students?" Now that I'm a college writing teacher, I see reading choices as so much more complex: What do I want them to read? How do I want them to read it? How do I want them to engage with the ideas in the text? Is the text a springboard for student thinking? Is it a model of academic discourse that I want them to emulate? How will this reading connect to all the other reading and writing we will be doing? There's so much more to think about and map out.

—*Tara*

- Consider using a favorite text or two, but be mindful of how it connects to your course's intellectual project and assigned writing.
- Subscribe to interesting news feeds (RSS feeds) to start building a collection of pertinent and current essays or articles.
- Consider allowing students to choose some texts—perhaps for book clubs or to bolster their own writing projects.

Not all of these sources will provide readings that are appropriate to your class and your choices. However, knowing that there are many places to find readings can help alleviate a common worry teachers have when planning their courses.

How will you integrate reading and writing?

As much contemporary composition research tells us, reading and writing are overlapping, interpretive processes that benefit each other. (See especially the works by Vivian Zamel and Donna Qualley in the "Further Reading" list.) We can thus use one process to teach and enhance the other. For example, having students write as they are reading can help their comprehension and engagement; similarly, having students use reading to learn writing techniques, investigate style, or learn new rhetorical moves can help them become stronger, more flexible writers.

In the activities in this chapter, you have already brainstormed some readings that could serve not only as "content" for your students to respond to, but also as lessons in writing or models for student writing (Activity 7.3). Now you are ready to take your thinking further by considering how to design pedagogical practices that help students read to write *and* write to read.

Activity 7.9 Reading to write and writing to read

In this activity, we ask you to think about pedagogical practices—questions, exercises, or activities—that can help students integrate reading and writing and strengthen both processes. Focus on a particular unit you have in mind for your course (refer perhaps to Activity 6.8).

What writing tasks or strategies can help students become stronger readers?	What reading tasks or strategies can help students become more aware and flexible writers? How might you ask students to read as writers?

As you continue selecting readings, you will want to continue brainstorming about how readings can productively interact and be in dialogue in your class. Especially if you assign a few texts for a particular unit, or if all of your texts for a class engage similar inquiry questions, you will want to help students put those texts in conversation instead of treating them as discrete sets of words. For example, having students write to engage a text is a way of integrating their reading and writing practices in order to strengthen both.

 Activity 7.10 Putting readings in conversation with one another

With two particular readings in mind (perhaps two texts to be read together, or one text that follows and builds on another), explore how you might put them in conversation in your class. Activities 6.8, 7.2, and 7.3 might be helpful. For this activity, conversation may mean questions asked outside of class in writing assignments or during class via class discussion.

Highlighting overlap and differences:	Engaging and applying ideas:	Getting on the same page:
Questions that get students thinking about connections between the texts:	Key concepts/quotes to explore how the texts are in dialogue:	Identifying and comparing key terms, concepts, structure, or tone:
Questions that get students thinking about the differences or dissonances between the texts:	Ways to apply the texts or their ideas in some concrete fashion (perhaps applying them to students' experience):	Connecting the reading to an upcoming reading or writing task (bridges between texts):

As you completed the activity, you may have found that certain readings that initially seemed promising fell flat. Perhaps there were not enough "meaty ideas" or enough of a distinct or complex perspective in a certain reading to warrant its inclusion. Perhaps you noticed that there was not enough diversity in the types of texts, authors, or views you were asking students to read. Getting the big-picture view of the range and types of readings you assign is extremely useful before you start teaching so you can ensure you have a diversity of texts and perspectives. (See Chapter 15 for more on choosing diverse readings.)

Taking it further:
Writing to read and reading to write

Ultimately, we want students to see reading and writing as integrative processes that help them make meaning in the world. This can sometimes be difficult if students have had a rocky relationship with reading, writing, or both. Connecting reading to writing in explicit ways can help reassure students that practicing one process will benefit the other process as well.

For us, as teachers, to take the same advice means being aware of when we have unreflexively put writing solely in service of reading, or vice versa. Neither should the reading dominate (with the writing just "reporting" instead of engaging), nor should the writing dominate (writing in a vacuum without engaging the texts and ideas of others). Striking a productive and generative balance between reading and writing is one of the ongoing challenges writing teachers face.

For many teachers, especially those who are voracious readers, literature lovers, or who have backgrounds and training primarily in literature instead of composition, it can be tempting to focus only on the content, or ideas, of a reading. The next activity asks you to practice also attending to the style and rhetorical features of a given reading, as well as to brainstorm how students can connect writing tasks based on a reading to writing tasks concerning their own prose. We use Amy Tan's short essay "Mother Tongue" as our model, before asking you to practice with two of the key readings for your course.

📁 **Activity 7.11   Using reading to teach writing**

Select two of your course's possible readings. Then use the following chart to map out how these readings can be used to teach writing, not only in terms of ideas, but also in terms of rhetoric.

Questions about the reading's ideas:	Student writing connections:	Questions about the reading's rhetoric:	Student writing connections:
<ul><li>What are the many "Englishes" Tan speaks and uses?</li><li>What features do your "languages of intimacy" with family, friends, or partners contain?</li><li>How have Tan's experiences with language and her mother shaped her larger view of language?</li></ul>	<ul><li>Students prewrite on what the term *mother tongue* means in the essay and to them.</li><li>Students write in response to two or three key quotes they found in the reading.</li><li>Students write their own literacy narrative, highlighting someone who has shaped their view of language.</li></ul>	<ul><li>What compelled Tan to write this piece? What was her purpose?</li><li>What transitional phrases signal reflection on Tan's part? How, when, and where does she use reflection to make a larger point in this essay?</li><li>Which sentences in this essay are grammatically most complex? Do the ideas expressed necessitate this complexity?</li></ul>	<ul><li>Reverse outlining helps students pinpoint the structure of their writing and whether it helps them achieve their purpose.</li><li>Using Tan's structure as a model, students revise their literacy narrative, weaving in more reflection.</li><li>Students write a complex sentence (with their own content) using Tan's semicolon-driven list as a model (next to last paragraph). Then they reflect: What did this listing structure make you do as a writer?</li></ul>

Reflections from experienced teachers

We have often seen teachers who are designing a new class become overwhelmed or panicked about finding readings for the course. We hope that the activities in this chapter have helped dampen that anxiety somewhat. Obviously, the more time you have to collect a wide range of readings and then cull and curate them for specific purposes in your class, the better; that is why many teachers continually collect, copy, and bookmark interesting texts and ask other teachers for their ideas and recommendations.

As you work to create your own ongoing "library" of reading selections, we offer these perspectives from experienced teachers:

- Cherished readings can be both a boon and a liability. They can help us show our enthusiasm for written texts, but we can also be disappointed if students do not respond as we expect or do not admire the text as much as we do.

- Experienced teachers often select readings not only based on how they will help stimulate thought on the class's key inquiry questions or project, but also based on how they will be useful in terms of teaching something about writing. Questions like these are helpful in determining the difference: Does the text provide a model of how to write in a specific genre? Does it use a variety of sentence structures that students can identify and practice? Does it provide examples of what analysis or deep reflection looks like?

- Informal responses or creative applications can help students more deeply understand and even start to use the ideas they encounter in their reading. A variety of writing tasks will get students to anticipate, engage, understand, question, critique, and put readings in dialogue.

Putting it together: Articulating your approach to reading

Finding interesting, engaging, and productive readings for your writing class is an ongoing project. Many teachers consistently read with an eye toward whether materials might be used in a future class and file away readings for possible later use. In this way, selecting and curating readings can be one of the true joys of planning a course, although it might take a few semesters of experimentation to find how to best make use of the readings you have selected. As you work to gather possible readings, consider the following questions:

- Have I assigned students a range of texts (genres, lengths, complexity, perspectives, purposes)?
- Have I fleshed out how my key reading goals directly connect to writing goals?

Activity 7.12　Explaining your choices about readings

Imagine that you are preparing for a job interview. Use the following chart to write down key terms about reading that you want to bring up in the interview.

Terms describing the types or genres of readings you chose:	Terms describing the role readings play in your class:	Terms describing how and why you chose particular readings:

In the next activity, you will discuss in detail a specific example of how reading and writing are connected in the course you are teaching (or will be teaching). Be sure to anchor this discussion in how your choices exemplify your philosophy of reading, writing, and teaching.

Activity 7.13   Articulating your philosophy of reading and writing

In your teaching journal, discuss the following questions. Be sure to note any questions or issues that you are still wrestling with.

- What is your philosophy regarding the connections between reading and writing?
- How will you integrate reading and writing activities in your course? Provide a specific example.

Now that you have worked through this chapter, the readings for your course—and how they fit with the writing you will assign—should be coming into focus. Finding, selecting, and updating readings is, for most teachers, an ongoing process, so remain alert to potential readings you encounter in your daily life or studies. As you read the next two chapters on planning, keep in mind the reading-writing connections you hope to foster in your class. Chapter 8 and Chapter 9 will help you begin to plan both the big-picture arc of your course and the day-to-day activities that will help students practice the reading and writing tasks you have designed and, ultimately, fulfill your overall course goals.

Further Reading

- Bartholomae, David. "The Study of Error." *Writing on the Margins*. Ed. David Bartholomae. Boston: Bedford/St. Martin's, 2005. 19–35. Print.
- Hull, Glynda. "Youth Culture and Digital Media: New Literacies for New Times." *Research in the Teaching of English* 38.2 (2003): 229–33. Print.
- Lauer, Claire. "Contending with Terms: 'Multimodal' and 'Multimedia' in the Academic and Public Spheres." *Computers and Composition* 26.4 (2009): 229–39. Print.
- Lindblom, Kenneth, and Patricia Dunn. "Analyzing Grammar Rants: An Alternative to Traditional Grammar Instruction." *English Journal* 95.5 (2006): 71–77. Print.
- O'Brien, Annemaree. *Creating Multimodal Texts*. 2013. Web. 29 Sept. 2014. <http://www.creatingmultimodaltexts.com>.
- Orwell, George. "Politics and the English Language." *Language Awareness: Readings for College Writers*. 11th ed. Ed. Paul Eschholz, Alfred Rosa, and Virginia Clark. Boston: Bedford/St. Martin's, 2013. 234–44. Print.
- Poole, Steven. "Steven Poole: My Problem with George Orwell." *Guardian*. 17 Jan. 2013. Web. 29 Sept. 2014. <http://www.theguardian.com/books/2013/jan/17/my-problem-with-george-orwell>.
- Qualley, Donna. "Using Reading in the Writing Classroom." *Nuts and Bolts: A Practical Guide for Teaching College Composition*. Ed. Thomas Newkirk. Portsmouth, NH: Heinemann, 1993. 101–26. Print.
- Salvatori, Mariolina. "Conversations with Texts: Reading in the Teaching of Composition." *The Writing Teacher's Sourcebook*. 4th ed. Ed. Edward P. J. Corbett, Nancy Myers, and Gary Tate. Oxford: Oxford UP, 1999. 163–74. Print.
- Selfe, Richard J., and Cynthia L. Selfe. "'Convince Me!' Valuing Multimodal Literacies and Composing Public Service Announcements." *Theory into Practice* 47.2 (2008): 83–93. Print.
- Tan, Amy. "Mother Tongue." *Threepenny Review* 43 (1990): 7–8. Print.
- Zamel, Vivian. "Writing One's Way into Reading." *TESOL Quarterly* 26.3 (1992): 463–85. Print.

CHAPTER 8

Choices about Big-Picture Planning

This chapter will get you thinking about different big-picture ways to organize and map out your course, including working backward from your end goals (called "backward planning"), to ensure that your plans will help you and your students achieve the larger goals and objectives of your course (see Chapter 5). You will want to have your assignments from Chapter 6 (writing) and Chapter 7 (reading) at the ready as you work to construct your plans.

How will you manage the complexities of course design?

Course planning can be daunting for new composition teachers for a number of reasons:

- If you have read scholarship in the field of composition (e.g., articles listed at the end of Chapter 1 or the collections of essays listed in "Suggested Reading" at the back of this book), you have probably noticed that much of the scholarship deals with big-picture issues of philosophy and approach, but very little of it deals with the nuts and bolts of day-to-day planning.

- If you have taken teacher-training classes, you have probably written highly idealized course plans to demonstrate your mastery of theory, research, and pedagogical approaches. In fact, you may have spent hours planning just a single fifty-minute lesson. Now you are wondering, "How am I going to plan a whole course if it takes me so long just to plan a single lesson?"

- Your department may have given you a set of course learning objectives that appear both overly ambitious and frustratingly vague (e.g., "Students will write a variety of analytical texts in varied genres, for varied contexts, and for varied audiences"). You are wondering how you are going to turn these objectives into a cohesive writing course and actual day-to-day lesson plans.

- Your colleagues may have generously offered you some of their own course plans, assignments, or materials. Yet you find these difficult to decipher, intimidatingly complex, or puzzlingly sparse. When you try to teach from another teacher's plans, you discover that lessons or activities that supposedly "work wonders" for other teachers fall flat when you try to do them in your class.

When I first started teaching, I was overwhelmed by all the great things that my colleagues were doing in their classes. Everyone seemed to have awesome writing assignments and teaching activities. But when I borrowed something, it would fall flat in my class. I eventually realized that I can't just take other people's materials "as is"; I need to adapt them to my own teaching philosophy and my own teaching style.

—*Mark*

- You may be struggling with department-assigned textbooks and materials that do not seem to fit your teaching philosophy, style, or goals.

- And finally, you may be so anxious about the practical day-to-day questions (e.g., "What should I do in class on Monday morning?") that you have little energy to focus on the big picture.

As you will learn in this chapter's activities, an effective teacher is not someone who follows one particular planning practice, but rather someone who reflects and makes thoughtful, informed choices. As you will see later in this chapter, a good teacher is also someone who knows his or her particular planning style and can optimize that planning style.

When people think of planning, they often imagine a teacher filling in a calendar, moving chronologically, Monday to Friday, asking, "And what do I do after that?" However, effective planning is actually more like using the zoom lens on a camera: As a teacher, you zoom in close to examine an individual activity or assignment, you zoom out to see the whole course in one view, and you do a lot of moving back and forth between the big picture and the little details.

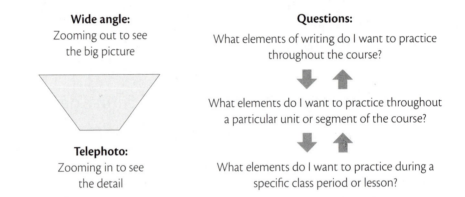

Wide angle:
Zooming out to see the big picture

Telephoto:
Zooming in to see the detail

Questions:

What elements of writing do I want to practice throughout the course?

What elements do I want to practice throughout a particular unit or segment of the course?

What elements do I want to practice during a specific class period or lesson?

To illustrate this, we will look at the following learning objective, taken from the *Framework for Success in Postsecondary Writing*'s recommendations on composing in electronic environments: Students will "select, evaluate, and use information and ideas from electronic sources responsibly in their own documents (whether by citation, hotlink, commentary, or other means)." Composition teachers cannot simply pencil this objective into a single class period, give a lecture on it, and then be done with it. Instead, teachers need to think about how this learning will take place through the entire course. Important questions include the following:

1. How will I integrate this learning objective throughout the course?

   - When do I want to introduce it? How do I want to introduce it?

   - How much of it do I want to teach and practice during each essay assignment, unit, or segment of the semester?

   - How will students build on what they know as the semester progresses?

   - By the end of the semester, what do I want students to have achieved? Where do I want them to be?

2. How will I integrate this learning objective into a particular unit, segment, or assignment?

   - When I am planning a series of class meetings that culminate in a specific writing assignment, where should I address the learning objective? Near the beginning? After discussing the readings? After students start drafting? After students have a complete draft?

   - How will I draw on what students have already learned in their prior writing assignments when introducing this new objective?

3. How will I plan a lesson or class period around this learning objective?

   - Can I break this objective down into smaller pieces in order to scaffold or "step out" the learning process?

   - How much can my students actually do in one class period?

   - How will I balance teacher-centered activity (explanation) with student-centered activity (discovery, experimentation, and practice)?

4. How will I set up specific activities within a lesson or class period to work on this learning objective?

   - Will I have students work in groups or alone?

   - Will I have students work on their own writing or on example texts?

   - What technology might be necessary to practice these activities?

Herein lies the challenge: Each of these choices is interdependent, and each question is embedded in your larger philosophies of teaching and writing. In short, you are always juggling and navigating through choices. In this chapter, we will focus on the big-picture choices about course planning. In the following chapter, we will look at some up-close choices about class planning. By the end of this book, you should feel more confident about making informed choices at all levels and navigating the terrain of teaching.

Fortunately, when you plan a college composition course, you are rarely starting from scratch. There are many conventional course designs you may want to draw on, especially if you are a new teacher. For example, regardless of your teaching philosophy or your level of expertise, you will probably divide the semester into several segments (or units, topics, or assignments), each of which will probably culminate in some sort of writing project. In the simplest and most conventional design, each of these segments culminates in an individual essay. For example, a fifteen-week semester might be divided into three-week segments, each of which culminates in a traditional essay, as shown in the following example.

> "I wish I'd learned more about nuts-and-bolts planning before I started teaching. I knew the big theories and controversies in the field of writing, but I didn't know to use that knowledge to create a course that was more than just "assorted activities." It took a lot of trial and error to figure out how my planning could make all the parts of my course fit together logically and cohesively.
>
> —*Tara*

Weeks	Writing projects
1–3	Essay 1
4–6	Essay 2
7–9	Essay 3
10–12	Essay 4
13–15	Essay 5

In more complex course designs, the writing projects might be interconnected. For instance, you could have students do a larger writing project that builds over many weeks, rather than write discrete essays, as shown in the following example.

Weeks	Writing projects
1–3	Choose a political, social, or economic problem that is being sidelined by mainstream media, and write a position paper arguing that we should address the problem.
4–6	Research the causes of the problem you selected, and write an essay that lays out your analysis. Draw on your position paper.
7–9	Write an essay in which you argue for a particular solution or a "way forward." Then combine your position paper, your analysis paper, and your solution paper into a single portfolio. Do a class presentation on what you have found.
10–12	(Additional assignments)
13–15	(Additional assignments)

In fact, this larger project could be even more complex; it might include multiple pieces of informal exploratory writing, data gathering (e.g., interviewing students on campus about the topic), multimedia presentations, blogging, or other assignments.

A common variation on traditional course design is the portfolio-based course. (We will discuss the logistics of portfolio assignments and grading in Chapter 14.) In such a design, students write multiple essays and then select certain essays for further revision. Students create a portfolio of revised essays, usually with an additional reflective piece of writing, such as a cover memo detailing their growth as writers. Portfolio-based classes commonly include time for "workshopping," revising, and conferencing so that students can assemble, reflect on, and polish their portfolio. In the following example, the teacher has students create both a midsemester portfolio and a final portfolio.

Weeks	Writing projects
1–2	Essay 1
3–4	Essay 2
5–6	Essay 3
7	Work on midsemester portfolio; include two revised pieces of writing.
8–9	Essay 4
10–11	Essay 5
12–13	Essay 6
14–15	Work on final portfolio; include four revised pieces of writing.

Another common variation on conventional course design includes an ongoing, semester-long project, along with shorter writing projects. This longer assignment might be an in-depth research paper, some sort of data-based project (e.g., interviews or observations), a semester-long blogging project, or a "book club," as in the next example.

Weeks	Individual writing projects	Ongoing project
1–3	Essay 1	"Book club": Groups of students choose a novel, meet throughout the semester to discuss it, and write short reflections. In weeks 13 through 15, they do presentations and write an essay about the novel.
4–6	Essay 2	
7–9	Essay 3	
10–12	Essay 4	
13–15	Presentations and essay on book club novel	

The best way to become comfortable with big-picture planning is to experiment with various course designs. Think of a specific course that you will teach or that you would like to teach. In the following activity you explore a couple of different ways that you might arrange the "big picture" of that course.

 Activity 8.1   Exploring possible course designs

Fill in the following chart. Feel free to draw on the assignments and course objectives that you created in prior chapters. If you have department-mandated requirements (e.g., a certain number of essays or in-class writing assignments), try to include them in your designs. We are assuming a fifteen-week semester here, but you should tailor the chart to your own teaching context.

Week	Writing projects for design 1:	Writing projects for design 2:
1		
2		
3		
4		
5		
6		
7		
8		
9		
10		
11		
12		
13		
14		
15		

Activity 8.2   Reflecting on alternative course designs

You now have two different possible course designs. Consider how each of the designs fits with your teaching philosophy. Fill in the following chart.

How does design 1 fit with your philosophies of writing, writing processes, and teaching?	How does design 2 fit with your philosophies of writing, writing processes, and teaching?
What tensions does design 1 create?	**What tensions does design 2 create?**

In thinking about the two course designs, you noted tensions between the many things that you want to accomplish during a single semester. In the next activity, we list some common tensions. Try to position yourself among these tensions.

 Activity 8.3   Examining tensions in course design

Circle any ideas that resonate with you, and mark with an asterisk any ideas that cause tension. Unpack at least one of the tensions in your teaching journal.

Where do you fall in these competing tensions?		
I want to emphasize the long-term developmental process of drafting, experimentation, and discovery.	←→	I only have a limited amount of time in the semester.
I want to include lots of informal, low-stakes writing in the class — so students can develop confidence as writers.	←→	I want to include lots of formal writing — which takes a lot of time, energy, and stepped-out instructional scaffolding.
I want to include lots of workshop time in the semester.	←→	I want to include lots of time for the discussion of readings, strategies, and other activities.
I want to help students work independently on longer writing projects.	←→	I want to scaffold and support students throughout the semester.
I want to meet university expectations about the amount of "polished" final draft writing that students will produce.	←→	I want to hold true to our philosophy that drafting is valuable and that not every draft will become a final product.

YOUR TEACHING JOURNAL: Engaging with tensions

Choose the pair of ideas that causes the most tension for you, and brainstorm about it in your teaching journal. Consider the following questions:

- Why does the pair of ideas cause tension?
- How does the left side of the pair fit with your teaching philosophy?
- How does the right side of the pair fit with your teaching philosophy?
- How might you find a middle ground between the two sides?

How will you achieve specific learning objectives?

In prior chapters, you looked at big course goals and divided them into smaller learning objectives. You also began to practice looking at individual assignments and breaking them down into components or skills that students will need to be successful in the assignments. Now we will focus on mapping out course objectives over the semester.

It is tempting to start the mapping process at the beginning of the semester and work through it sequentially, week by week. This is especially true if you conceive of writing as a set of discrete skills that build sequentially. However, the planning process is generally easier (and produces more coherent results) if you start at the end. In other words, think about what you want students to have accomplished by the end of your course.

There are many ways to figure out what you want students to have accomplished:

- If your department has specific learning outcomes or learning objectives for the course, that is a good starting point for your planning.

- If your course is a prerequisite to another course, you can look at that course's syllabus or talk to its teachers to determine what skills your students need to master by the end of your course.

- If the department or your fellow faculty have sample student essays from prior semesters, you can use those as "anchors" to determine where students should be at the end of the semester.

- If students have written a diagnostic essay or produced an early writing sample, you can work from that, creating a list of objectives that you want students to attain.

- If your department uses a portfolio (or other assessment) at the end of each semester, you can look at the rubric for evaluating it.

In fact, teachers often use several of these methods, as well as their own experience, when honing a course plan.

Let us take some learning objectives and experiment with backward planning. Imagine that you are teaching a course with a relatively conventional design: You have divided your semester into five teaching segments, about three weeks each, and each segment culminates in a piece of formal writing. How do you map out learning objectives across such a course?

In the following chart, we map out a common learning objective, "Address writing to a range of audiences using a range of discourse strategies," across sequential essays. In the first segment ("Writing assignment 1"), students are introduced to the notion of audience and they write to a familiar audience — their classmates. By the time they reach the final segment ("Writing assignment 5"), they are writing to a much less familiar audience (one that they have researched themselves in "Writing assignment 4") and the students are doing a rhetorical analysis of their own writing. Note how the course builds toward the objective with each subsequent assignment.

Sample objective: Address writing to a range of audiences using a range of discourse/stylistic strategies

Assignment	How the assignment contributes to the objective
Writing assignment 1 Students each identify a problem in the community and write an essay about how they are personally affected. Classmates are the audience.	*Students see how a familiar audience reacts to their writing.*
Writing assignment 2 Students identify a problem in the community (e.g., lack of a children's playground) and write two "letters" about that problem — each letter directed to a different audience (e.g., neighbors vs. local government officials). Students also write a cover memo in which they reflect on the different approaches they took in addressing the two audiences.	*Students explore how they use different strategies and styles to address different audiences.*
Writing assignment 3 The whole class focuses on a single problem in the community (e.g., gentrification). The teacher provides a variety of articles from a variety of viewpoints directed to a variety of audiences (e.g., real estate developers, homeless advocates, homeowners). Students select two of the articles and compare how the authors use rhetorical and stylistic strategies to address their intended audiences.	*Students examine the variety of rhetorical strategies that authors use to address different audiences.*
Writing assignment 4 Students research a problem in the community to determine the "stakeholders" and explore the political, social, and economic interests of those stakeholders. Students write an essay presenting the results of the research.	*Students explore the characteristics and interests of audiences that they will address in Writing assignment 5.*
Writing assignment 5 Students write an essay addressed to one of the stakeholders in Writing assignment 4, arguing for a solution to the problem. Students also write a rhetorical analysis of their own essay, discussing the rhetorical strategies they used to appeal to that audience.	*Students produce writing directed toward an audience that they have researched and students consciously reflect on their rhetorical choices in addressing that audience.*

Activity 8.4   Mapping a learning objective across assignments

Now we ask you to select one of your own course learning objectives (Activity 5.9 and Activity 5.12) and map it out across assignments. How will each assignment contribute to that objective? Fill in the following chart.

Assignment:	How will each assignment contribute to the objective?
Writing assignment 1:	
Writing assignment 2:	
Writing assignment 3:	
Writing assignment 4:	
Writing assignment 5:	

Because writing courses have more than one learning objective, we must also think about how a single assignment can fulfill multiple learning objectives. The following example shows how a literary narrative assignment might touch on four different learning objectives.

Objective 1: Engage in writing as a creative, disciplined form of critical inquiry.	**Objective 2:** Address challenging questions about the consequences of their own writing.	**Objective 3:** Compose thoughtfully crafted essays that position the writer's ideas among other views.	**Objective 4:** Write with precision, nuance, and awareness of textual conventions.
How will the assignment contribute to each of the four objectives?			
Writing assignment: personal narrative about literacy learning	Students will learn to use brainstorming strategies, journaling, and freewriting to inquire into their own literacy experiences.	Students will learn to use peer response and critical reading strategies to develop and clarify their reflections about literacy learning.	Students will learn to integrate source texts on literacy into their narratives.	Students will note stylistic features in sample literacy narratives. Students will learn revision and editing strategies they can use to strengthen their narrative.

Activity 8.5   Negotiating multiple learning objectives

In this activity, you will use one of your own assignments to practice negotiating multiple learning objectives. List several course objectives across the top row of the chart, and then note how your assignment might contribute to each objective.

Objective 1:	Objective 2:	Objective 3:	Objective 4:
How will the assignment contribute to each of the four objectives?			
Your writing assignment:			

Of course, the biggest challenge in planning is juggling *multiple* learning objectives across *multiple* assignments. When you map learning objectives onto an entire writing course, you must do both longitudinal planning as you did in Activity 8.4 (i.e., planning across time) and latitudinal planning as you did in Activity 8.5 (i.e., planning for a single point in time, in this case a single writing assignment).

Juggling multiple objectives is challenging, and it almost always involves trade-offs. It is impossible for every writing assignment to contribute to every learning objective in a robust way. And planning becomes even more complex when you map multiple objectives across assignments. In the next activity you will explore these challenges.

 Activity 8.6   Aligning objectives and assignments

List four of your main learning objectives at the top of the chart, and list your major essay assignments down the left side. Then brainstorm about how each assignment will contribute to each objective. Remember that an assignment might not target or directly contribute to all four objectives. For example, if your first assignment is a personal narrative, it would probably contribute toward an objective such as "Practice various writing processes," but it would not necessarily contribute to an objective such as "Synthesize multiple source texts."

	Objective 1:	Objective 2:	Objective 3:	Objective 4:
How will the assignment contribute to each of the objectives?				
Writing assignment 1:				
Writing assignment 2:				
Writing assignment 3:				
Writing assignment 4:				
Writing assignment 5:				

YOUR TEACHING JOURNAL: Engaging with tensions

As you mapped multiple learning objectives onto multiple assignments across the arc of your course, you surely experienced challenges and tensions. In your teaching journal, address the following questions:

- Which learning objectives were most difficult to map onto assignments? Why do you think this is so?

- Which assignments were best at meeting multiple learning objectives? Why? Which assignments created tensions or conflicts between learning objectives? Why?

- Finally, reflect a bit on your own planning style: Did you begin with the objectives or did you begin with the assignments? Why? Did you start at the end of the course and work backward or did you start at the beginning and work forward? Why?

As you likely noticed while doing Activity 8.6, brainstorming and connecting your assignments to your objectives is by no means a linear process. At times, you sketch out the ways you would touch on each objective with a single writing assignment (working horizontally across the chart). At other times, you take one objective and see how it plays out in multiple assignments (working vertically down the chart). Sometimes, you start somewhere in the middle with a particular set of objectives that seem to cluster together in a single writing assignment, or you adapt a colleague's assignment (as in Activity 6.11) to more clearly fit your objectives and to complement your other assignments.

The important thing to remember in big-picture planning is that it is an iterative process of brainstorming and experimentation. Each time you add an objective or an assignment to your semester plan, new questions, tensions, and contradictions will arise. The goal is not to "solve the equation" or to create the "definitive" semester plan, but rather to see choices that you have in designing assignments and think about trade-offs that each choice entails.

How will you map out specific teaching activities onto your course plan?

Thus far, we have focused on the big picture of connecting major writing assignments with major course objectives. However, we now need to zoom in on particular teaching activities and map those onto your calendar for the semester.

The first step is to think about the skills students will need for a particular assignment and the activities that you will do in class to help students practice those skills.

Here is a sample assignment and a breakdown of the individual skills that students will need to practice in order to complete the assignment successfully:

Assignment	Academic, rhetorical, and critical thinking skills
Rhetorical analysis of an advertisement Choose a print ad that contains both image and text, and write a rhetorical analysis of that ad. Make sure your analysis goes deeper than mere description and that you go beyond things that are obvious (e.g., the delicious-looking hamburger makes you hungry). Your goal is to show the reader subtle or even covert ways that the ad creates an appeal. Be sure to draw on the readings that we have done.	• Note taking (especially for visuals) • Description • Finding something meaningful to say through critical and rhetorical reading • Supporting claims with examples • Planning and organizing the writing process • Integrating source materials (articles we have read about advertising) • Revising • Editing and proofreading

This list of skills may seem a bit overwhelming. You are probably asking, "How am I going to teach all that in three weeks?" However, you are not starting from scratch; students bring many academic, rhetorical, and critical thinking skills from prior writing experiences. For example, students surely acquired some useful note-taking skills before coming into your course. So your "lesson" on note taking might consist of simply giving a few tips about how to take notes on a visual print ad (because students probably have not done this before). Also, some of the skills in the preceding example are things that you may have introduced or practiced in prior units; for this unit, you may simply need to remind students to transfer those skills, or you may give students time in class to "do" the skill (e.g., editing).

After you have a list of skills required for an assignment, you can plot out teaching activities for the unit on a calendar grid. The following example considers a three-week unit for a class that meets three days a week.

Monday	Wednesday	Friday
1 (Start unit)	2	3
4	5	6
7	8	9 (Turn in final draft of essay)

This gives you a total of nine class meetings to fill with teaching activities that will help students write a successful paper—an often daunting prospect for new teachers. For some new teachers, this may seem like a huge amount of time; they may be wondering, "How am I going to create enough material to fill nine classes?" For other new teachers, this may seem like too little time; they may be wondering, "How am I going to squeeze everything into nine classes?" And for most new teachers, these nine classes will seem like a puzzle to be solved: "What do I do, and when do I do it?"

In mapping out these nine class meetings, however, teachers do not start from scratch. In fact, teaching units often follow a fairly consistent sequence of activities:

- Activities to introduce the topic or issue (e.g., brainstorming, discussions)
- Activities to prepare students for the readings (especially if the readings are difficult)
- Activities to work through the assigned readings (e.g., small-group discussions, whole-class discussions, reader-response journals, online discussion postings)
- Activities to start the writing process (e.g., freewriting, planning, brainstorming)
- Activities to support revision (e.g., peer response)
- Activities to support editing

We can map these activities onto our nine class meetings as follows:

Monday	Wednesday	Friday
1 Introduce the topic or issue Lead a pre-reading discussion	2 Discuss the reading Do reader-response journals Assign another reading	3 Discuss the reading Assign another reading
4 Discuss the reading Start the writing process	5 Create a first draft	6 Lead revision workshop Circle back to the readings
7 Conduct peer-response activities	8 Practice editing activities and apply to an "almost-final" draft	9 Allow students class time to compose a "cover memo" for the essay, in which they reflect on their writing processes, strengths, and challenges Turn in final draft of essay

Activity 8.7 Mapping a writing assignment across a unit

Now we ask you to take one of your own writing assignments (Activity 6.8) and attempt to map it out across a three-week unit. If you will be teaching a class that meets fewer or more days per week, adjust the chart.

Monday	Wednesday	Friday
1 (Start unit)	2	3
4	5	6
7	8	9 (Turn in unit assignment)

Turning to the field: Planning with assessment in mind

A last component of your successful big-picture planning will inevitably be assessment. Assessment is a way of gathering information to make decisions about learning and to inform teaching. It is integral for both you and your students so both parties know what has been learned and what remains to be done. In this way, assessment is more than just evaluation (or grading)—it also means using the assessment to gain valuable information about the teaching and learning that should come next.

We typically think about two major categories of assessment: formative and summative. *Formative assessments* provide in-process feedback to students that they can directly apply to a reading or writing project as they move forward on that project. Formative assessments might include responses to drafts, ungraded learning checklists or quizzes, or even asking students to explain in their own words a concept or process. Essentially, when a teacher asks students to check their understanding and provides feedback about that understanding, the teacher has conducted a formative assessment and is monitoring student learning and intervening to help. In the writing class, whenever you offer feedback for revision, you are conducting a formative assessment and offering formative feedback.

A *summative assessment*, instead of being in-process, usually concludes a unit, a course, or even a school year. It offers a summary of learning. Final drafts of papers or projects, final exams, and even standardized tests are thus summative assessments (and indeed, it is from summative assessments that we sometimes draw a negative connotation with the word *assessment*). Summative assessments are usually designed to be more comprehensive, to promote accountability for both students and teachers, and to be used as essential information to gauge how successfully course goals and outcomes have been met.

We will return to issues of assessment in the next several chapters, particularly Chapter 13 and Chapter 14. But for now, we will consider the field's best-practice principles about assessment so you can begin to imagine the types of assessment that will be most important in your course.

The *CCCC Position Statement on Writing Assessment* (revised 2009) states:

> In a course context, writing assessment should be part of the highly social activity within the community of faculty and students in the class. This social activity includes:
>
> - a period of ungraded work (prior to the completion of graded work) that receives response from multiple readers, including peer reviewers
> - assessment of texts—from initial through to final drafts—from human readers, and
> - more than one opportunity to demonstrate outcomes

The CCCC offers additional practices, listed in Activity 8.8, which are slightly more specific and which will help you further explore the ways that assessment will play out in your classes.

📁 Activity 8.8 Applying principles to assignments

Looking at your plans, and thinking perhaps about one key assignment from Activity 6.8, consider how you will use or adapt the WPA best-practice assessment principles. Fill in the following chart.

Best-practice assessment principle:	How will this play out for your assignment?
Self-assessment should be encouraged.	
Assessment practices and criteria should match the particular kind of text being created and its purpose.	
These criteria should be clearly communicated to students in advance so that the students can be guided by the criteria while writing.	

Lastly, your big-picture plans can begin to account for the larger assessment plan for your class. Consider the principle excerpted in Activity 8.9, as well as the pedagogical results that stem from that principle.

Activity 8.9 Pondering assessment principles

Circle any ideas that resonate with you, and mark with an asterisk any ideas that cause tension. Unpack at least one of the tensions in your teaching journal.

WPA Principle 3 for writing assessment

> Any individual's writing ability is a sum of a variety of skills employed in a diversity of contexts, and individual ability fluctuates unevenly among these varieties.
> As a result . . .
>
> **A.** Best assessment practice uses multiple measures. One piece of writing — even if it is generated under the most desirable conditions — can never serve as an indicator of overall writing ability, particularly for high-stakes decisions. Ideally, writing ability must be assessed by more than one piece of writing, in more than one genre, written on different occasions, for different audiences, and responded to and evaluated by multiple readers as part of a substantial and sustained writing process.
>
> **B.** Best assessment practice respects language variety and diversity and assesses writing on the basis of effectiveness for readers, acknowledging that as purposes vary, criteria will as well. Standardized tests that rely more on identifying grammatical and stylistic errors than authentic rhetorical choices disadvantage students whose home dialect is not the dominant dialect. Assessing authentic acts of writing simultaneously raises performance standards and provides multiple avenues to success. Thus students are not arbitrarily punished for linguistic differences that in some contexts make them more, not less, effective communicators. Furthermore, assessments that are keyed closely to an American cultural context may disadvantage second language writers. The CCCC Statement on Second Language Writing and Writers calls on us "to recognize the regular presence of second-language writers in writing classes, to understand their characteristics, and to develop instructional and administrative practices that are sensitive to their linguistic and cultural needs." Best assessment practice responds to this call by creating assessments that are sensitive to the language varieties in use among the local population and sensitive to the context-specific outcomes being assessed.
>
> **C.** Best assessment practice includes assessment by peers, instructors, and the student writer himself or herself. Valid assessment requires combining multiple perspectives on a performance and generating an overall assessment out of the combined descriptions of those multiple perspectives. As a result, assessments should include formative and summative assessments from all these kinds of readers. Reflection by the writer on her or his own writing processes and performances holds particular promise as a way of generating knowledge about writing and increasing the ability to write successfully.

Source: CCCC Executive Committee, "Writing Assessment: A Position Statement." Copyright © 2009 by National Council of Teachers of English. www.ncte.org/cccc/resources/positions/writingassessment.

YOUR TEACHING JOURNAL: Engaging with tensions
In dialogue with WPA Principle 3, jot down planning notes, pose questions, or engage with the big-picture ideas about assessment that will affect your planning. In your teaching journal, note the tensions that you are seeing in your beliefs about assessment.

Taking it further:
Examining alternative course designs

While teachers most commonly think of their semester in terms of discrete units, each typically lasting two to four weeks and culminating in a single piece of formal writing, there are certainly ways to break out of this "one paper per unit" box. Experimenting with alternative course designs can push your thinking further; even if you do not adopt a radically different course design, many of these experimental ideas can enrich your current course design and might allow you to be more responsive to student needs. In the next activities, we will ask you to experiment with two very different course designs: one that forgoes longer pieces of writing altogether in favor of shorter writing assignments or blogs, and another that places a heavy emphasis on in-class writing.

Imagine that instead of assigning four to six formal full-length papers, you are going to have your students write a series of ten to twenty blog entries throughout the semester. These blog entries will be shorter and less formal than traditional academic papers. (We will discuss blogging more in Chapter 16; if you are unfamiliar with blogs, you can think of this activity simply in terms of assigning shorter informal pieces of writing.)

📁 **Activity 8.10**   Mapping out blog assignments

Select one of the learning objectives that you worked with earlier in the chapter (Activities 8.4 through 8.6), and map it onto the types of blog entries that you might assign students. Fill in the following chart.

Learning objective:		
Blog	**What will you have students write about? What will be your writing prompt?**	**How will students build toward, practice, and demonstrate this learning objective?**
1		
2		
3		
4		
5		
6		
7		
8		
9		
10		

Activity 8.11 Mapping out a course with in-class exams

Now imagine that you are teaching in a program that requires you to do at least two in-class writing assignments (a midterm and a final), which must comprise a major portion of the course grade. Return to one of the course designs that you prepared in Activity 8.1, and rework this design to incorporate the in-class writing. Fill in the following chart.

Week	Activity
1	Essay 1 assignment:
2	
3	
4	Essay 2 assignment:
5	
6	
7	Midterm exam
8	Essay 3 assignment:
9	
10	
11	Essay 4 assignment:
12	
13	
14	
15	Final exam

What kind of writing task will you assign for the midterm?

What learning objectives will the midterm demonstrate?

How will the prior essays build toward or connect to the midterm?

What kind of writing task will you assign for the final?

What learning objectives will the final demonstrate?

How will the prior essays build toward or connect to the final?

Reflections from experienced teachers

Much of the "art" of planning comes through experience, including trial and error. New teachers can turn to their experienced colleagues for some shared wisdom on planning:

- Consider how you can "set the stage" with plans like these to move to more complex or more independent (less scaffolded) work later in the term. Teachers often begin with general critical reading skills, idea-generation skills, and prewriting skills for the first unit and focus more heavily on revision and editing skills toward the end of the semester; this is especially true in a portfolio-based course.

- Be cautious about introducing too many writing skills in a single course segment. Experienced teachers often introduce a small repertoire of skills for the first assignment and then reinforce those skills throughout the course. With each subsequent assignment, skills can be added to students' repertoires.

- Some activities will surely take longer than planned. You may want to consider building a bit of flexibility into course segments, and sometimes a bit of buffer time between course segments, just in case an assignment takes longer than expected.

- Once they have been planning for a while, seasoned teachers can identify their planning style and their level of comfort with structure. You can start by reflecting on questions and strategies such as the following: Are you anxious if you do not plan everything out ahead of time? Then get an early start, and allow yourself time to plan. Do you feel constricted if things are overplanned? Then build a loose structure based on course goals, and fill in the teaching activities as you go. Being aware of your planning style, and following it when you can, can help you feel more confident when you walk into the classroom.

- Most important, remember that planning gets easier each semester. During your first few semesters you may feel that you are reinventing the wheel with each assignment; however, as you gain experience, planning will become second nature to you.

Putting it together:
Explaining your course design process

Over the course of your career, you will likely be asked to teach many different courses as well as revise courses that you have already taught. Use the following activities to crystallize the processes and steps you will use in planning a course.

Activity 8.12   Creating a course-planning checklist

Imagine that you are preparing for an interview. The interview committee will ask you about the steps that you go through when planning a course. Brainstorm a checklist of steps. Your checklist should make it clear that you make thoughtful choices that are informed by the field and by your own philosophy of reading, writing, and teaching.

In addition to being a useful guide to help you think about how you would talk about course planning with others, the checklist you just generated will serve as an important tool that you can return to each time you plan a course. We recommend that you continue to revise it as you become a more expert planner.

In the next activity, you will think about a course that you are teaching (or one that you hope to teach). Discuss your plans and your rationale, referencing your own developing teaching philosophy (Activities 1.12, 2.10, 5.11, 6.15, and 6.16).

 Activity 8.13 Articulating the philosophical rationale for your course

In your teaching journal, discuss the following questions. Be sure to note any questions or issues that you are still wrestling with.

- What is the big-picture plan for the course?
- What is the rationale for the major planning decisions that you have made?
- How is your plan grounded in your philosophy of good writing, writing processes, and effective teaching?

In this chapter, we have explored big-picture planning, including the overall arc of your class and how to backward-plan to ensure you reach key course goals. Some of this planning will inevitably shift as you work on day-to-day lesson plans in Chapter 9; you may want to move back and forth between this chapter and the next as you continue to refine your course. And you will want to continue to return to early chapters of this book to check in with your overall philosophies about writing and teaching (Chapter 1 and Chapter 2), ensuring that your plans are indeed in line with the larger course goals you hope to achieve as well as your commitments to how you want to achieve them (Chapter 5).

Further Reading

- CCCC Committee on Assessment. "Writing Assessment: A Position Statement." National Council of Teachers of English/Conference on College Composition and Communication. March 2009. Web. 30 Sept. 2014. <http://www.ncte.org/cccc/resources/positions/writingassessment>.
- Ferris, Dana R., and John Hedgcock. *Teaching L2 Composition: Purpose, Process, and Practice.* New York: Routledge, 2013. 146–84. Print.
- Lindemann, Erika, and Daniel Anderson. *A Rhetoric for Writing Teachers.* 4th ed. New York: Oxford UP, 2001. 252–79. Print.
- Smagorinsky, P. *Teaching English by Design.* Portsmouth, NH: Heinemann, 2008. Print.
- Wiggins, G., and J. McTighe. *Understanding by Design.* Alexandria, VA: ASCD, 2005. Print.

CHAPTER 9

Choices about Day-to-Day Planning

Now we turn to the quintessential teacher question, "What am I going to do in class on Monday morning?" You are well prepared to answer this question and plan your lessons because you have articulated your course goals (Chapter 5) and your big-picture vision of the class (Chapter 8). More specifically, you have practiced dividing the semester into segments, units, or assignments (Activity 6.8 and Activity 8.1), you have plotted out your objectives over the semester (Activity 8.4 and Activity 8.6), and you have practiced plotting out the rough progression of a unit (Activity 8.7). This chapter asks you to build on this work to think more specifically about your day-to-day plans and the choices you will need to make to ensure productive class sessions.

How will you structure individual class periods?

If you have taken courses about teaching, you probably have experience writing out long, detailed lesson plans with objectives, scripted teacher dialogues, rationales, outcomes, and all sorts of other things that display your understanding of pedagogy for your professor. And if you have worked in the K–12 school system, you probably have experience writing out lesson plans that display for the administration how your teaching activities are linked to mandated learning outcomes. In contrast, in this chapter you will learn how to craft lesson plans for yourself. You are your own audience for your lesson plan.

We find some lesson-planning guides from graduate-level pedagogy classes to be overly complicated for everyday use. Here are a couple of examples:

Example 1	Example 2
Stage 1: Pre-lesson preparation	Sections
• Goals	• Subject of lesson
• Content	• Instructional aids, materials, or tools needed
• Student entry level	• References
Stage 2: Lesson planning and implementation	• Lesson outline
• Unit title	• Assignment
• Instructional goals	Notes
• Objectives	
• Rationale	
• Content	
• Instructional procedures	
• Evaluation procedures	
• Materials	
Stage 3: Post-lesson activities	
• Lesson evaluation and revision	

Rather than prescribe a set formula, we want to stress that teachers' lesson-planning styles vary greatly: Some write out lesson plans in great detail, scripting everything they are going to say; some sketch out only parts of a lesson; and some go into a class with just one or two bullet points scribbled on a piece of paper. Compare, for example, these two lesson plans, each for a seventy-five-minute period in which students will read and respond to one another's papers:

Teacher A's lesson plan	Teacher B's lesson plan
• 15 min: Elicit principles of good peer response, put on board; go over goals of peer response	• Do peer response — focus on organization and develop (whole class period)
• 5 min: Assign peer-response groups; remind students to focus on content not grammar	
• 25 min: First round of response — 10 min to read and 15 min to discuss w/partner	
• 25 min: Second round of peer response (w/new partner) — 10 min to read, 15 min to discuss w/partner	
• 5 min: Discussion; revision homework	

Which teacher's plan is better? How much detail is "enough"? And how should you construct your own lesson plans? The short answer is that you should write as much detail as you—yourself—need for that particular lesson or activity.

For example, if students have practiced peer response many times and have the routine down, teacher B's single bullet point might suffice as your lesson plan. If you are introducing peer response for the first time, you probably need an even more detailed plan than teacher A's plan. Keep in mind, though, that even well-seasoned teachers still script out individual parts of a lesson plan when they integrate new material, new skills, or new activities into their teaching.

As a general rule, we recommend that you create more detailed lesson plans during your first few semesters of teaching; you will naturally taper the amount of detail as you build up your repertoire of familiar teaching activities.

In previous chapters, we noted that you are not starting from scratch each time you plan a writing unit. Similarly, you are not starting from scratch each time you plan a lesson. Class periods generally follow a rough pattern or arc that includes some or all of these elements:

- Write a brief outline of today's activities and tomorrow's homework on the board.
- Give some sort of greeting or opener.
- Take attendance.
- Collect homework.
- Make general announcements.
- Explain the activity or activities of the day.
- Explain the rationale for the day's work.
- Do the activity.
- Summarize what students have done.
- Assign homework.

Much of this may be obvious, but it can still be helpful to have a checklist handy when planning. Even experienced teachers forget important items of a lesson—especially when they are very intellectually involved in what they are teaching.

📁 Activity 9.1 Outlining an individual class period

Select a day from the course or unit that you have been planning, and fully map out the sequence of activities for the class period. Include both the "business items," such as taking attendance and assigning homework, as well as the teaching activities. Adapt the following chart to your particular teaching context. For example, if you will be teaching a ninety-minute class, plan for ninety minutes. In the right-hand column, estimate how many minutes each activity will take.

Detailed sequence of activities:	Estimated time:

If you are a completely new teacher, you will want to repeat this planning process to cover the first several days—or even several weeks—of the semester. As you progress through the semester and as sequencing becomes more automatic, your daily lesson plans will become shorter, perhaps even resembling very briefly the lesson plan of "Teacher B" depicted earlier in the chapter, which simply said, "Do peer response—focus on organization and develop."

How will you effectively explain goals and activities?

By now, you have practiced mapping out your semester, your teaching units, and your individual class periods; you also have a fairly clear idea about what you will be doing and why you will be doing it. However, it is important to remember that your plans and goals are not automatically clear to students, even if you outlined them on the syllabus.

It is a good idea to continually remind students of where they are on any given day. We have noticed that the most effective teachers tend to write a few bullet points on the board telling students what they will be doing that day and what the homework will be for the next class. From a cognitive perspective, students are "juggling a lot of balls" as they work on your class activities (and the activities in their other classes). A simple visual reference can help them stay on track. The bullet points can also make the purpose of the lesson clear. If students know what they are going to do and why, they will be more invested in your lesson and will pay greater attention. Finally, even in an advanced class, you may have students with special learning styles or needs; writing a brief outline on the board is one way to build in reinforcement and redundancy to help them. Here are a couple of examples:

Today:
Discuss readings. Explain essay assignment.
Homework:
Write first draft of essay.

Goals for the week:
Today: Select a general topic for your paper. Wednesday: Explore topic in an "idea draft," and find a "kernel" of an idea you want to focus on. Friday: Develop the "kernel" into a first draft.

Activity 9.2   Practicing board work for a lesson

Now look back at some of your evolving unit plans (such as in Activity 8.7), select a couple of class periods, and sketch out the notes that you will write on the board at the beginning of those class periods. Fill in the following chart.

Example 1:	**Example 2:**

If you are a new teacher, you will want to do this for many classes, perhaps sketching out the first several days—or even several weeks—of the semester. In time, the process of writing board notes becomes more automatic, decreasing your need to script board notes. However, a bit of scripting can help even an experienced teacher stay focused on the progression of the lesson and the rationale for specific teaching activities within that lesson.

Scripting your rationale for activities

To help students understand what they should be doing at any given time in your class, it is important to share with them your rationale for activities or assignments, telling *why* they should be doing something, and *how* a given activity or exercise connects to their learning. Things that are obvious to us, as teachers, are not always obvious to students (e.g., that class discussions should somehow lead into the thinking that students do for their essays). Students often do not see the connection between what they have already done in your class and what they are doing today. And students are often confused about how today's activity will relate to subsequent work. This is why explaining the rationale for particular activities is so important.

Although it may seem awkward or unnecessary, we recommend scripting the rationale of the lesson—both so that you can remember to do it and so that you can figure out clear and succinct language that will be accessible to all students. Here are some examples of short "scripts" from various teachers:

> Over the past couple of weeks, we've read a variety of pro and con articles about our topic. Today we're going to summarize the pro and con arguments so that you can draw on them when you write your essay over the weekend.

> Over the weekend, you worked on your first draft to get some ideas down on paper. Today you're going to share those ideas with a partner to get some feedback from the perspective of a reader. This feedback will help you when you revise your draft for Friday.

> We have practiced several revision strategies so far this semester. Today we're going to add yet another strategy to your repertoire so that you'll have lots of techniques to use when you revise your drafts next week.

While reading these scripts, you may think, "Of course I'm going to explain what we've done and what we're going to do, so why should I script it?" But you would be surprised at how many experienced teachers—even superb teachers— forget to explain to students the rationale for what they are doing, how it builds on what students have done already, and how it will contribute to what they are going to do in subsequent writing.

Similarly, at the end of an activity, you should return to the overall purpose and rationale. Here are two short scripts from teachers:

> In our discussion today, we fleshed out descriptions of the most important characters in the story. This will help you when you do the homework assignment, which is to choose one character and show how the author portrays that character.

> Today we did lots of brainstorming and wrote a lot of potential research paper topics on the board. This gives you a wide range of topics to choose

from. The next step, for homework, is to freewrite about two or three of these topics to test them out and see if they interest you.

How will you plan for contingencies?

Thus far, we have assumed that your teaching lessons will go exactly according to plan. Unfortunately, this is seldom the case, even for experienced teachers. Therefore you must build flexibility into your teaching plans. It can be helpful to think about these two questions:

- What will I do if the lesson or activity takes much less time than expected?
- What will I do if the lesson or activity takes much more time than expected?

The answer to the first question is simple: Always have a backup activity in mind for each class period. Here are some common options:

- Preview the next class's lesson.
- Have students get a head start on their homework assignment.
- Do a quick review of lessons that you have already covered.
- Practice strategies such as freewriting, brainstorming, or proofreading.

The second question can be thornier, especially when the lesson of the day is a prerequisite to the homework assignment. Here are a few particularly challenging examples:

- You are doing peer response in pairs. Only half of the students have given feedback to their partners, but class time has run out.
- You are working on a rhetorical, stylistic, or grammatical point that is a prerequisite for the homework. Students are confused, but class time has run out.
- You need to complete an in-class activity today so that students can write the first draft of their essay over the weekend, but class time has run out.

An inexperienced teacher might become flustered when situations like these occur—we certainly did during our first semesters of teaching! However, with experience you will build up a repertoire of contingency plans for such scenarios. Here are a few examples:

- Push the remainder of the activity to the next class meeting, and postpone the related homework assignment. This works especially well for a class that meets frequently because little time is lost.
- Have students continue the activity electronically. For example, group members can e-mail their feedback to students who did not receive it or can continue the activity through an online discussion during peer response.
- Reframe the instructions for the activity. For example, if you ask your students to analyze three sample essays in class but they only manage to get through one, you can simply reframe the instructions as follows: "We've discussed one sample essay together, and now I'd like you to analyze the remaining essays for homework."

Turning to the field:
Planning across different modes of teaching and learning

As teaching and learning continue to span different modalities, the features and opportunities of these modalities can shape our planning, resulting in more effective pedagogy. As we consider the different ways that students learn, and the different learning opportunities afforded to them via different modes, we can make more subtle choices in our day-to-day plans.

First, consider how you might plan to incorporate learning across the various modalities of *listening* (to classmates, the teacher, podcasts, videos), *speaking* (in small-group and whole-class settings), *reading* (student work, the work of professional authors, one's own work), and *writing* (formal and informal, in-class, at home, online).

Activity 9.3 Planning for multimodal learning

Using a daily plan, such as the one you created for Activity 9.1, consider how you might plan to have students learning through listening, speaking, reading, and writing. Fill in the following chart.

	How will you use this modality in the lesson?	How will it aid learning in this lesson?
Listening		
Speaking		
Reading		
Writing		
	What are the benefits of incorporating all four modes of learning in each lesson?	What are the challenges of incorporating all four modes of learning in each lesson?

Now we will further extend this reflective planning across modes. A CCCC committee has recently created a document outlining the best practices for online writing instruction ("A Position Statement of Principles and Example Effective Practices for Online Writing Instruction [OWI]"). As the modes of learning and teaching increase to include fully online writing courses, hybrid courses (with both online and face-to-face interactions), distance learning, and even massive open online courses (MOOCs), teachers need to consider how they can take advantage of the features of these new modes.

Activity 9.4 Applying effective online practices

Some of the practices articulated in the CCCC document are particularly relevant to day-to-day planning. The following chart summarizes them. Jot down notes about how you might apply each practice to your course plan and daily lesson plans. We have filled in the first box as an example.

Practices for online and hybrid teaching:	How I might integrate this practice:
Text-based instruction should be supplemented with oral and/or video instruction in keeping with the need for presenting instruction in different and redundant modalities.	When I assign online texts for homework, I will also give students links to relevant news clips or podcasts to diversify the modalities students can use to access key content information.
Teachers should provide students with additional and supportive course materials through hyperlinks, electronic documents, and access to databases.	
The concept of the "classroom" can be expanded productively to include time when students and teacher are not physically present in a room. For example, discussions, collaborative work, research, invention activities, and individual and group instruction and guidance begun in class can continue beyond that point using both asynchronous and synchronous modalities.	
The inherently archival nature of the online environment should be used for learning. To this end, teachers should use the digital setting to encourage students to rhetorically and metacognitively analyze their own learning/writing processes and progress.	

Source: CCCC Committee on Best Practices for Online Instruction, "A Position Statement of Principles and Example Effective Practices for Online Writing Instruction (OWI)." Copyright © 2013 by National Council of Teachers of English. www.ncte.org/cccc/resources/positions/owiprinciples.

Taking it further: Planning for multiple class formats

In the coming years, many of us will be called on to teach some form of hybrid course—one that meets for fewer hours in a physical classroom and has online activities that complement the in-class work. Even those who never teach an actual hybrid course will probably be expected to extend their in-class teaching with online activities via a course-management system like Blackboard or Moodle. In fact, the use of course-management systems has become the norm in composition teaching, and it is particularly important when a faculty member will be absent for several class periods (to attend a conference, for example).

Designing a hybrid course can be challenging. Consider, for example, the following unit plan that a writing instructor might use in a Monday–Wednesday–Friday class that meets for a total of three hours a week. Imagine now that the instructor has been asked to teach a *hybrid version* of the course that will meet only once a week for an hour on Mondays with the rest of the teaching and learning taking place online. As a first step in planning the instructor has crossed out the Wednesday and Friday class meetings.

Monday (face-to-face)	Wednesday (no class meeting)	Friday (no class meeting)
1 Introduce the topic or issue Lead a pre-reading discussion	2 Discuss the reading Do reader-response journals Assign another reading	3 Discuss the reading Assign another reading
4 Discuss the reading Start the writing process	5 Create a first draft	6 Do revision activities Circle back to the readings
7 Do peer response	8 Do editing activities	9 Turn in the paper

As you can see from the unit plan, the teacher cannot simply move all Wednesday and Friday activities to an online discussion forum. Instead, the teacher must think carefully about what activities are most usefully done in a face-to-face forum, what activities can be done online, and what form the online activities will take.

Activity 9.5   Restructuring a unit plan for a hybrid course

Select one of the unit plans that you designed in the last chapter, or a plan for a course that you are already teaching. Now imagine that you have been assigned to teach a hybrid version of the course that meets only on Mondays; you must do the remaining teaching through online activities. Think about how you could rearrange the activities so that you can make the most productive use of face-to-face time with students. What would the new unit plan look like? Fill in the following chart.

Monday (face-to-face) *What might you do in class?*	Wednesday (no class meeting) *What might you do online?*	Friday (no class meeting) *What might you do online?*
1	2	3
4	5	6
7	8	9

Now consider in more detail how you might plan those three days that you are going to meet face-to-face. Because you and the students will only see each other three times during the unit, it is critical that you plan—and use—this in-class time judiciously.

It is also essential that you have a contingency plan for each of the three meetings, because activities cannot easily be postponed from one class meeting to the next as one might do in a regular Monday–Wednesday–Friday class. Most of the online activities will be contingent on the in-class activities; therefore, if you run out of time in class, you cannot simply say, "We'll continue this on Wednesday." While less of a problem, the contingency plan should also include ideas about what to do if the in-class activities go more quickly than expected. In a regular class, you would likely dismiss the students a few minutes early; however, in a hybrid class you will want to make full use of the precious face-to-face time.

 Activity 9.6   Planning in-class meetings for a hybrid course

Create a detailed plan for each of the three Mondays, mapping out what you will do in class (as you did in Activity 9.1).

	Essential face-to-face activities:	**Contingency plan:**	**Optional activities:**
First Monday			
Second Monday			
Third Monday			

Reflections from experienced teachers

One of the trickiest challenges related to planning is knowing how much planning is enough. Individual teachers often need a few semesters to figure this out, and many times the amount of planning they need as a new teacher will change as they become more seasoned. Ultimately, you will find that planning comes down to striking a balance between focus and spontaneity, all the while helping you (and your students) feel confident that you have a plan and know where you are headed.

As you continue to explore the amount and types of planning that work best for you, consider the following ideas and wisdom from your experienced colleagues:

- Many teachers find that a key part of planning is making clear connections, or bridges, between different aspects of the lesson. This means (when you are planning a lesson for the first time) often ordering and reordering activities until you feel confident that the parts of the lesson will achieve the desired goals and will help students learn effectively. Some teachers find it useful to write out the transitions between different class segments.

- Similarly, many teachers write notes about the rationale for activities. Since it is essential to explain why students are doing what they are doing, it is important to include this explicit teaching. Having some notes can help remind you.

- You may find that your time estimates for activities become more precise as you gain more experience. To help develop this precision, teachers often find it helpful to try to discover patterns in their timing. Are you a teacher who always moves too fast and has extra time? Or do you find yourself running out of time in every class? Why do you think this might be?

- As you become more experienced, you will likely experiment with how much planning you need. Although it is helpful (and reassuring) to have a plan (and even a backup plan or some "extra" activities), it can also be nice to build a lesson directly out of what happened in the previous class. Good teachers try both approaches, and some approaches in between, to see what works best.

- Experimenting often by generating a few options for a given part of the class will allow you to choose the option that seems most natural or useful in the moment—or even to ask students which activity they would find most useful.

Putting it together:
Articulating your approach to lesson planning

Now that you have worked through a chapter on big-picture planning (Chapter 8) and this chapter on day-to-day planning, use the activities that follow to distill and describe the type of planner you are and the role that planning plays in your course and teaching philosophy.

Activity 9.7   Explaining your planning process in the context of your philosophy

Imagine that you are preparing for a job interview. The interview committee will ask you about your lesson-planning process—how you plan, why you plan that way, and what you keep in mind while planning. In the space provided, jot down several phrases you could use to describe your personal lesson-planning style. Include notes about how your planning style fits with your teaching persona and philosophy.

In the final activity, you will further develop your ideas in your teaching journal and begin some introspection about possible tensions between the way that you plan and your philosophy of teaching.

Activity 9.8   Articulating the philosophical rationale for your course

In your teaching journal, discuss the following questions. Be sure to note any questions or issues that you are still wrestling with.

- What is your lesson-planning style?
- In what ways does this style come out of your philosophy of teaching?
- In what ways does this style come out of your personal work style?
- Are there contradictions or tensions between your planning style and your philosophy of teaching?

At this point, you have thought about how your writing and reading assignments (Chapter 6 and Chapter 7) will play out in your course through both big-picture and daily plans. The next chapter adds a last piece of the puzzle to your planning: the use of textbooks. As you finish Part 2 of the book and move into Part 3, you will find many opportunities to revisit and revise the plans you have begun to make. Use your reflections from Chapter 8 and Chapter 9 about what type of planner you are to help support your ongoing planning as you continue to work through the rest of *Informed Choices*.

Further Reading

- CCCC Committee for Best Practices in Online Writing Instruction. "A Position Statement of Principles and Example Effective Practices for Online Writing Instruction." National Council of Teachers of English — Conference on College Composition and Communication. March 2013. Web. 30 Sept. 2014. <http://www.ncte.org/library/NCTEFiles/Groups/CCCC/OWIPrinciples.pdf>.

- Glenn, Cheryl, and Melissa A. Goldthwaite. *The St. Martin's Guide to Teaching Writing.* 7th ed. Boston: Bedford/St. Martin's, 2014. Print.

- Milkova, Stiliana. *Strategies for Effective Lesson Planning.* Center for Research on Learning and Teaching, University of Michigan. Web. 30 Sept. 2014. <http://www.crlt.umich.edu/gsis/p2_5>.

- Teaching Guide: Writing Lesson Plans. Writing@CSU, The Writing Studio. Web. 30 Sept. 2014. <http://writing.colostate.edu/guides/teaching/lesson_plans/>.

CHAPTER 10

Choices about Using a Textbook

Textbooks, handbooks, and digital resources for first-year composition are abundant, as are the ways you may choose to use such materials. Some teachers are assigned a particular textbook or set of materials by their department or program; other teachers have a great deal of freedom in choosing which textbook to adopt and even whether to use a textbook at all. Many teachers find themselves in between these two poles: Their departments have a list of commonly used or "endorsed" textbooks, but they still have leeway in making individual course adoptions. As you consider either your requirements or your freedoms, you might look back at the major writing assignments you generated in Activity 6.8, the readings you brainstormed about in Activity 7.2 and Activity 7.3, and the overall course designs you proposed in Activity 8.1 to consider what role a textbook might productively play in your class. Then use this chapter to help you practice analyzing the different views of writing that various textbooks present, so that any textbook you use will be integrated with your evolving philosophy of teaching writing.

What role will textbooks play in your course?

This chapter explores what textbooks can offer, and it presents some suggestions for assessing textbooks and implementing them in the writing classroom. Of course, much of this book also encourages teachers to use their autonomy and expertise to develop their own assignments that best serve their particular students and their goals. Knowing when a textbook might be useful, or how to best implement a required textbook, is thus a helpful complement to earlier chapters about developing individualized materials. Before we discuss textbook choices, we will define several categories that often organize textbooks that will be helpful in our discussion.

Readers.   Textbooks that consist mainly of readings—rather than pedagogical activities—are generally referred to as *readers*. They typically contain essays, but sometimes literature, excerpts from longer nonfiction works, or pieces from other genres, such as blog posts and images. Because students and instructors have different strengths and interests, the selections in readers can range from extremely brief (only a page or two) to quite long (ten or twenty pages), from easy to very challenging, and may include very contemporary or mostly classic essays.

Publishers usually divide readers into two broad categories by their organization: rhetorical readers and thematic readers. (A small number of readers are organized alphabetically or by purpose.) Rhetorical readers organize the selections by chapter categories that describe types or features of writing: narration, description, cause/effect, and so on. Thematic readers are organized by subject; chapters of thematic readers may focus on topics such as family, education, and gender.

Whether rhetorical or thematic, a good reader not only collects readings but ties them together with a pedagogical focus. This focus is referred to as the *apparatus* and often may include an introduction for students, chapter introductions, headnotes, and post-reading questions. Rhetorically organized readers generally have more apparatus than do thematic readers—that is, rhetorical readers often aim to teach students more about writing as well as presenting readings. On the whole, readers typically have less of this apparatus than do *rhetorics*.

Rhetorics.   In comparison to a reader, the rhetoric's primary goal is to teach students about writing. Whether its approach is classically rhetorical, process-oriented, genre-based, or argument-based, a rhetoric presents both information and guided opportunities for students to practice writing (through assignments, questions, sample student writing, and the like). So although a rhetoric may also contain readings, it differs from a reader in the amount of teaching material it presents.

Handbooks.   Handbooks are usually shorter texts designed primarily to explain writing conventions. Handbooks can range from short "pocket" volumes with brief style lessons, usage rules, and convention guidelines, to longer texts that also include information about writing processes, research, and the like. Style manuals, such as those for MLA or APA styles, are also considered handbooks.

Custom textbook.   It is now fairly easy to create a custom textbook with your own materials, apparatus, and readings (or some combination thereof). Most major publishers offer this option.

What can a textbook offer you and your students?

There are four main benefits that most textbooks offer: structure and support, a wide range of readings and assignments, a coherent philosophy of writing, and auxiliary materials—including online materials—to support students. Let us explore each of these potential benefits in depth.

Structure and support

One of the primary benefits of using a textbook is that someone has done most of the thinking about your course structure for you; the author has spent significant time choosing readings, writing assignments, and discussion questions and may have created cohesive sequences of assignments. Usually, a textbook also explores a particular topic or approach (e.g., a writing process approach, a focus on argument, an exploration of multiculturalism, a Writing about Writing approach).

For new teachers, and for those teaching a new class or in a new program, reliance on a textbook can be useful, grounding, and reassuring.

A good textbook will also often have an instructor's manual, sometimes called *Resources for Teaching*. A manual may offer tips for using the textbook, correlations to WPA guidelines, additional activities and assignments, sample syllabi and student writing, and summaries of readings. You can often find the manual either bound into the text as an instructor's edition or as a PDF that can be downloaded for free from the publisher's catalog site; these resources can support teachers, as well as help them to explore new ideas and approaches.

This grounding force is, in fact, why many programs suggest or require that teachers use a particular textbook or one from an "approved" textbook list. Requiring that all teachers use the same textbook supports cohesion within a writing program. Writing program directors know that many instructors are teaching multiple sections, sometimes at multiple schools; requiring the use of a common textbook helps ensure that all teachers are working with similar materials and toward similar goals and outcomes. A required or approved textbook can also help new teachers be in sync with their colleagues or students more easily, particularly if they are new to a program. And of course, using a textbook helps students stay organized because all their materials and readings are located in the same place.

Teachers who use textbooks can rely on them (to differing degrees, depending on the book) to collate readings, provide discussion questions, offer a range of writing assignments, and even do some of the "instructing" about writing processes, revision, or other common writing topics. For busy or new teachers, this structure and support can be invaluable. It can also allow teachers to ascertain how a full course that promotes a particular approach to writing might play out.

A wide range of readings and assignments

Similarly, one of the key benefits that a textbook offers is a large menu of both readings and assignments from which a teacher may choose. Instead of collecting readings on your own, asking colleagues for suggestions, or searching at the bookstore or online, you can select from the materials that the textbook author has already collected and feel assured that the authors of those materials have been fairly compensated. Typically, textbooks offer a range of materials from the tried-and-true to new favorites—that is, they will collect canonical favorites, as well as try to update popular issues, themes, or genres with more contemporary selections. For teachers who are pressed for time, who are looking to explore new issues or topics, or who want to revitalize their practice, textbooks can offer new, productive materials for teaching without requiring a lot of legwork finding or creating materials. In fact, textbooks can be one of the best resources to explore to discover new readings, new assignments, or new genres.

Many teachers also appreciate the range of assignments that textbooks contain. Some textbooks offer support at many levels of instruction—from in-class discussion questions or writing prompts to major assignments and revision projects. This ready supply of effective teaching materials can save teachers from having to create their own materials.

A coherent philosophy of writing

One strength of good textbooks that may be less obvious than the abundance of structured materials they offer is a coherent and cohesive philosophy of writing. As we have argued throughout this book, having a coherent philosophy for teaching writing—for why you are doing what you are doing—is essential. What this means in practical terms is that good textbooks present a clearly articulated view of writing that is expressed in the assignments and structure of the book. This can be greatly beneficial to new teachers, since it makes clear how a consistent view of writing can play out throughout a term; teachers can see how a strong belief in revision, for example, can be integrated at every level of the class. However, it is also important for teachers to be able to assess if the textbook's philosophy is, indeed, consistent, while also reflecting on whether the textbook's philosophy is a strong fit for them and their students. We will work with such assessment later in this chapter.

Auxiliary materials

A more recent benefit of adopting a textbook is the wealth of supplementary materials and support accompanying the textbook. Many publishers have created online resources that may include teachers' manuals, additional reading, or even support-based instruction, such as grammar exercises or portfolio tools. Depending on your plans for your semester and your particular students, these online materials may or may not be useful to you—it is usually difficult to get to all the materials in a given textbook as it is! But online materials can help diversify your teaching platforms and the ways and places your students interact with course material, which can be very attractive to both teachers and students.

> When choosing a textbook for my writing class, I used to start by looking at the readings to see if they were interesting and engaging. This was helpful, as I was trying to gather new readings for my course. Now I do just the opposite; I start by looking at the writing activities structured around the readings, and I ask myself if the activities fit my philosophy of teaching. Whether the philosophy of the textbook "matches" my key values about writing has become my new benchmark for selecting a textbook.
>
> —*Tara*

Turning to the field:
Analyzing writing ideologies in textbooks

Whether you are exploring a textbook you have been assigned to teach from or are surveying textbooks on your own for possible adoption, having ways to assess a textbook, its goals, and its philosophy is key. You will need to identify a given textbook's view of writing, ascertain how that fits with your philosophy, decide which reading and writing assignments to use, and make any adaptations or modifications necessary for your students and your goals.

In his seminal work about composition, scholar James Berlin argues that our different views of writing are informed by the different beliefs we have about four interconnected elements: who the writer is, who the audience is (and how they interact with the writer), what language is and how it works, and what reality consists of (as well as how we perceive and communicate reality). Consider two different views on meaning: (1) Meaning is created by the author and resides primarily in the text, and (2) meaning is negotiated between writer and reader via the mediating (and constructing) force of language. Each of these views would result in very different approaches to teaching both reading and writing. As you are assessing a textbook, it is helpful to look for the view of writing, or ideology, that the textbook promotes. For example, consider the different views of writing present in the following prompts.

Prompt 1	Prompt 2
Now that we have read several current articles on the state of education and its problems, it is time to make your voice heard. Write an essay in which you describe a pressing problem in education, and use your experiences to offer concrete solutions.	Mary Louise Pratt draws on Benedict Anderson's idea of "imagined communities" to describe her own idea of contact zones. Analyze Pratt's use of Anderson's concept: How does it help her make her argument?

	Prompt 1	Prompt 2
View of writing	• Writing is communication; clear communication is possible between the writer and the audience (the writer can make a recommendation that an audience can follow). • Experience is valued in making arguments.	• Writing provides a way of thinking critically or "analyzing." • Writers use writing to examine ideas. • Writing is about more than communicating an argument to an outside audience; it is also a way to think and reflect.
View of students	• Students have ideas worth communicating. • Students can draw on their experience to argue for change and to solve problems.	• Students need practice analyzing concepts and how they fit together. • Students can use writing to help read and understand more deeply. • Students can be a primary audience for their own writing.

Now try your hand at performing the same analysis with a textbook prompt.

 Activity 10.1 Analyzing views of writing in a textbook

Use a prompt from a textbook that you have already, or go online to find a writing prompt. Fill in the following chart.

	Brief summary of the prompt:
View of writing	
View of students	

How will you decide if a textbook is right for you and your course?

In line with examining a textbook's view of writing, there are two good places to start your initial assessment of a textbook. The first is the introduction to the textbook—whether it is addressed to teachers or students. Here the authors will often lay out any guiding principles or philosophies that have shaped the book. A rhetorically oriented textbook may begin by giving an example of a rhetorical situation and foregrounding how the text will ask students to pay attention to audience and purpose throughout. An inquiry-based textbook might extol the value of critical thinking—of asking good questions and being able to pursue and answer those questions through different types of writing and research. Literature-based textbooks might discuss the importance of reading or might highlight contemporary themes or questions that will introduce students to literary study. Whatever the approach, figuring out the view of writing that the textbook presents will help you make an initial decision about whether to continue assessing the text. You may be able to eliminate the textbook from consideration, or you may determine that you will have to adapt it if it is an assigned text.

📁 Activity 10.2   Analyzing a textbook you are considering using

In this activity, we ask you to analyze a textbook that you are considering, one that a colleague uses, or one that is mandated by your program. Answer the following questions.

---

1. What theoretical assumptions or beliefs seem to inform this textbook?

2. How are these theoretical beliefs connected to, or played out in, the textbook's pedagogy or approach?

3. How would you describe how this textbook views students (e.g., what they are capable of, interested in, in need of)? How does it address students? What kinds of students might benefit most from this textbook?

4. How would you describe how this textbook views teachers? How does it address teachers?

A second way to begin assessing and analyzing a particular textbook is to survey the major writing assignments the text offers. You should examine several of the major writing prompts, looking for patterns and analyzing the view of writing (as you practiced in Activity 10.1 and Activity 10.2). For example, you should consider the following:

- Your general impression of the writing prompts, including the level of difficulty and sophistication they demand
- The length of the prompts
- The kinds of questions that are asked (e.g., inquiry-based, project-based, creative, centered on reporting back information, and so on)
- Your impressions about what the textbook seems to be encouraging students to practice, including any implicit habits of mind or worldviews
- Your assessment of whether the assignments are useful, engaging, and pertinent

You might also consider whether the assignments offer a good fit for your specific student population. By investigating a textbook using the two approaches above, as well as taking time to identify the textbook's ideology and the subsequent fit with your teaching philosophy, you will have a solid sense of whether you would like to adopt (or adapt) it.

 Activity 10.3 Exploring the implementation of a textbook in your class

As you think about implementing a particular textbook in your class, consider the modifications you might need to make to match the textbook to your philosophy, your course goals, and the needs of your students. Answer the following questions to make a final assessment of a textbook you are considering.

1. What would be the benefits and limitations of using this textbook in your class?

2. What elements of the textbook would you have to supplement or revise?

3. What theoretical or pedagogical dissonances exist between this textbook and your philosophy, your course goals, and the needs of your students? What might you do to resolve or bridge those disagreements?

As you can see, many of the questions you will use to analyze a textbook are questions you have dealt with in terms of creating your own writing assignments and assignment sequence (see, for example, Activities 6.7, 6.10, and 6.11). You can use the questions in both this chapter and Chapter 6 to clarify the rationale behind particular assignments.

How will you adapt the textbook to better fit your philosophy?

There are many ways that you can use a textbook, from adopting the book and its philosophy wholesale, to using a textbook only for readings and providing your own writing assignments, to picking and choosing materials from the book and supplementing at each stage. As you begin working with a textbook, you might try the three strategies described in this section to pinpoint how you might use the textbook most effectively in your class. Of course, you will want to draw on your work in Activity 10.3, where you identified adaptations and modifications you think you might need to make to ensure your textbook will work for you and your students.

Find your path or trajectory

Textbooks offer a wealth of materials—often far more than any teacher could use. This is so teachers can choose the options that both appeal to and are most appropriate for their class, students, and program. With your goals and your students in mind, you will want to be selective (and realistic) about the material you would like to cover.

Once you have a sense of the reading and writing assignments you would like to use or adapt, take a step back to make sure there is a thread or path through the semester. In essence, you will probably use the textbook as a buffet of possibilities—but you want to make sure that it is a "connected buffet" that holds together as a whole course. Can you construct a sequence of assignments that makes sense in its progression? What are the themes and inquiries that you will explore across units? Or, to put this another way, do you have a clear sense of the larger intellectual or writing project your class will be working on by using the selected materials in the textbook? Look back at the earlier chapters of this book if you get stuck.

Adapt assignments to meet your outcomes

Once you have selected the materials you will use from the textbook and decided how they will fit together in a logical and appropriate progression, consider how the textbook and its assignments will help your students fulfill the learning outcomes for the class. You may find that the premade assignments in the textbook will not address all of the outcomes you are responsible for. If this is the case, identify the missing outcomes and add or tweak assignments to make sure they are addressed. Similarly, you will want to decide whether there are any necessary tweaks or clarifications you will need to make in working inside the textbook's view of writing. Are you fully on the same page philosophically and pedagogically? If not, or if the textbook largely matches your philosophy but differs in some small areas, you will need to outline any differences so you can clarify or discuss them with your students.

Adapt assignments for your class culture and tone

Finally, you might need to adapt assignments to match your class culture, the common practices within your classroom, and your tone. For example, if your textbook tends toward black-and-white, pro/con assignments but you want to encourage students to deal with more complexity and ambiguity, you will need to adapt assignments to reflect this different orientation. If your textbook tends to ask more content-based discussion questions but your approach is more rhetorical (focusing on what the writer did in the text and whether it is effective), you will need to revise those questions. Also consider the "voice" or tone of your

> "There's no perfect textbook. Even when I find a book that has readings I like and has activities that fit my teaching philosophy, I'm still going to need to adapt it heavily. I guess I've discovered that textbooks can never "teach themselves."
>
> —*Mark*

textbook and its writing prompts: Is it a voice you feel comfortable aligning yourself with? If not, adapt the prompts so that they fit better with the ethos of your course.

Taking it further:
Working with a mandated textbook

Not all teachers have the luxury (and responsibility) of choosing their own textbook or materials; sometimes this choice has already been made by a writing program director or a faculty committee. What can you do if your writing program's required textbook is not the one you would have chosen yourself? How can you adapt the textbook (and perhaps yourself) to make it work?

To practice adapting a mandated textbook to your teaching philosophy, you will begin by identifying a textbook that would not be your first choice for your course. This might be a textbook you have come across in your own education, one currently used in your department by some (or all) faculty, or one that you find online. (You can scroll through current releases at a Web site such as http://macmillanhighered.com/Catalog/discipline/English/Composition.) Likewise, if you are new to teaching or have not looked at many textbooks before, we suggest surveying four books from this link that are quite different, choosing the one that least appeals to you. (Try *Understanding Rhetoric*, *Ways of Reading*, *Writing about Writing*, and *Writer/Designer* to get a good variety.)

 Activity 10.4   Analyzing a textbook

Flip through the textbook (or explore the table of contents and samples available online), and make notes about your assessment of the book. Draw on the questions and interpretive strategies you practiced in Activity 10.1 and Activity 10.2 as you try to ascertain this textbook's philosophy and orientation. Then fill in the following chart.

The organization or philosophy of this textbook seems to privilege or value . . .	The readings and accompanying activities in this textbook seem to privilege or value . . .	The writing assignments in this textbook seem to privilege or value . . .

Now that you have ascertained some of the general values or principles of the textbook, you can begin to assess whether those values match your own.

Activity 10.5   Integrating a textbook with your philosophy

With the textbook's values or ideology now squarely in mind, compare how it fits with your views about writing, writing processes, and teaching. Fill in the following chart.

What aspects of this textbook overlap or mesh with your philosophy of writing?	How might you actively draw on these overlaps in your course?
What aspects of this textbook contradict or conflict with your philosophy of writing?	How might you adapt, reframe, or use these differences to your benefit?
Questions you would need to resolve if you were to use this textbook:	Resources that could help you plan how to productively use this book in your course:

Reflections from experienced teachers

Perhaps the most enduring question about using textbooks is whether the benefits are worth the cost. Will the time savings and cohesion offered by a textbook be worth the trade-offs of cost to students and perhaps tension between the textbook and the instructor's philosophies of writing and teaching? Often, adaptations can make a textbook work. But many teachers are left wondering whether they would not be better off creating custom materials to suit their students and their preferred pedagogies.

Whatever your stance on adopting textbooks for your course, they nonetheless offer a wealth of new ideas, new readings, and new approaches—as well as some of the rationale that allows you to understand their choices. Whether you use textbooks to gain fresh ideas, try out a new kind of assignment, support yourself when teaching for the first time or when teaching a new class, or in other ways, textbooks create the best partnership when you use them mindfully, maximizing their strengths while remaining alert to inconsistencies with your own practice and philosophy. As you consider where you stand regarding textbook adoption, the following reflections from experienced colleagues may aid you.

- A practical consideration that teachers often weigh in adopting a textbook is the ratio of price to how much students will use the book. If you are only using a handful of materials from a book, you should consider whether you can legally obtain those materials from somewhere else or perhaps assemble a custom reader. Students appreciate teachers' consideration of their budgets when making adoption decisions.

- Although there are many economical handbooks, many students will not know how to use a handbook effectively unless it is integrated into class instruction. Experienced teachers find that when requiring a handbook, it is essential to spend some time working with it in class so that it becomes a usable resource for students. Similarly, many teachers find that students will use the handbook more regularly when they are given time in class to work with it to address feedback; this is particularly true for teachers who refer to the handbook explicitly in their written feedback.

- Experienced teachers know that they will inevitably need to adapt, revise, or modify assignments to create their own cohesive trajectory through any textbook. This might mean creating a new prompt for some assignments, noting that the assignment was adapted from the textbook.

Putting it together:
Articulating your approach to textbooks

Textbooks can be a terrific resource and a reassuring support. Like any resource you use, however, they cannot teach your writing class for you. It will be up to you to curate a cohesive set of materials and assignments from the textbook, to have a clear rationale, and to understand how the textbook does and does not mesh with your philosophy. Take the next step by trying to articulate your philosophy with regard to textbook use, drawing on what you have practiced in this chapter.

 Activity 10.6   Explaining your use of a textbook

Imagine that an interview committee will ask the following questions about your textbook use: Which textbook do you use in your first-year composition course? Why? What do you like about it? Does it have any limitations? If you do not use a textbook, why not? In the space provided, brainstorm some notes that you could use to answer these questions.

Now turn to your teaching journal, and think about the fit between your choices about textbook use and your course goals, your student population and their needs, and your developing philosophy of teaching.

Activity 10.7 Connecting your philosophy, your textbook choices, and your students

In your teaching journal, discuss the following questions. Be sure to note any questions or issues that you are still wrestling with.

- How will you match your choice of textbook and materials to your course goals?
- How will you match your choice of textbook and materials to your students' needs?
- How do these choices reflect your developing teaching philosophy?

This final chapter in Part 2 of *Informed Choices* has given you the opportunity to assess textbooks you may (or must) use and has helped you start thinking about either adoption decisions or adaptations. If you do adopt a textbook, you can use it to help strengthen your assignments (Activities 6.8, 7.2, and 7.3) and to shape both your big-picture unit planning (Chapter 8) and your day-to-day lesson plans (Chapter 9). However, you should also use the thinking and composing you have done in those activities and chapters to thoughtfully and strategically inform how you will use the textbook. That is, you should be guided by your own ideas for assignments and plans, along with your course goals (Chapter 5) and developing teaching philosophy (Chapter 1, Chapter 2, and the concluding activities of many chapters), in determining how a textbook fits with your course design.

The significant work you have already completed will be further developed as you turn to Parts 3 and 4. These parts ask you to deepen your understanding of the many ways to support student writing and to teach composition in the twenty-first century—what it means to teach in a diverse, technologically rich world and how you can continue to grow and develop as a teacher.

Further Reading

- Berlin, James. "Contemporary Composition: The Major Pedagogical Theories." *College English* 44.8 (1982): 765–77. Print.

- Connors, Robert J. "The Rise and Fall of the Modes of Discourse." *College Composition and Communication* 32.4 (1981): 444–55. Print.

- Hawhee, Debra. "Composition History and the Harbrace College Handbook." *College Composition and Communication* 50.3 (1999): 504–23. Print.

- Knoblauch, Abby. "A Textbook Argument: Definitions of Argument in Leading Composition Textbooks." *College Composition and Communication* 63.2 (2011): 244–68. Print.

- Rendleman, Eliot. "Balancing Act: Student Valuation and Cultural Studies Composition Textbooks." *Composition Forum* 24 (2011): n. pag. Web. 30 Sept. 2014. <http://compositionforum.com/issue/24/balancing-act-textbooks.php>.

PART 3

Supporting Student Writing

CHAPTER 11

Opportunities for Writing and Writing Instruction

One of the central goals for us as writing teachers is just to get students writing. We hope that, as students write more, they also begin to write more fluently and with less fear. Given these goals, it is important to build writing into nearly every class session and to encourage writing for different purposes (including generating or processing ideas—or "writing to learn"—instead of just reporting ideas). This chapter offers strategies for integrating more writing into your class not only to get students writing frequently and regularly, but also to help create productive classroom learning experiences centered on writing and writing instruction—that is, to keep writing at the center of your class. Before you begin this chapter, you may want to circle back to your work with the first two chapters of this book. Recalling your definitions of good writing and good teaching—even if those definitions are still evolving and changing—can help you tackle the activities in this chapter with more purpose.

How will your students use writing to generate ideas and explore topics?

One of the primary reasons we write is to generate ideas. Many writers agree that often we do not know what we really think about a topic until we begin writing. Writing helps us articulate our thoughts, discover additional ideas, and refine our thinking. Giving students class time to practice using writing for invention will help demonstrate this fact and reinforce the use of this strategy. Consider how you might have students explore a new concept or theme through informal writing. Likewise, writing provides a wonderful way for students to engage difficult ideas or concepts, puzzling through them as it were. In the middle of a unit, informal writing can help students clarify their thinking or their position. And of course, writing can be used to brainstorm or map out topics, examples, and evidence as students move into more formal writing.

> I'll always remember a quote I heard in a composition pedagogy seminar: "If you actually have time to read and comment on everything that your students write, then you aren't assigning anywhere near enough writing." It took me a long time to realize what that meant: that students should be doing all kinds of writing and that I needed to be strategic about when my feedback was most helpful and needed.
>
> —*Mark*

Writing to engage ideas or texts

Teachers almost always use writing in their classes to get students to engage ideas and texts. Whether students are writing to summarize a text or to make an argument in response, whether they are freewriting to generate ideas or revising to expand and deepen ideas, they are using writing to think through concepts, questions, their own writing, and the writing of others. Exploring the options for writing can help you design meaningful writing activities to support various thinking and reading practices.

Teachers can consider the spectrum of writing (from summary to invention to integration to negotiation) when planning ways to get students engaged with ideas. Popular writing textbooks, like *Joining the Conversation*, offer a framework for thinking about this spectrum under the premise that academic writing can be thought of as representing an ongoing conversation. Thus, when students write, they are joining a conversation already in progress and are offering their thoughts and perspectives in return. To this end, the model teaches students how to effectively summarize others' ideas and how to respond with their own ideas. Writing becomes a way to negotiate different voices and viewpoints.

Activity 11.1   Creating engaging questions for students

Consider the different types of questions you might ask students to respond to in order to engage a complex idea like "Identity is socially constructed." See if you can fill in an additional question for each approach listed in the following chart.

Reading: _____

Idea: Identity is socially constructed.

Approach:	Question:	Additional question:
Personal experience with an aspect of this idea	Think about a time when you became aware of how others viewed you. Did their version of who you were differ from how you perceived yourself?	
Definitional work or conceptual work	Where do our identities come from? How do others help shape who we are, our goals, and our beliefs? Provide concrete examples.	
Clarifying understanding	What language does X use to explain how identity is socially constructed? Analyze his description. Why do you think he uses the words he does to describe this phenomenon? Paraphrase his argument in your own words.	
Exploring your stance in relationship to an author's ideas	To what extent do you agree with X's claim? What evidence can you offer from your own life to confirm or dispute his argument?	

Now take this exercise a bit further by investigating one of the readings you selected for your class in Chapter 7. (You might build on the inquiry questions you developed in Activity 7.2 or any of the readings you pinpointed in Activity 7.3.)

📁 Activity 11.2   Creating additional engaging questions for students

In the following chart, brainstorm a list of questions that you can use to engage students in an exploration of one of your course readings.

Reading: _____

Idea: _____

Approach:	Question:	Additional question or connection:
Personal experience with an aspect of this idea		
Definitional work or conceptual work		
Clarifying understanding		
Exploring your stance in relationship to an author's ideas		

Writing to begin, end, or structure discussion

A productive way to integrate more opportunities for writing into your class is to think strategically about how writing can further your pedagogical goals for a particular class. Writing provides rich opportunities for structuring your class, linking activities together, bridging different segments of your class, and applying learning.

Writing to begin a class or discussion	Writing to bridge activities	Writing to end a class or discussion
• Students write about a key question or term and then discuss it. • Students write about how ideas or issues apply to their lives and then discuss their ideas. • Students write the questions they have; they swap and try to answer; then swap back and respond. • Students write in response to an excerpt of student writing.	• Students apply the lesson or discussion to their own writing or draft. • Students write in response to a model or example. • Students write to problematize, ask questions. • Students write to develop examples or evidence.	• Students summarize takeaway points or strategies from the lesson. • Students use writing to prioritize tasks or goals for the next assignment. • Students write (and submit) their unanswered questions. • Students write to reflect on how their thinking has evolved or shifted.

Activity 11.3   Creating writing activities for a lesson or an assignment

Now you will apply these ideas to one of your lessons or assignments. Think about the specific activities that you will do to encourage writing. Fill in the following chart.

Lesson or assignment: _____

Writing to begin a class or discussion:	Writing to bridge activities:	Writing to end a class or discussion:

As a teacher, you should determine how you can most productively use the writing you ask students to generate in class. Often you will not collect or read the informal writing students complete. This writing is primarily to get them engaged and using writing to learn. It also provides a way to get students talking to one another. After students complete their writing, you might ask them to pair up to discuss their ideas, or you might have them talk in small groups if you have asked them a particularly rich or complex question. Or you might move directly into a full-class conversation after students have spent some time writing individually. Whatever configuration you choose on a given day should fit the instructional goals for that segment of the class. You should consider how students will learn or practice most productively—on their own, with a partner, in small groups, or as a whole class? Often some combination of these groupings will work best.

Writing to reflect

Many teachers find that reflective writing promotes some of the strongest gains for their students. By asking students to write reflectively, teachers can encourage them to

- Become more aware of their reading and writing processes and themselves as readers and writers
- Assess their strengths and weaknesses as writers, or assess the strengths and weaknesses of a piece of writing
- Strategize about how to continue to build on their strengths and address challenges
- Pinpoint the strategies or processes that work best for them, and develop metacognition
- Reflect on how ideas connect to or can be used to analyze their own experiences

- Reflect on how students can transfer their learning to other classes, contexts, or assignments
- Consider the many ideas they are encountering in class (or the university), and reflect on their college experience as a whole
- Set goals for themselves, and construct plans to reach those goals

If we want to help students develop the ability to reflect and build their capacity for metacognition, we must ask them to practice reflective writing regularly throughout the semester. Key moments to reflect are listed in the chart in Activity 11.4.

Activity 11.4   Considering key moments to reflect

Circle any ideas that resonate with you, and mark with an asterisk any ideas that cause tension. Unpack at least one of the tensions in your teaching journal.

Key moment for reflection	Questions for reflection
When submitting written work	What were you trying to accomplish in this draft? Where were you successful? What would you work on if you had more time? How have you applied feedback in this draft?
At the end of a challenging class or discussion	What will you take away from this discussion? What questions do you still have? How has your thinking or position shifted from the beginning of class?
At the end of a lesson or unit	How can you apply X to your own writing? How can this lesson help you revise your draft or begin making those changes? What do you need to do by the next time we meet?
When building or presenting a portfolio	Why have you selected the work you have? How does it represent you as a writer and student? What would you like readers to notice in your portfolio? How have you grown as a writer? Discuss using evidence from your portfolio.
At the beginning, middle, and end of the semester	*Beginning:* How would you describe yourself as a writer and reader? What would you like to learn or improve this semester? *Middle:* Looking back to your earlier writing, what progress do you see? Where have you improved? What are you still working on? What strategies are most useful to you? What else do you need to do to accomplish your learning goals? *End:* What have you learned this term? What processes and strategies will you continue to use? How does your work show how you have met the learning outcomes for this class? What can you use in other classes? How have you grown as a writer, reader, or student?

Looking at your notations above, brainstorm in your teaching journal. Consider the following questions:

- Which questions do you think would produce the strongest reflective writing? Why?
- Which questions seem less productive to you? Why?

Writing to self-assess, set goals, or strategize

In the preceding section, we suggested some questions that can help students use writing to set goals, check their progress, and make plans or strategize to achieve both short-term goals (What do I need to do to revise this paper for Monday?) and long-term goals (What strategies work best for me? What strategies can I use in other classes?). In these ways, students are also practicing metacognition: They are beginning to notice and direct their ways of thinking to better achieve their goals.

Notice how many of these reflective questions ask students to assess themselves—their writing and indeed their learning. This is an extremely valuable kind of writing (and thinking) exercise for students, since it encourages and rewards them for being responsible for their own learning. Additionally, it allows students agency in the assessment process, putting the teacher in the position of affirming or responding to students' self-assessments rather than being the sole assessor. Many teachers find that encouraging student self-assessment—asking students to write reflective cover memos to present their work, reflecting in writing on their progress and goals, or using rubrics to demonstrate how their work has met the required outcomes—puts students in the driver's seat. This can free up time for teachers in that they do not need to work as hard to justify their grades; indeed, feedback can become more streamlined as well, since students have already done a lot of the work. And it can help create a more positive environment with regard to evaluation and grading (issues we explore further in Chapter 14). When asked to be honest about their progress, effort, and performance—and to provide evidence from their writing—students often give themselves a grade that is very close to what the teacher would give, producing fewer surprises and more satisfaction with the evaluation process.

Writing dialogically

We might think of a productive writing class as a space for cross-fertilization: Ideas and words are exchanged and continue to influence everyone in an ongoing, generative way. As the teacher, you are a central facilitator in this cross-fertilization in the ways that you structure and encourage dialogue. By this we mean not only dialogue between yourself and the students, as well as among the students themselves, but also dialogue between ideas, methods, texts, and perspectives. By creating a dialogic classroom, you can model how scholars contend with ideas and use writing to add their voices to the mix.

To illustrate what we mean, consider how "dialogue" can serve as a useful metaphor across a unit on literacy narratives.

> "I've noticed that it can often take new teachers a long time to break out of the "teaching unit" mind-set—the idea that a "writing unit" consists mainly of rough draft, revision draft, and final draft with a little grammar and style instruction mixed in. Shifting new teachers' emphasis from these discrete products to students' overall development as academic readers and writers can help them focus on achieving their overall course goals and begin to experiment with assigning a range of writing that can help students succeed.
>
> —*Mark*

Dialogue between texts	Dialogue between ideas
How are the authors we have read exploring similar ideas? Why did their experiences differ? How does your experience compare to your classmates' narratives? Why did your experiences differ?	What questions do all of these texts (the authors we read and the student literacy narratives) raise about education? How should education change to promote more of the positive experiences and diminish the negative experiences? What does *literacy* mean, and what does it look like? Whose responsibility is literacy?
Dialogue between perspectives	**Dialogue between methods**
Malcolm X gives us a portrait of self-directed literacy, while Deborah Brandt explores how our "subject positions" (race, class, gender) shape the access we have to literacy. What would these two authors say to each other? What is the balance between individual motivation and societal structures/injustices in developing literacy? Amy Tan seems to promote the many "Englishes" she has learned and uses, while Richard Rodriguez details his pursuit of academic English (and, ultimately, his argument against bilingual education). Describe their different stances and their reasons for them. Then decide where you stand in response.	How does each writer go about relaying his or her story? How does each use both narrative and reflection effectively? Given these texts, what features of the literacy narrative genre can we discern? What is the purpose of the genre, and who are the audiences these texts address? Stylistically, what do you like about each author's writing style? What strategies do you see in these texts that you might try out in your own writing?

Of course, there is actual dialogue happening across all of these dimensions—real talk between students and real talk between you and your class. Foregrounding how we learn from talking with others—bouncing our ideas off others, testing or changing or refining our ideas in response to others—can highlight how much learning is dialogic in nature. And it can encourage students to be open to revising both their words and their ideas in ongoing and recursive ways, using dialogue as a generative strategy.

Activity 11.5 Brainstorming dialogic connections for an assignment

Select one of the assignments you have created, and fill in the following chart.

Dialogue between texts:	Dialogue between ideas:
Dialogue between perspectives:	**Dialogue between methods:**

How will student writing build throughout the semester?

With all the writing that students are doing, one of your challenges becomes finding ways to build on students' work instead of letting it fall to the side. There are real benefits to using student writing in class. Students appreciate seeing how their peers write or how they have approached an assignment. Students also appreciate seeing models of successful student writing and discussing how and why they work. The frequent sharing of writing in class shows that you value students' ideas and perspectives, promoting students' ownership over both their writing and their learning. And as students share and work on their writing with one another, they become more skilled at reading their own work critically and more comfortable with sharing their writing and receiving feedback.

One of the mainstays of your writing class will thus be looking at and discussing student writing. This can of course happen in peer review, but it can also happen as a whole-class discussion (or group work/discussion that then builds to a whole-class discussion) about how student writing works and how it could be productively revised. By bringing in excerpts of student work, as well as full essays, you can ask students to focus on particular elements of writing: One class might focus on several introductions or conclusions so students can work on strengthening these crucial elements of the essay; a workshop might pinpoint how writers use evidence to support their claims. The effective use of student writing means selecting samples from all students throughout the term, providing "representative" samples to work on together (samples in the midrange of performance that address issues that all or most students need to work on), and using everything from individual sentences culled from student work all the way up to full essays.

Another way to weave student writing into the class is to use it not only to discuss writing, but to discuss ideas. This might mean putting a few student sentences on the board, or bringing sample student work to class, and asking students to write in response to the ideas they see their peers discussing. When used in this way, the question shifts from "What do we notice about X in this piece of writing?" to "What do we make of the idea that Y is exploring in this writing?" This can be a productive way of beginning a conversation or introducing different opinions or positions in the classroom; it values students' ideas by engaging them, and it begins to put student texts and published texts on equal ground.

How will you teach writing rather than simply assign writing?

Even though we use writing in many ways throughout our courses, we must make sure that we are not merely *assigning* writing tasks but rather *using* writing tasks in ways that will help students grow as writers. Consider the following chart.

When writing is assigned . . .	When writing is taught . . .
Students are asked to write only on the teacher's topics.	Students have opportunities to create topics that matter to them.
The teacher selects writing topics for papers without consideration of audience and purpose.	Assignments specifically identify the audience and purpose for papers.
Most of a teacher's time is spent correcting papers.	Most of a teacher's time is spent in class teaching writing skills and strategies.
Students are asked to analyze, compare, describe, narrate, review, and summarize, without the strategies they need to successfully complete these tasks.	Students are given writing models, assignments, and strategies to guide each of their different writing tasks.
Students are not aware of significant improvement in their writing.	Students reflect on significant growth — or lack of it — in specific writing skills.
Students are sometimes required to rewrite, but rewriting usually is limited to correcting grammar, usage, and so on.	Students are encouraged to revise, edit, and improve — and to correct and resubmit their drafts.
Students are required to write without much forethought.	Students think about what they will write through brainstorming, freewriting, role playing, discussion, and other prewriting activities.
Students and teachers are bored by what students write.	Students and teachers are excited about what students write and make efforts to display and publish it.

Source: National Writing Project and Carl Nagin, from *Because Writing Matters: Improving Student Writing in Our Schools*. Copyright © 2003 by Jossey-Bass.

Activity 11.6   Investigating a writing assignment

Choose one of your writing assignments, and think about how you can teach rather than assign writing. Fill in the following chart.

Key writing tasks that are assigned in this prompt:	Ways to teach these assigned tasks:

When you find continuing opportunities to use writing in your class—and adopt the orientation of *teaching* writing (instead of just *assigning* it)—you help students grow as writers, gain confidence, and even perceive themselves more as writers and less as dutiful students. And this practice can help you pedagogically in terms of creating connections and bridges between the elements of a particular lesson or between classes. Using writing as the connective tissue that binds your in-class work, students' at-home work, and even the different parts of your lesson together relays the message that writing is, indeed, a crucial and useful way of making and communicating meaning in the world.

Turning to the field:
Metacognition and flexible writing processes

One of the reasons writing teachers advocate consistent and varied writing tasks throughout the semester is to help students become more astute observers and more successful managers of their own writing processes. Students often need several experiences to help them draw conclusions about their strengths and weaknesses, hone effective writing practices that work for them, or be able to stand back from themselves and think metacognitively. In the following activities, we first ask you to think concretely about how you can encourage students to develop their metacognition—one of the eight key habits of mind identified by the *Framework for Success in Postsecondary Writing*. We then ask you to think about how such metacognition can play a role as you and your students work together to achieve one of the main goals of any writing class: developing flexible writing processes. The *Framework for Success* defines *metacognition* as follows:

> **Metacognition**—the ability to reflect on one's own thinking as well as on the individual and cultural processes and systems used to structure knowledge. Metacognition is fostered when writers are encouraged to:
>
> - examine processes they use to think and write in a variety of disciplines and contexts
> - reflect on the texts that they have produced in a variety of contexts
> - connect choices they have made in texts to audiences and purposes for which texts are intended
> - use what they learn from reflections on one writing project to improve writing on subsequent projects

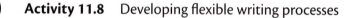

Activity 11.7   Promoting metacognition

What are some specific ways to promote metacognition in your course (questions to ask, tasks to assign, and so on)? Brainstorm in the space provided.

In the next activity, you will take a look at the suggestions that the *Framework for Success* provides for developing flexible writing practices.

Activity 11.8   Developing flexible writing processes

Circle any ideas that resonate with you, and mark with an asterisk any ideas that cause tension. Unpack at least one of the tensions in your teaching journal.

Developing flexible writing processes

Writing processes are the multiple strategies writers use to approach and undertake writing and research. Writing processes are not linear. Successful writers use different processes that vary over time and depend on the particular task. For example, a writer may research a topic before drafting, then after receiving feedback conduct additional research as part of revising. Writers learn to move back and forth through different stages of writing, adapting those stages to the situation. This ability to employ flexible writing processes is important as students encounter different types of writing tasks that require them to work through the various stages independently to produce final, polished texts. Teachers can help writers develop flexible processes by having students:

- practice all aspects of writing processes including invention, research, drafting, sharing with others, revising in response to reviews, and editing
- generate ideas and texts using a variety of processes and situate those ideas within different academic disciplines and contexts
- incorporate evidence and ideas from written, visual, graphic, verbal, and other kinds of texts
- use feedback to revise texts to make them appropriate for the academic discipline or context for which the writing is intended
- work with others in various stages of writing
- reflect on how different writing tasks and elements of the writing process contribute to their development as a writer

Source: Council of Writing Program Administrators, National Council of Teachers of English, and the National Writing Project, "Framework for Success in Postsecondary Writing." Copyright © 2011 by CWPA, NCTE, and NWP. Reprinted by permission. http://wpacouncil.org/framework.

YOUR TEACHING JOURNAL: Engaging with tensions

Select one of the ideas that causes tension for you, and brainstorm about it in your teaching journal. Consider the following questions:

- Why did it cause tension for you?
- In what ways does it conflict with your evolving teaching philosophy or your notions about what a college writing course should accomplish?

As a last step in thinking through how metacognition and a rich repertoire of flexible writing practices can serve your students, you will reflect on how these goals pertain to or play out in your specific class.

 Activity 11.9 Identifying ways to encourage metacognition

Fill in the following chart, identifying first the ways that you encourage flexible writing processes and then brainstorming about how you encourage metacognition about that flexibility.

	Assignments/units:	Elements/practices of the course:	Elements of your pedagogy:
Name specific facets of your course that encourage flexible writing processes for each category:			
Describe the flexibility each facet encourages or *how* it helps students develop flexible writing practices:			
Bullet strategies or questions to help students become metacognitively aware of the flexibility they are developing:			

Taking it further:
Incorporating writing frequently, consistently, and strategically

As we have started to explore, an important part of any writing class is the frequent and consistent use of writing. In short, we want to use writing as often as we can to help students both initiate learning and apply instruction. Asking students to write for a range of purposes—from exploring their ideas to engaging others' ideas to reflecting on their learning and processes—ensures that they develop and practice a range of writing strategies.

The list of writing practices in Activity 11.10 can help you think about how you might offer students additional opportunities to write, including writing to learn. But what does this look like in practice, in your specific classroom? Looking back at one of the units you planned in Chapter 8 and Chapter 9, think about the possibilities for ongoing, sustained writing. How might you use writing even more frequently and strategically in your course?

 Activity 11.10 Creating opportunities for ongoing sustained writing

Select one of the units you have planned, and fill in the following chart. Then brainstorm answers to the questions that follow.

Writing for different kinds of learning:	Ideas for using writing in this way throughout the course:
Writing to "prime the pump"—to help students engage a key issue, question, term, or piece of text	
Writing for a range of purposes—to find, explore, analyze, complicate, and communicate ideas	
Process writing—to reflect, strategize, set goals, plan	
Reflective writing—to consider learning, self-assess, determine how to apply strategies in future assignments	

What other types of writing might you integrate into various parts of the unit?	How could you structure some of these writing tasks so that students write collaboratively?

Reflections from experienced teachers

In this chapter, you have explored the many possibilities that exist for using writing in diverse ways in your class. Using writing throughout the writing process allows writing to be a tool for ongoing learning and discovery in your classroom, in addition to a tool for communication. One of the enduring challenges of a writing classroom is finding ways to weave writing and talking about writing throughout the class in a sustained way.

As you continue to explore this challenge, consider these ideas from veteran teachers:

- To get in the rhythm of including diverse types of writing throughout the course, experienced teachers often find themselves examining their lesson plans and asking questions like these: Have I scheduled in-class writing time throughout most stages of the process? Are students using writing to help with reading? Have I planned some writing or discussion of writing in every class?

- Experienced teachers know that experimentation—followed by observation and reflection—can lead to surprising and exciting results. Explore the many uses of writing in your classes and pay attention to how students respond to each. Do students come to rely on having time to write at the beginning of class? Do their attitudes about writing seem to be changing? Do they have a more engaged discussion if they have first written in response to a related question or concept? Discussing such questions with students will help them practice metacognition.

- It is important to take time to talk about words, sentences, structures, genres, and purposes—both in terms of what students have read and in terms of what they are writing. As a more experienced reader and writer, you can model your own thinking processes and challenge students to articulate "what works" in a piece of writing and how they might use similar strategies in their own work.

- Some veteran teachers enjoy writing alongside their students; you might consider whether this practice matches your philosophy of writing.

Putting it together:
Articulating your approach to ongoing student writing

Now that you have explored several ways to incorporate more writing throughout every stage of the writing process and have capitalized on the many diverse purposes for writing—from invention to strategic goal setting to reflection—try to pinpoint those practices that best fit with your own philosophy of writing and teaching.

Activity 11.11   Including more writing in your class

Imagine that an interview committee asks you the following question: What are the ways you include writing in your class—ways that go beyond just the formal full-length essay assignments? Brainstorm some possibilities in the space provided, and jot notes about how you would explain and justify these additional kinds of writing.

Given both the descriptive notes you have just made and the strategies you brainstormed in this chapter, consider the extent to which your course includes ongoing opportunities for writing. How do the choices you have made fit with and support your overall teaching philosophy?

Activity 11.12   Articulating your philosophy of ongoing writing

In your teaching journal, discuss the following questions. Be sure to note any questions or issues that you are still wrestling with.

- How will you use writing in an ongoing way in your class?
- How does this approach connect to your philosophy of good teaching?

In this chapter, you have explored how to ensure that writing is truly at the center of your class by asking students to write in multiple ways and for multiple kinds of learning, thinking, and processing. Writing in such ways—instead of on demand—is one of the characteristics that distinguishes writers from those who write only when they have to. Accordingly, if you can help students get in the habit of writing frequently, they too might come to see themselves more as writers and feel they have more confidence and control over their writing processes. As you move to the next chapter on peer collaboration, you might consider how the social component of your class can help reinforce understanding and build both self-directed and collaborative learning processes. In Chapter 13 and Chapter 14, you will gain a better sense of how revision and assessment practices, like the writing practices you explored in this chapter, are also ongoing.

Further Reading

- Fishman, Jenn, et al. "Performing Writing, Performing Literacy." *College Composition and Communication* 57.2 (2005): 224–52. Print.

- Gordon, Heather G. "Using a Reader Response Journal." *Teaching English in the Two-Year College* 28.1 (2000): 41–43. Print.

- Roozen, Kevin. "From Journals to Journalism: Tracing Trajectories of Literate Development." *College Composition and Communication* 60.3 (2009): 541–72. Print.

- Sommers, Nancy. "Across the Drafts." *College Composition and Communication* 58.2 (2006): 248–57. Print.

- ---. "Between the Drafts." *College Composition and Communication* 43.1 (1992): 23–31. Print.

CHAPTER 12

Choices about Peer Collaboration, Response, and Support in Your Class

One of the best resources students have for learning is one another. Many teachers want to capitalize on this resource while simultaneously creating a "student-centered classroom" where much of the learning takes place between students rather than in a unidirectional path from teacher to student. Yet it is sometimes challenging to find ways to make group work, especially peer review, be productive and feel useful for students. This chapter discusses issues related to community building, choosing appropriate levels of peer interaction for specific instructional goals, and selecting strategies for successful peer review. As in previous chapters, you will be guided by the philosophies of good writing and good teaching that you constructed in Chapter 1 and Chapter 2, as well as your overall course goals (Chapter 5) and the specific assignments and plans you created in Chapters 6 through 9. In this chapter, you will explore how you can capitalize on the social dimensions of learning and classrooms throughout the term.

What kind of classroom community will you create?

Preparing for successful peer interactions and support often begins on the very first day of the semester. Although much of this day is taken up with the logistics of managing the roster and going over the syllabus, try to find time on the first day—and over the next few class periods—to allow students to get to know one another and interact. From large-group introductions, which allow students to learn one another's names, where they are from, and what their majors are, to icebreakers that stimulate interaction and engagement, some initial community building can pay substantial dividends in the future. Of course, you will also be beginning the intellectual work of the class in these first days; however, finding ways to merge the two can be a useful strategy. Get students talking, learning about one another, and sharing a bit of writing. (Let them know when they will be sharing before they start writing so they can maintain some autonomy over what they share.) Do your part by learning students' names as quickly as you can. Circulate around the class often to engage students, and make your enthusiasm and interest evident. Ask colleagues for icebreakers they have used effectively, check out the resources at the end of this chapter, or search the many ideas available online. However you decide to build community, the goal is to start to get to know one another, to help students feel comfortable sharing ideas and questions (and even writing!), and to begin to construct and practice a shared vision of the course.

> I always believed that group collaboration, sharing ideas, and peer support were good things. But I quickly found out that a lot more goes into it than just putting students in groups and saying, "Discuss." After a lot of trial and error, I found that having clear but challenging questions, giving students time to warm up (sometimes by writing first), and making collaboration a regular part of our classroom activities seemed to help students feel comfortable sharing their ideas with one another.
>
> —*Tara*

One way teachers build community at a small-group level is to place students in writing groups. These groups allow students to get to know a handful of students more deeply, and they provide a structured support system for students as they begin the class (and perhaps college).

 Activity 12.1 Examining different group configurations

Your philosophy about writing and teaching will help you determine the types of writing groups that will fit your class, as well as how to create the groups and select the work that group members will do together. The following chart lists the potential benefits of different group configurations; complete the chart by listing the potential drawbacks.

	Potential benefits:	Potential drawbacks:
Same writing group all term	• The continuity of working with the same students all term can provide continuous, known support that can help students become accountable to one another. • Working with the same group can allow students to know several peers quite well and to observe their progress.	
Different writing groups during term	• Students can get to know more of their peers and have a wider audience for their work. • New groups can keep things fresh and challenge students in new ways.	
Ability-based groups: mixed	• Students can practice supporting one another and drawing on the group's resources. • These groups can raise students' awareness about their own strengths and weaknesses, as they work to recognize these traits in others.	
Ability-based groups: same	• Students can draw on their shared ability level to challenge one another. • Students may feel more comfortable in ability-based groups.	
Diversity-based groups	• The focus is more on gaining new viewpoints and audiences rather than on ability. • Students can learn from others who are different from them in terms of ethnicity, race, gender, majors, age, and so on.	
Interest-based groups	• Students can build on shared interests inside and outside of class. • For some projects, students may have similar audiences, purposes, or resources.	

Teacher-created groups	<ul><li>The teacher can tailor groups based on pedagogical goals.</li><li>The teacher can separate students who do not work well together.</li><li>The teacher can group students who will work well together.</li><li>The teacher can push students to move beyond their comfort zone, ensuring that they do not work with the same group of friends or like-minded classmates for each activity.</li></ul>	
Student-created groups	<ul><li>Students can choose others they know they will work well with.</li><li>Students can choose others they are comfortable with.</li><li>Students have some autonomy in who they work with.</li></ul>	

Of course, combinations of these configurations are possible. You can assign students to semester-long writing groups and have these groups perform consistent tasks (like responding to one another online or being a primary audience for one another's portfolios) while still using mixed groups occasionally in class. You can create groups for some tasks while allowing students to create their own groups for others. And you can always opt to change things up if you sense that the current groups are not working. Some teachers ask students in the middle of the term whether they want to change their groups or not (or if they are okay either way), and then they rearrange the groups accordingly.

How will you use collaboration in your classroom?

Successful teachers often use a range of collaborative strategies and groupings to keep the class moving, to change things up, and of course to meet different pedagogical and instructional objectives. As you explored in Chapter 11, many of these interactions begin by having students first do some individual writing. This gives students a chance to collect their thoughts and to deepen their ideas beyond their first impressions or reactions. It also helps to prevent students from immediately agreeing with one another when they move into groups. And it gives students something concrete that they can share with others; this can be especially helpful for students who are shy or reluctant to speak. The following chart compares the advantages of various grouping configurations.

Partners	**Small groups**	**Writing groups**	**Whole class**
<ul><li>"Safer" to share more personal writing or less-developed, riskier ideas</li><li>Easiest to manage logistically</li><li>Have more time to talk in depth about a piece of writing</li></ul>	<ul><li>Offer a wider range of responses and ideas</li><li>Challenge students to take on different roles and communicate differently than they do one-to-one</li><li>Useful for hashing out big ideas and exploring new concepts</li></ul>	<ul><li>Allow students to continue or build on earlier conversations since these groups are ongoing</li><li>Can track progress in members' growth</li><li>Can strengthen the existing rapport between students</li></ul>	<ul><li>Most efficient in sharing information and making sure everyone has a similar understanding</li><li>Often least interactive in terms of individual student contributions</li><li>Tends to be controlled by teacher's agenda</li></ul>

Now try your hand at pinpointing which levels of peer interaction might best support particular activities.

Activity 12.2   Creating a fit between tasks and levels of interaction

Using a unit from your developing course (perhaps a unit or group of lessons you created in Chapter 8 or Chapter 9), map out when you would like to use each type of interaction. Within that unit, which reading or idea activities work best at each level? Which writing activities work best at each level? Complete the following charts.

Exploring a key idea or reading

Inquiry question or reading: _____

Individual activities	Partners	Small groups	Writing groups	Whole class

Practicing writing

Lesson, writing strategy, or genre to practice: _____

Individual activities	Partners	Small groups	Writing groups	Whole class

Once you have a sense of these options, explore additional options that are in between or that combine different group configurations. For example, if you are moving from a paired talk to a whole-class discussion, perhaps it would make sense for students to return to their partners to debrief and strategize. After working with partners, perhaps two pairs could join to make a foursome; what types of activities might this configuration support?

How will you use collaboration online?

Many teachers are taking some of their class work online. Whether you use online resources and work spaces to help students stay engaged (particularly if you meet only once or twice a week), to allow them to connect and write in different ways, or to help you track where students are in terms of their reading, writing, or thinking, you can create online groups of different levels and organizational principles, depending on your goals.

Activity 12.3   Brainstorming possibilities for online work

List several teaching activities that you might do collaboratively online (e.g., group discussions, online reviewing and commenting on written work, blogs, e-folios) and list the pedagogical goals for those activities. Then brainstorm about possible group configurations for those activities as well as the resulting benefits for students.

Types of online activities or work:	Your pedagogical goals for the work:	Group configuration that makes sense given your goals:	Benefits of doing this work online in this format:

How will you structure effective peer review?

Structuring peer feedback is one of a writing teacher's main challenges. When peer review goes right, students teach themselves, become self-motivated, and practice becoming stronger critical readers of text—an essential skill that helps them revise their own work effectively, particularly in future classes or contexts where they will be working on their own. When peer review goes wrong, however, students learn little, they give and act on bad advice, and they are frustrated by a process that wastes their time and hurts their feelings.

So what can you do to ensure the first scenario instead of the second? First, embrace your role as facilitator and more experienced writer, and use peer review to work on specific issues that you see in student work. Teaching students how to read and respond to one another's work, while specifying what they are reading for, can help ensure a more focused and productive review session. We will now take a closer look at three modes of peer response.

Reader response

This mode of response asks students to focus on their experience of the text as readers. Typical questions focus on where readers were most engaged or interested in the text (and why), which parts of the text they admired or liked, which examples stayed with them, where they were confused, and where they

> "Peer response is one of those things that every teacher does because it's an expected part of teaching writing. But I think we all wrestle with the question, "Does it really help students?" I've discovered that it can help students if you really prepare them. You can't just tell them to exchange drafts with a partner and give each other advice.
>
> —*Mark*

wanted more information or wished the writer had said more. Reader response can also productively include "mirroring"—a strategy where readers state what they understand the writer to be saying. Especially for developing writers or those writers who do not yet have much self-awareness, a mirroring exercise can be clarifying and can point both reader and writer back to the text ("Hey! That's not what I meant at all! Why did you understand it that way?"). Reader response mimics one of the ways teachers often respond to student writing, particularly when reading more personal writing or when responding to writing early in the semester. Thus this mode of response is often very useful for the first rounds of peer review: It sets a positive tone for future peer review, it shows students that they are engaging ideas instead of correcting mistakes, and it gets them talking about the relationship between reader and writer.

Activity 12.4   Responding to a piece of writing

Test out these ideas by responding to a piece of student writing. (If you do not have any student writing handy, try searching "student essay" plus a broad topic or author to find a sample student essay to practice with.) Read the student work, and then answer the following questions.

1. What did you like or admire in this essay?

2. Where, specifically, were you most drawn in and engaged? Why did that passage or moment work well for you?

3. What will you take away from this essay — an impression, an idea, a question, an argument?

4. What questions would you have for this writer? What were you wondering as you read? Where did you want (or need) to know more?

Then reflect on the following questions:

1. What did you notice about responding to student writing using this framework?

2. To what extent was your interaction or intention different from the way you usually read student work?

3. What differences do you notice in responding as a reader versus responding in a more traditional sense?

4. To what extent did responding as a reader help you fulfill your course goals and allow you to enact your desired teacher persona? Look back to Chapter 1 and Chapter 5; consider adding to or revising your work in those chapters in light of what you have learned through this activity.

Task-specific peer response

This mode of response often draws on either your expertise in terms of what you know will be challenging about a given assignment or your conclusions about what most students need to spend time working on in their writing. In either case, you are asking students to work on their challenges together in the review session so that their drafts will be stronger by the time they make it to you. Peer-review questions thus ask students to complete specific tasks or answer specific questions, and they often connect directly to lessons you have been working on in class.

For example, if you find that students have trouble introducing a quotation, integrating it into their text, and then analyzing the quote, you will probably want to teach a mini-lesson or mini-workshop on these three skills. The next peer-review session would then focus on exactly this issue: Readers would answer specific questions about how well the writer has achieved each of the three desired goals (introducing, integrating, and analyzing quotes) and where he or she might need to revise. Students would work together to discuss these skills and start addressing them, offering suggestions to one another.

Another approach is to backward-plan from your assignment to determine where you think students will struggle, either conceptually or in terms of their writing. Generate peer-review questions that ask them to focus on these areas so that they can work together on the more challenging aspects of an assignment before being held individually accountable for their work.

Now it is time to practice constructing a task-specific peer-review session that gets students working collaboratively on the challenges of a particular writing assignment.

Activity 12.5   Constructing a task-specific peer-review session

Select one of your major writing assignments (use Activity 6.8, a draft of a writing prompt, or a plan from Chapter 8 or Chapter 9), and answer the following questions.

1. What is most challenging about this assignment? Where do you think students might struggle?

2. What can students identify or describe in one another's written work to help them focus on this issue?

3. What questions can you ask — or what tasks can you assign — to ensure that students work productively on the issue? If you have already taught a lesson on this issue, how might students apply that lesson by reading their peers' drafts? Generate some questions or tasks here:

Writer-driven peer response

Writer-driven response sessions require that all of the writers in the group have a high (and accurate) sense of awareness about their writing. Thus these sessions are often most useful toward the end of the semester or as students are working on self-designed projects where they have a clear sense of their goal or purpose. These sessions usually begin with the writer reflecting on the type of feedback that would be most useful; the writer then poses questions to the group. The group is thus guided by the writer's own concerns, including attending to any part of the draft that the writer knows needs more work or has been struggling with.

 Activity 12.6   Deciding what and when to do peer review

Look at one of your more challenging or complex writing assignments, and map three different options for peer review: one early in the process, one in the middle of the process, and one later in the process. What would be productive to focus on at each stage? Use your writing prompt to help you backward-plan to generate specific peer-review questions appropriate to each stage. Complete the following chart.

Early peer-review questions:	Mid-process peer-review questions:	Later peer-review questions:

Turning to the field:
Best practices for peer review and group work

You will notice that each of the models we have described—reader-response, task-specific, and writer-based—is more specific than the familiar (and usually too generic) writer workshop model, which asks some version of two questions: What is working? And what is not working? Your students may have enough practice with giving feedback by the end of the term to answer these questions productively, but few students entering your class will have enough context about academic, college-level writing to be able to offer sound advice. Additionally, this mode is sometimes the least effective in terms of efficiency and quality of conversation. Although this model may work well in other contexts, like creative writing classes or advanced writing classes, many first-year composition teachers will opt for one of the methods described earlier—or some combination or progression of those methods—instead of a less guided approach.

Whatever approach or combination of approaches you choose, remember that much of the benefit of peer review is actually in terms of teaching reading (not in offering writing advice). Although writers will walk away with some concrete feedback that can assist their revision, much of the learning happens when students read for particular things and in particular ways. Peer review is thus, in many ways, about students' development of awareness as readers so that, ultimately, they will become better readers of their own work by practicing on texts from which they have more distance.

The practice of using peer review or response, or group work more broadly, has been studied widely over the years. Composition scholar Wendy Bishop, for example, provides a good overview and synthesis of what we know in her article "Helping Peer Writing Groups Succeed." Specifically, she draws on previous research (cited in her article) to outline five major principles on which most successful peer groups are based. Bishop concludes that the following is true of successful peer groups:

- All members of the group are included in the task.
- Group members work together to clarify the task or assignment.
- The group uses a common vocabulary to describe writing.
- The group works on big-picture writing issues (such as argument, organization, or focus), not just minor writing issues.
- Group members come to value group work and see the instructor as a resource.

Although guidelines and goals such as these are helpful in planning your group activities, sometimes things will not go as planned when you ask students to learn and work collaboratively. Thus, having in mind Bishop's larger pedagogical principles for group work—understanding the theories behind group work, having clear uses of peer support in your class, and knowing your goals for having students work together—can help ground you and help you readjust when needed. Based on your knowledge about peer groups and your goals, you can then begin to anticipate common problems, think critically about what the possible causes are, and be prepared with responses (and know why you will make them).

Activity 12.7   Troubleshooting peer response

What will you do if a student does not bring a draft to peer review? (Will the student still offer feedback to others? Work alone on a draft in class? Brainstorm and map with other students with no draft?) How would knowing the possible causes of the student's action guide you in making a choice? And why, pedagogically, does that choice make sense for your class and philosophy? Consider how you will handle questions like these by completing the following chart.

Scenario:	Possible causes of this issue:	Strategies to address this issue:	Rationale for strategies, given your philosophy:
Students do not go beyond surface-level issues.			
One student dominates the group.			
No one has a clear understanding of the prompt.			
Students insist on defaulting to the teacher.			

Taking it further:
Comparing face-to-face and online responses

Although generally the same principles apply to peer review that takes place online (or via computer-mediated communication, or CMC), research is beginning to show us that peer interactions that take place via CMC might differ from face-to-face interactions. Composition scholar Beth Hewett has shown that the medium shapes both the kinds of responses that are given and how students revise in light of the feedback they receive. You can probably think of similar experiences of your own: How is the kind of response you give different if you are talking to someone directly, versus chatting with them online (synchronous communication), versus responding electronically via e-mail (asynchronous communication)?

 Activity 12.8 Comparing types of responses

To explore the dimensions of responses given via different media, complete the following chart.

	Face-to-face response:	Synchronous CMC response:	Asynchronous CMC response:
Possible benefits of this mode of response:			
Possible challenges or limitations of this mode:			
This mode seems best for . . .			

Now expand on what you learned in Activity 12.8 to investigate and complicate common beliefs about peer review.

Activity 12.9 Unpacking common notions of peer review

Fill in the following chart, pondering when the common notions may or may not be true.

Common beliefs about effective peer review:	In what situations might this be true?	In what situations might this *not* be true?
Students benefit from being taught how to do peer review effectively.		
Structured peer review is often better, especially initially. Know what you want students to work on, and focus their task.		
Peer feedback is best used to ask students to engage ideas and practice complex tasks (like integrating quotations or marshaling evidence), not correct mistakes.		
Peer review is useful when it is directly connected to recent lessons or things students have been practicing.		
Peer review often benefits the reader more than the writer. Through peer review, readers learn how to better read their own written work as they offer advice to the writer.		

Reflections from experienced teachers

In this chapter, you have explored the benefits, as well as some of the challenges, of cultivating peer relationships and support in your class. As you experiment with different types of peer review, continue to contemplate the trade-offs between student-directed collaborative learning (which generally takes more time) and more teacher-directed learning (which may be time-efficient and consistent but which allows students less agency). Between these two poles you may find a compromise, such as "structured freedom" in peer review or group work.

Lastly, do not hesitate to change tactics when necessary. For example, you may have started off intending to keep students in semester-long writing groups. But if that does not seem to be working (or you ask students and they say it is not working), you will need to adapt. Do not let an existing structure derail students or determine your pedagogy; stay flexible, not locked in. Students are usually pretty amenable if you say, "You know what? This isn't working. Let's make a change."

As you move forward, keep the following veteran-teacher strategies in mind for further reflection and action. Since peer review is one of those practices that new teachers often struggle with, we offer a slightly longer list of best practices culled from the field.

- Experienced teachers have a clear purpose for group work; they give their rationale to students and try to cultivate the classroom culture that serves their purpose. For example, if you encourage responsibility and frame getting peer feedback as a privilege, you may choose to make participation less about earning points and more about learning or practicing the skills that will help students reach a clear end goal (e.g., writing a successful essay with evidence, choosing the best examples of their work for their portfolio). How you frame the session is thus quite important and should match the larger goals of your class.

- Teachers often rely heavily on their own goals and philosophy of teaching to decide how structured to make peer-review sessions. Do you want students to mainly build community and enjoy reading one another's work? Do you want them to practice specific strategies? Or do you want writers to pinpoint the help they need and ask for support? Priorities will vary at different points in the semester, at different stages of the writing process, or for different assignments.

- Gathering information about how peer review is going allows teachers to redirect and readjust as necessary. Walk around to look at peer-review sheets and listen in on conversations. Occasionally collect peer-review sheets to ascertain the quality of the feedback, or ask students to write exit tickets about the most helpful piece of feedback they got from peer review as well as any questions that were not answered.

- Student conferences offer a good opportunity to check in with individuals about peer review or writing groups. During conferences, students can give you specific information about what is helpful and what is not.

- Sometimes ways of interacting that seem off-base may actually be important to building group rapport and community. There will inevitably be some off-topic chatter. With practice and judiciousness, teachers learn to discriminate between when this is okay and when groups need to be redirected.

- Experienced teachers find creative ways to foster group accountability and responsibility. The more students get to know one another, the more they may be called on to help one another, be accountable to one another, and go out of their way to ensure one another's success.

- Peer review is often most helpful when used consistently throughout the term. Frequently balancing this general consistency with additional sessions specifically aimed at addressing the challenges of upcoming assignments or incorporating new lessons or strategies will help keep peer review focused, useful, and fresh.

- Lastly, with experience, teachers come to recognize that for students to take seriously their jobs as peer reviewers and supporters, and to respect the responsibility it carries, teachers cannot undermine (or overwrite) the process. Do not, for example, offer your own feedback on the same drafts that students are peer reviewing—a move that might lead some students to disregard the process and their peers and focus solely on what you want or say. Instead, veteran teachers trust the process they have intentionally set up and wait to weigh in until the next draft.

Putting it together: Articulating your approach to student collaboration

Many teachers come to a rich understanding of the benefits and possibilities of group work through trial and error, but we hope that this chapter has given you a more informed foundation from which to begin exploring productive group dynamics and tasks. To synthesize the exploration and application you have completed in this chapter, try to outline the principles that will be most central to your philosophy of peer review, peer support, and group work in your first-year composition class.

 Activity 12.10   Using peer review in your course

Imagine that an interview committee will ask you the following questions: Do you use peer review in your class? If so, how? If you do not use peer review, why not? In the space provided, brainstorm key concepts, examples, or reasons to help you answer their questions.

Now you will take your answers a bit further by directly connecting your views on peer review, group work, and collaboration to your teaching philosophy. The next activity asks you to describe how peer support functions in your class and how it connects to your philosophy of teaching writing.

Activity 12.11 Articulating your philosophy of collaboration

In your teaching journal, discuss the following questions. Be sure to note any questions or issues that you are still wrestling with.

- What is your philosophy of student collaboration?
- How does it relate to your philosophy of good writing, the writing process, and effective teaching?
- How will you use collaboration in your classes?

You have now dug more deeply into specific classroom practices that will help students develop and strengthen their writing. Although ongoing opportunities to write are crucial for individual development (as we explored in Chapter 11), having an audience is a crucial part of learning how to be an effective writer. The work you have done in mapping opportunities for collaboration and peer support will also pay dividends, then, in helping students attend to both peer feedback as well as your feedback. The next two chapters thus take up these crucial components of the writing process loop: revision and feedback in Chapter 13 and assessment and evaluation in Chapter 14.

Further Reading

- Bishop, Wendy. "Helping Peer Writing Groups Succeed." *Teaching English in the Two-Year College* 15 (1988): 120–25. Print.
- Ching, Kory Lawson. "Peer Response in the Composition Classroom: An Alternative Genealogy." *Rhetoric Review* 26.3 (2007): 303–19. Print.
- Hewett, Beth L. "Characteristics of Interactive Oral and Computer-Mediated Peer Group Talk and Its Influence on Revision." *Computers and Composition* 17.3 (2000): 265–88. Print.
- Lockhart, Tara. *Sustained Peer Response for Active Engagement.* CSU Pachyderm. 2010. Web. 29 Sept. 2014. <http://pachyderm.csuprojects.org/pachyderm/presos/legacy /SustainedPeerResponseforActiveEngagement354/>.
- Roskelly, Hephzibah. "The Risky Business of Group Work." *The Writing Teacher's Sourcebook.* 3rd ed. Ed. Gary Tate et al. New York: Oxford UP, 1994. 141–46. Print.
- Strasma, Kip. "'Spotlighting': Peer-Response in Digitally Supported First-Year Writing Courses." *Teaching English in the Two-Year College* 37.2 (2009): 153–60. Print.

CHAPTER 13

Choices about Feedback and Revision

In the first chapter of this book, you began by exploring answers to the question "What is good writing?" Now that you have explored your role as a writing teacher (Chapters 2 through 4), the specific assignments that will drive your class (Chapter 6 and Chapter 7), and the ongoing practices that will shape your classroom (writing in Chapter 11 and peer support in Chapter 12), you are ready to consider the specific roles that feedback and revision will play in your course. As all writers know, both feedback from readers and purposeful revision are often needed to produce effective writing. This chapter asks you to first draw from your significant experiences as a writer and as a student to inform your own beliefs about constructive feedback and useful revision practices. As in other chapters, we then ask you to explore different perspectives from the field, practice composing different types of feedback, and ultimately align your views about feedback and revision with your evolving philosophy of how best to teach writing.

> "All through my own education, my professors gave me written feedback on my final draft, as an explanation or justification for the grade. It took me a few semesters of teaching to realize that feedback during the writing process is much more useful, especially when working with developing writers.
>
> —Mark

Activity 13.1 Reflecting on feedback you have received

Think about the feedback that teachers gave you about your writing in high school and college, and complete the following chart. Address the questions in the first column, and note anything else that you can remember about the feedback you received. Then fill in the second column with "do's and don'ts" about teacher feedback that you can derive from your experience.

Your experience:	Do's and don'ts drawn from your experience:
What kind of feedback did you get on your writing?	
At what stage in the writing process did your teachers provide feedback?	
What types of issues did the teachers comment on?	

What was the tone of the feedback?	
What did the teachers expect you to do with the feedback?	
What was your reaction to the feedback?	
Did you understand all the feedback?	

These do's and don'ts are a good starting point. We now ask you to flesh out more of your beliefs about feedback in the next activity.

 Activity 13.2   Examining feedback terminology

Circle any ideas that resonate with you, and mark with an asterisk any ideas that cause tension. Unpack at least one of the tensions in your teaching journal.

Terms that describe feedback . . .

support   holistic   grades   examples   editing
        critique   encouragement   red ink   "painful process"
improvement   dialogue   margin notes   office hours   grammar
        reader response   reflection   gatekeeping   peer groups
revision   writing tips   growth   "do's and don'ts"   assessment
        "awkward"   questioning   "pushing you"   help
errors   correction   evaluation   standards   typos

Additional terms that come to mind . . .

YOUR TEACHING JOURNAL: Engaging with tensions

Choose the term that you feel most uncomfortable with, and brainstorm about it in your teaching journal. Consider the following questions:

- Why does this idea create tension for you?

- In what ways does it clash with your teaching philosophy?

- How might you modify this term (rather than discard it) to make it fit better with your philosophy?

How will your feedback strategies reflect your teaching philosophy?

Now we will begin connecting feedback to specific teacher strategies. The chart in Activity 13.3 presents what four hypothetical teachers might say about the feedback they give to students.

 Activity 13.3 Examining notions of feedback

Circle any ideas that resonate with you, and mark with an asterisk any ideas that cause tension. Unpack at least one of the tensions in your teaching journal.

A more text-oriented teacher might say:	**A more context/culture-oriented teacher might say:**
I teach students how to write a well-crafted essay. My class focuses on essay organization, paragraph structure, stylistically and grammatically correct sentences, and writing conventions like MLA. Students write essays to demonstrate that they've learned these things. So my feedback tells them where they are in terms of their learning. My feedback essentially says, "These are the skills that you've mastered, and these are the skills that you still need to learn."	Of course, I give students some feedback on stylistic and grammatical things because I want them to write in a clear, academic, professional way. But most of my feedback is on their ideas. This is a college class, and I want my students to be thinking like college students — thinking critically, examining their own assumptions, looking at issues through various ideological and cultural lenses. My feedback is probably a lot like what a student would receive in any course across this curriculum. Students are writing complex analyses, and I respond to those analyses as a fellow academic would.
A more writer-oriented teacher might say:	**A more reader-oriented teacher might say:**
I want to encourage my students to see themselves as real writers, so I respond as a real reader, not as a teacher or editor. When I respond to student writing, I'm in dialogue with students, as if we're in a conversation. I respond to their ideas. I tell them my thoughts and personal reactions as a reader. I tell them what I'm enjoying in their text, and I tell them why I'm enjoying it. And I focus a lot on what's unique about each student's individual voice, point of view, and experience. My feedback is never generic or didactic.	My students are writing (as much as possible) for real audiences — I'm not the only, or primary, audience. But in my feedback, I can act like a debate coach, helping students hone their arguments for a real audience. I can point out rhetorical weaknesses in their arguments. I can ask them to think about how specific audiences would react to their arguments, style, and tone. And I can even "put on the hat" of possible audiences, saying, for example, "As a general reader I'm confused when you write X because. . . ." Or as a reader with a different political viewpoint, I might react to your argument this way. . . ."

YOUR TEACHING JOURNAL: Engaging with tensions

Choose the idea that you feel most uncomfortable with, and brainstorm about it in your teaching journal. Consider the following questions:

- How does this idea clash with your own experience or philosophy about feedback?
- How might this type of feedback be useful for certain teaching contexts, classes, levels, or with certain student populations?
- How might you bridge this notion of feedback and your own?

Return to the developing teaching philosophy that you sketched out in earlier chapters (Activities 1.12, 2.10, 5.11, 6.14, and 6.15, for example), and review your notes from the three activities in this chapter thus far. Now link your notions about feedback to your teaching philosophy.

Activity 13.4   Creating your own definition of useful feedback

In your teaching journal, discuss the following questions. Be sure to note any questions or issues that you are still wrestling with.

- According to your teaching philosophy, what kind of feedback is useful?
- According to your teaching philosophy, what kind of feedback is not useful (or perhaps even detrimental)?

You now have the beginnings of a general philosophy of feedback, but you need to think about how to enact this philosophy in your teaching. The next activity asks you to articulate your approach.

Activity 13.5   Creating a feedback plan

In your teaching journal, discuss the following questions, perhaps with a particular unit in mind. Be sure to note any questions or issues that you are still wrestling with.

- Who will give feedback at various times throughout the teaching segment/unit (teacher, peers, tutor)? Why?
- When will they give feedback (on initial ideas, on intermediate drafts, on final drafts)? Why?
- What kind of feedback will they give (content, organization, style, grammar)? Why?
- What will be the goal of the feedback (to promote revision, to evaluate)? Why?
- How will they give feedback (an endnote, margin comments, corrections, a matrix or rubric, oral feedback, online comments)? Why?
- Where will they give feedback (in class, at home, online)? Why?

When and how will you give feedback to students?

Now we will specifically address the question of when to give feedback. Think back to your writing experiences in high school and college English classes. If you are like most of us, you worked on a paper by yourself, then perhaps did some sort of peer-response activity, and then handed the paper in. The teacher took this paper—the final "product" of your labor—and gave you feedback (perhaps in red ink) and a grade.

Some compositionists refer to this process as a "postmortem"—the paper is already dead in the sense that it will not be revised any further, and the teacher takes on the role of medical examiner, determining what went wrong in the paper.

What are teachers trying to achieve with this postmortem? If you look at examples of many teachers' feedback, you probably will be able to infer only a fuzzy rationale: Much of the feedback seems to be a mixture of liking/disliking, evaluating, ranking, and offering sage advice. Underlying their feedback is the dubious assumption that the feedback will somehow transfer to students' writing of subsequent essays.

Unfortunately, not much evidence exists that this sort of feedback helps students. During the 1980s and 1990s, there was great interest in measuring the effects of this feedback on student writing. However, most studies pointed to three discouraging truths:

> "When I first started teaching, I was overwhelmed by the task of commenting on papers. I eventually realized that I was giving students way too much feedback. Now I just focus my comments on the main issues in a paper. I pay attention to what information is most important for students to receive right now, given where they are in the writing process.
>
> —*Tara*

- Often students do not understand the teacher comments that they receive on essays.

- Even when they do understand the comments, they often do not know how to turn those evaluative comments into strategies for improving their writing.

- Even if they do know how to turn the comments into strategies, they often may not apply those strategies in subsequent essays.

So is it hopeless? We can say from our own experiences that today's teachers comment much more effectively on student essays. However, we still notice teachers giving feedback at the "already too late" stage—that is, after the final draft.

Here are some ways that you can shift feedback to earlier stages of the drafting process.

- Feedback at the predrafting stage: You can respond to journal entries, free-writing, or brainstorming that the students do to help them focus their ideas.

- Feedback on the first draft: First drafts are generally "idea drafts"—an exploratory attempt to get thoughts down on paper. You can respond to these ideas in writing or in conference, giving the student motivation to continue the drafting process.

- Feedback on an intermediate draft: Once the paper has taken shape, you can help the student come up with a revision plan to move to the final draft.

- Feedback right before the final editing process: When the paper is essentially done, you can give it a quick read and tell the student what grammatical or stylistic issues to proofread for. By establishing proofreading priorities, you focus the student's efforts.

A teacher trainer at our school used to caution us against writing what she called "endnote mush." Throughout her many years of mentoring and coaching, she found that new teachers' endnotes tended to be a confusing stew of praise, criticism, and suggestions—something that was difficult or impossible for students to decode. For example, we have seen endnotes much like this one:

> Dear _____,
> I really enjoyed your paper, but it has some significant weaknesses that
> brought down the grade. There were a lot of grammar errors, but you did
> put forth some thought-provoking ideas. Next time you might want to think
> about your audience more. Overall you have got a handle on essay structure,
> but you might want to work on topic sentences. So overall—good job! Spend
> a bit more time on revision for the next essay. Grade: B–

This endnote seems to randomly alternate between (1) things the student did well, (2) things the student still needs to work on, (3) the teacher's affective and intellectual reactions to the content, and (4) "tips" for the next assignment. Even a highly skilled student would have trouble sorting out the main message of this endnote; an inexperienced writer would surely be baffled.

A revised version of the endnote might look something like this:

> Dear _____,
> I really enjoyed your paper. You put forth thought-provoking ideas, and it
> was easy to follow your line of argument because the paper is well structured
> overall.

Your arguments, while thought-provoking, might be lost on a general readership that doesn't know as much about your topic as you do. On the next essay, think about what kinds of arguments would appeal to a broader audience.

When you edit your next essay, you should also check that you give readers a clear signpost for each paragraph in the form of a topic sentence. Grade: B–

In this revised endnote, the teacher has begun with a positive response to the paper and has offered some global comments. The teacher has then given the student two concrete strategies to use on the next paper. The endnote thus provides a "plan" for the student as he or she moves forward in the course.

An alternative form of endnote is a T chart, such as the following example. It is especially useful when grading huge batches of papers: It is fast because it encourages you to write bullet points rather than prose, and the form itself encourages you to stick to the most essential points.

Strengths	Things to work on

By now you realize that our own approach to writing focuses heavily on revision because that is where the real learning takes place; making time for revision is one of the most important parts of creating a successful writing class. As you work through the next activity, which offers suggestions for building more revision into your course, you might look back to earlier activities that have asked you to think about how revision fits into your class (Activities 6.5, 6.8, and 6.9, for example).

 Activity 13.6   Integrating revision practices with your philosophy

Think about how you might draw on or apply each suggestion in the following chart, keeping in mind ways that the suggestion might fit (or not fit) with your teaching philosophy.

Common suggestions regarding revision practices:	How does this suggestion fit with your philosophy?	How might you apply this in your teaching?
Scaffold or step out the writing process during each teaching unit to give students more time and structure to write and revise each paper.		
Build in a portfolio assignment at the end of the course. Have students select essays from the course, work on revising those essays, and then compile a final portfolio.		
Use the last segment of your course as an opportunity to revise an essay of the student's choosing. This is a particularly useful strategy if you have run out of time in the semester and only have a week or so left. That week can serve as a "revision unit."		

Turning to the field:
Developing knowledge of conventions

One of the primary areas of research in the field of composition centers on revision practices. Those who have taught even one semester of first-year composition know that students' ideas about what "revision" entails often do not align with the more substantial revision that academic writing (or professional writing) necessitates. When teachers or professional writers talk about revision, they usually mean the significant reworking of a text—actually re-viewing or re-seeing what a text accomplishes and where it falls short, in order to consider the many options available to move the draft forward. Revision in this sense can also mean scrapping a draft entirely and starting fresh, doing a major reorganization, adding a significant amount of new material, or completely revising the approach, tone, or style that the draft pursues. When students hear the word *revision*, however, they often think of just tidying up their draft and correcting small mistakes or (worse) just fixing the errors that someone else—usually a teacher—has already identified.

Composition scholar Nancy Sommers's early work on revision is instructive in this sense. In her article "Revision Strategies of Student Writers and Experienced Adult Writers," she notes that experienced writers tend to see revision as an opportunity to do the following:

- Recursively and strategically revise to attend to both big-picture issues and sentence-level issues.
- Generate new meaning through revision (instead of remaining tied to already established or predetermined meaning).
- Discover the best form for a piece of writing, find the best shape of an argument, or discover what it is they want to say through the process of drafting and revision.
- Discover how the whole of a piece of writing and the parts can better fit together, often by restructuring, adding, or deleting.
- Imagine or communicate with an audience purposefully; use revision as a way to reframe writing by viewing it through an audience's eyes.

By contrast, students tend to work much more on the level of changing particular words and phrases, often because they do not have strategies for figuring out how to fix larger issues in a draft. Students often view revision as a linear task of fixing (much more akin to editing) than a recursive task of rewriting and reimagining. And if they are thinking of an audience at all, it is often a teacher who is judging their performance instead of engaging with their ideas.

Sharing these practices of more experienced writers—and finding ways for students to explicitly practice them in the classroom—thus becomes one of the central ways we can help our students develop as writers.

> "The metaphor I remember most vividly from my composition training is the idea of a "postmortem" on a paper. An old-fashioned writing teacher acts a bit like a medical examiner and assesses the paper as if conducting an autopsy. "Cause of death: lack of clear thesis and insufficient supporting evidence." I realize now that assessment is a much more fluid process. In my comments I'm much more like a coach and much less like a medical examiner.
>
> —*Mark*

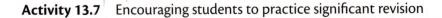

Activity 13.7 Encouraging students to practice significant revision

Brainstorm ways to ask students to practice these more sophisticated approaches to revision in your class through activities, lessons, or workshops.

Revision strategy or goal:	Specific ways to practice this strategy or goal:
Revise recursively and strategically to attend to both big-picture issues and sentence-level issues.	
Generate new meaning through revision (instead of remaining tied to already established or predetermined meaning).	
Discover the best form for a piece of writing, find the best shape of an argument, or discover what it is the writer wants to say through the process of drafting and revision.	
Discover how the whole of a piece of writing and the parts can better fit together, often by restructuring, adding, or deleting.	
Imagine or communicate with an audience purposefully; use revision as a way to reframe writing by viewing it through an audience's eyes.	
Other revision principles or strategies:	

Revision is essential to help students strengthen their writing in many areas, from ideas and analysis to polish and conventions. Conventions, however, are not static or singularly "correct" ways of writing. Just as the "correct" spelling of *colour/color* is specific to British versus American English, or the "correct" citation practice differs between APA and MLA styles, conventions are specific to particular groups of readers/writers, genres, and contexts or disciplines. Conventions change over time. Thus, as the *Framework for Success in Postsecondary Writing* states in its section "Developing Knowledge of Conventions": "The ability to understand, analyze, and make decisions about using conventions appropriate for the purpose, audience, and genre is important in writing."

With the understanding that conventions are historical (and changing) in nature, as well as site- and context-specific, the *Framework for Success* notes that there are still many "formal rules and informal guidelines that define what is considered to be correct (or appropriate) and incorrect (or inappropriate)" in any given piece of writing. From surface-level concerns such as punctuation, spelling, mechanics, and source citation, to more global concerns such as organization, style, tone, and the use of evidence, teachers want to help students develop knowledge of and facility with conventions so that their writing will be well received by readers.

How do we help students develop, understand, and perhaps even question (or break) writing conventions? A key way, of course, is through our feedback on student writing, our identification of patterns that students might address, and our provision of time to practice (with assistance as needed). The *Framework for Success* offers strategies, listed in Activity 13.8, for helping students develop knowledge of conventions, particularly knowledge that extends beyond "following a rule" to having a greater dexterity and resourcefulness in recognizing, analyzing, and performing conventions.

 Activity 13.8   Developing knowledge of conventions

Consider how you might employ in your class the strategies listed in the following chart. The first row has been completed as an example.

Practices from the *Framework for Success* for developing knowledge of conventions:	Specific ways this strategy might play out in your class:	Guiding questions to help students use this strategy to gain awareness:
Read and analyze print and multimodal texts composed in various styles, tones, and levels of formality.	Have students map comparisons of different texts. Have students adapt their own texts for different audiences, adjusting formality, tone, and style accordingly and explaining their decisions.	What differences do you note in the level of formality of these documents? How do you think each decision about formality, along with the tone the writer takes, is appropriate for the chosen audience?
Write, read, and analyze a variety of texts from various disciplines and perspectives in order to • Investigate the logic and implications of different conventions • Practice different conventions and analyze expectations for and effects on different audiences • Practice editing and proofreading one's own writing and explore the implications of editing choices • Explore the concept of intellectual property (i.e., ownership of ideas) as it is used in different disciplines and contexts • Identify differences between errors and intentional variations from expected conventions		
Use resources (such as print and online writing handbooks), with guidance, to edit drafts.		
Practice various approaches to the documentation and attribution of sources.		
Examine the underlying logic in commonly used citation systems (e.g., MLA and APA).		

It takes time to develop a sophisticated understanding of conventions and the reasons why particular conventions might exist (or change) in particular environments. Developing the flexibility to move between competing conventions also takes time, as well as two particular habits of mind: persistence and responsibility. Since these two habits of mind (drawn from the eight key academic habits of mind offered by the *Framework for Success*) are particularly relevant to the ongoing process of revision, they are worth exploring in more depth. The next activity asks you to explore how you can support students' development of these habits of mind. You will explore these habits further, in regard to your development, in Chapter 17.

 Activity 13.9 Encouraging persistence and responsibility in revision

Complete the following charts.

Persistence — the ability to sustain interest in and attention to short- and long-term projects.

Persistence is fostered when writers are encouraged to . . .	Supports you can offer to help students cultivate this habit:
Commit to exploring, in writing, a topic, idea, or demanding task	
Grapple with challenging ideas, texts, processes, or projects	
Follow through, over time, to complete tasks, processes, or projects	
Consistently take advantage of in-class feedback (peer and instructor responses) and out-of-class opportunities to improve and refine their work (writing or learning center support)	

Responsibility — the ability to take ownership of one's actions and understand the consequences of those actions for oneself and others.

Responsibility is fostered when writers are encouraged to . . .	Supports you can offer to help students cultivate this habit:
Recognize their own role in learning	
Act on the understanding that learning is shared among the writer and others — students, instructors, and the institution, as well as those engaged in the questions or fields in which the writer is interested	
Engage and incorporate the ideas of others, giving credit to those ideas by using appropriate attribution	

How will you avoid "feedback burnout"?

All teachers know that there is a very material and practical challenge related to feedback—handling the vast paper load. This is especially true if you are teaching multiple composition classes and must respond to multiple stacks of student writing every week. Students need consistent and thoughtful feedback about their writing to recognize their strengths and weaknesses, understand how their writing was received, and identify what they might try next time to better achieve their purposes; indeed, feedback is one of the main things students say helps them learn the most. But if you are teaching several classes with many students—or if you are just getting started teaching and offering feedback—the paper load can at times seem overwhelming.

In this section, we offer some tips derived from a seasoned teacher's practice. Carol Jago is a former high school teacher who is now active in the leadership of the National Council of Teachers of English (NCTE). High school writing teachers often have an incredibly challenging paper load, since they often serve over 150 students per semester. Jago's tips are connected not to any one specific philosophy of teaching but to being a strategic reader who, instead of commenting on everything (in a student paper or in a course as a whole), considers which interventions or feedback is most appropriate at any given time. Her suggestions span both the pedagogical and the practical facets of offering feedback, and they dovetail with some of the principles you practiced in Activity 13.5 and Activity 13.6.

Tips for balancing the paper load

- Decide what you need to respond to and what you do not. Remember, you do not need to evaluate or "touch" much of the writing that your students do, particularly when it is writing to learn or invention-based writing.

- Time your responses so that they can be the most useful interventions. When will individualized feedback be most useful, and when might peer feedback or a group comment do the trick?

- If you find yourself writing the same comment over and over, opt for a class comment or mini-lesson instead.

- Explore other ways to discuss a paper instead of writing comments, including recording audio feedback.

- Carry papers in your bag and write feedback when you have a spare moment: waiting in line, riding on the bus, and so on.

- Use a timer to get in the habit of spending a set amount of time on each paper.

For more tips, see Carol Jago's book *Papers, Papers, Papers*.

Source: Carol Jago, from *Papers, Papers, Papers: An English Teacher's Survival Guide*. Copyright © 2005 by Heinemann.

If the student has not met the basics of the assignment, just note that and move on. Do not spend more time giving feedback than a student spent writing the paper!

Taking it further:
Feedback on grammar

If you are a very new teacher, you may sometimes look at a student paper and see only a tangle of grammatically snarled sentences. Over time, as you read hundreds of student essays, you learn to read past the surface errors and find meaning in the students' texts. This ability to read past errors is especially important when you are commenting on early drafts of an essay. In the early drafts, your main concern should be steering the student in the right direction in terms of developing and organizing ideas.

However, the issue of grammar in the final draft remains. Your process for dealing with grammar in final drafts will be determined by your philosophy of good writing; your philosophy of language in general; institutional constraints, such as course learning objectives; and the environment "around the course"— for example, students' subsequent classes and subsequent career paths.

We can offer a few general principles for grammar feedback on individual essays:

- **Less is more.** Most teachers spend a huge amount of time extensively marking errors on papers. There is little evidence that error marking at this stage has any effect on students' grammatical development in subsequent essays. By cutting back, you can save yourself time and prevent burnout.

- **Restrict your marking to main patterns of error.** There is no use in marking twenty different types of errors on a single paper; it will be impossible for a student to learn from each error notation. Pedagogically, it is much more effective to focus on only three or so recurring patterns of error per paper. For example, an ESL student's main patterns of error might be verb problems, singular/plural problems, and sentence boundaries (fragments and run-ons). If you mark these three patterns and ask the student to do some follow-up work on these areas, there is a much better chance that the student will develop editing skills that he or she can apply in subsequent essays.

- **Have students do something with your markings.** You can ask students to self-correct the errors you have marked, work in groups to correct errors, keep an error log, or set proofreading goals. If students do not physically do something with the error markings, there is little chance that the process will have any long-term effect on students' writing.

Although this advice seems straightforward, as a teacher you will find that implementing it creates a challenging tension: If each student is working on his or her own patterns of error, how do you assess and grade students who are working at vastly different levels? For example, compare the patterns of error for three students:

Student A	Student B	Student C
• Basic sentence structure and sentence boundaries • Basic verb forms • Spelling (often incorrectly "corrected" with a spell-checker)	• Choppiness • Imprecise use of academic vocabulary • Integrating quotes into paragraphs	• Wordiness in complex academic sentences • Punctuation in MLA citations • Overuse of passive verbs

Use this chart to complete Activity 13.10.

 Activity 13.10   Evaluating students at different proficiency levels

In your teaching journal, discuss the following questions. Be sure to note any questions or issues that you are still wrestling with.

- How would grammar errors affect each student's overall grade on an essay? Would the errors of all three students count equally?
- Would certain types of errors lead automatically to a failing essay grade? Why?
- Would a certain number of errors lead automatically to a failing essay grade regardless of how small those errors are? Why?
- Imagine that you mark errors on intermediate drafts. When you receive students' final drafts, you notice that student A (the weaker writer) has made big editing improvements, while student C (the stronger writer) has made little or no editing improvement. How would this affect the grades you would give to each final draft? Why?
- Imagine that you are giving the final grade for the semester. Student A has improved greatly throughout the semester, while student C has improved very little. However, student A's writing is still weaker than student C's. Would you somehow give student A extra credit for all the improvement made? Or would you hold both students to the same absolute standard? Why?

Another challenge is knowing how to embed your grammar feedback into the larger framework of editing practice. Here are a few suggestions:

- Discuss and model editing strategies with your students.
- Have students practice editing and proofreading in class.
- Have students do an editing/proofreading draft—a pre-final draft that they mark up before they print the final draft.
- Give students time in class for proofreading. You can build this time into a grammar workshop day in which you introduce a grammatical or stylistic device, review proofreading strategies, and then have students work on their papers in class.

Again, this advice may seem straightforward. However, it raises a challenging tension: How do you balance this kind of grammar, editing, and proofreading work with all the other things that you are teaching and doing in class? There is no easy answer to this question; to answer it, you must somehow "triangulate" your students' writing needs, your institution's expectations, and your own teaching philosophy.

Activity 13.11   Navigating conflicting grammar demands

Complete the following chart. If you have taught already, work from your experience. If you have not taught yet, try asking a practicing teacher to see how he or she resolves these issues.

Where are your students in terms of grammar needs?	What are your institution's expectations?	What role should grammar play, according to your teaching philosophy?

What tensions emerge between these three things?	How might you deal with these tensions?

Reflections from experienced teachers

Offering feedback on student writing is one of the most crucial duties of a writing teacher. Indeed, many students find that the commentary they receive from their readers provides the strongest, most tangible learning opportunities for them about what works and what does not in their writing. As you continue thinking about revision and feedback, consider how these reflections from experienced teachers might inform your practice:

- Although they may have regular revision routines, experienced teachers also experiment with which readers (peers, teachers, tutors, or even the student via self-assessment) should give feedback and when. You can think about this in two ways: Which readers are most useful at which stage of writing? And how can we maximize efficiency in terms of getting students the feedback they need? Through experimentation, observation, and reflection, you can decide when in the writing process your expertise is most necessary and can intervene then.

- A central practice that connects to the first bullet point pertains to peer review. Seasoned teachers know not to undermine peer review by providing their own additional feedback at that stage. If students are doing peer review, have them apply peer-review comments before you review their materials; otherwise, your feedback might trump or overshadow the feedback from their peers. (You can explore peer-review practices in more depth in Chapter 12.)

- Much important learning happens when students become their own best readers and evaluators. Experienced teachers thus try to get students involved in the feedback process for their own writing. There are many useful ways of getting students involved in response and self-assessment: for example, having students self-assess their work using the assignment prompt or rubric; asking students to generate peer feedback questions they would like answered; and having students prioritize the issues or concerns that they would like you, as teachers, to respond to.

- Getting students to apply and capitalize on feedback—actually putting it to use—can be a challenge. Veteran teachers thus often create time in class for students to both read feedback and apply it, either by revising the draft they have just received back or by extrapolating comments and making a plan for applying them to the next writing project they will do. This practice emphasizes how important revision is, and it helps ensure that students actually use the feedback teachers have spent time writing for them.

Putting it together:
Articulating your approach to feedback

As we have explored in this chapter, revision is essential to learning to write; however, the word *revision* can mean many different things—especially to students, who often equate revision with correcting mistakes or editing.

In the next activity, we ask you to describe some central principles that will guide the revision practices in your own classes, including the role that grammar might play in revision.

Activity 13.12   Explaining your views on revision and grammar

Imagine that you will be interviewing for a teaching position and that the committee will ask you to explain how, when, and for what purposes students revise in your course. In the space provided, write out some notes, as well as concrete examples, that you might use to illustrate your definition of revision and how it would play out in your course. Be sure to address the role of grammar and editing in the revision process.

Now attempt to articulate your views in prose so that you can integrate them into your evolving and expanding teaching philosophy.

Activity 13.13   Anchoring feedback and revision in your teaching philosophy

In your teaching journal, discuss the ways that your revision and feedback practices intersect with or exemplify your overall philosophy of teaching writing. Be sure to note any questions or issues that you are still wrestling with.

In this chapter, you explored one of the primary responsibilities you have as a teacher: helping students revise and offering your feedback to help students develop their writing. You also explored how these practices are intimately connected to the larger practices of your course, such as ongoing writing opportunities (Chapter 11) and peer work, including peer review (Chapter 12). In the next chapter, you will connect the writing, revision, and feedback practices you have explored to the bigger picture of assessment and evaluation.

Further Reading

- Harris, Joseph. "Revision as a Critical Practice." *College English* 65.6 (2003): 577–92. Print.
- Knoblauch, C. H., and Lil Brannon. "On Students' Rights to Their Own Texts." *College Composition and Communication* 33.2 (1982): 157–66. Print.
- Sommers, Nancy. "Revision Strategies of Student Writers and Experienced Adult Writers." *College Composition and Communication* 31.4 (1980): 378–88. Print.

CHAPTER 14

Choices about Assessment and Evaluation

Newer teachers often have anxiety about assessment: How should work be evaluated? Is it better to be strict or encouraging? What if a student challenges his or her grade? Even seasoned teachers frequently have questions about the complexities of fair and useful assessment, particularly when assessment and learning seem disconnected or at odds or when assessment is mandated in certain ways (standardized tests might come to mind). In short, assessment can bring up a range of emotions depending on the context for the assessment, its goal, and how helpful teachers and students feel the assessment to be.

We explored several related dimensions of assessment in Chapter 13, as well as in Chapter 3 and Chapter 4 where you worked through your roles as a teacher and as an institutional authority. This chapter asks you to focus more specifically on assessment practices. It is no surprise that assessment often feels most useful for everyone when it is purposeful, when it is fair and accurate, and when it offers information about performance that can lead to improvement. In this way, assessment and feedback are intimately connected; in fact, teachers make "assessments" (of student learning, understanding, and reading/writing) all the time and offer "feedback" on what they see or hear.

🔦 Activity 14.1 Looking at your experience with assessment

Answer the following questions in order to reflect on your own experience with assessment.

---

1. Freewrite about a positive or negative experience with assessment that you had as a student.

2. What was good or bad about your experience? What did you learn? If you did not learn anything, what guidance do you feel you would have needed in order to learn?

3. What lessons can you draw from your experience that might inform your teaching?

Activity 14.2 lists common terms that come up in discussions about assessment and evaluation. To further explore what assessment means, look through the terms, and note your reactions to each. Think about how each term might fit into or conflict with your own philosophy of teaching.

 Activity 14.2   Examining assessment terms

Circle any ideas that resonate with you, and mark with an asterisk any ideas that cause tension. Unpack at least one of the tensions in your teaching journal.

Terms related to assessment . . .

high stakes   preparedness   accountability   mandates   support

    timed writing   performance   anxiety   learning outcomes   rubric

averages   norming   pressure   objectives

    grades   red ink   improvement   holistic   scoring

tests   failing   feedback   progress report

    bell curve   competition   excellence   gatekeeping   GPA

Additional terms that come to mind . . .

YOUR TEACHING JOURNAL: Engaging with tensions

Choose one of the terms that you feel most uncomfortable with, and brainstorm about it in your teaching journal. Consider the following questions:

- Why does it create tension for you?

- In what ways does it clash with your teaching philosophy?

- How might you modify this term (rather than discard it) to make it fit better with your philosophy?

Separating out assessment—our formative or summative evaluation of work—from grading and testing can be quite useful, particularly in the college context where "testing" in writing is less frequent. This separation can also help us reframe our attitudes about assessment in productive and positive ways along the lines of "sharing information" with students that is useful for their growth. The next several sections and activities elaborate these ideas.

How will you navigate assessment mandates and requirements?

If you are new to your program, assessment is perhaps the most challenging part of teaching. One way to begin, when thinking about assessment, is to get a handle on university, department, and program requirements. You may find it useful to return to Activities 5.3, 5.4, and 5.8 as you complete the next activity.

Complete the following chart to explore the amount of flexibility that you have with assessments as a teacher.

What assessments are used to place students into English courses?	What assessments will students face after your course (e.g., an exit exam)?	Does your program have clearly defined learning outcomes, and are you required to tie your assessment activities to those outcomes?	How much flexibility do teachers in your program have in assessing students? Is there a shared assessment (e.g., a common final exam, a course exit exam, or a collectively assessed portfolio)?

With this initial lay of the land in place, you can also use your colleagues to gauge the assessment landscape in your program. Ask colleagues to share syllabi, writing prompts, grading rubrics, and example anchor essays (a strong A essay, a weak passing essay, a non-passing essay).

During our first few semesters of teaching, we relied heavily on our colleagues when we were trying to figure out how to assess our students. In addition to collecting materials from our colleges, programs, and colleagues, we would often share student essays with our colleagues, particularly essays that seemed to be on the border of passing and failing. Talking through the merits of a specific paper with colleagues helped clarify programmatic expectations, the choices to be made in offering feedback, and the ultimate decision to be made about the paper's grade.

At times, such sharing of assessment practices will take place through faculty development (either mandated or optional). Look for opportunities to talk with others about how they would assess particular pieces of student writing in order to deepen your own knowledge and response. These opportunities range from informal brown-bag sessions where you read and discuss student work with colleagues, to more formal norming sessions where you practice evaluating student work and strive to reach agreement (often for placement decisions).

Most compositionists would argue that assessment should not be an after-the-fact part of your course. Instead, the best assessments are designed as you are crafting your assignments and your pedagogy. It will thus be particularly useful to return to the assignments you created in Chapter 6, revising them to integrate assessments based on the knowledge you gain from this chapter, your general understanding of how assessment works at your institution, and common practices gleaned from your colleagues.

> "*Assessment* is one of those buzzwords that initially intimidated me. However, once I reframed that term as "getting and giving information," I was able to wrap my head around its role in my classes.
>
> —*Tara*

But first it might be helpful to build further on the work you did in Chapter 13 concerning feedback and revision. In Chapter 13, you worked mainly on the types of formative assessment (feedback or written commentary) that you would provide on student drafts. *Feedback*—the word we most often use to describe our dialogues with students about their writing—is in many spheres the preferred way to describe assessment: It is friendlier and less unidirectional, and it connotes the way that good assessment "feeds back" into the writing task to shape the final performance. Feedback is, however, one of the ways we most often formatively assess our students. Even as we are offering them our impressions and advice, we are also gaining and giving information about where they are. Feedback often assumes (or is directed toward) the idea that students will have a chance to apply the comments they receive. By contrast, summative assessments offer a judgment on a final product or performance.

The following chart summarizes a few key differences between formative and summative assessments. The next activity asks you to think about the range of assessments you might generate for your own course.

Formative assessment . . .	Summative assessment . . .
Is provided in many ways (conferences, peer response, comments on essays)	Typically occurs only on "final products" such as final drafts and final portfolios
Helps students develop; offers assessment with an eye to future performance or revision	Documents (or "summarizes") student performance at a given point in time
Is often engaging for both teacher and student	Can be stressful or unenjoyable for teacher or student
Typically represents lower stakes	Typically represents higher stakes
Is aimed more at the learning that goes on in the classroom	Is aimed more at institutional demands and accountability
Is often broad or holistic	Is often narrow and focused on specific skills

Now you will apply these ideas in Activity 14.4 by looking at one of the units you developed in Chapter 8 or Chapter 9. The chart in Activity 14.4 is partially filled out with an example based on a unit on literacy narratives. As you can see, there are actually many small assessments you might make over the course of the unit. As the unit builds, you will want to check both individual and group understanding, often through verbal or informal assessments conducted in class (short writing, exit ticket with a takeaway or question from class, and so on). The larger formative assessments you offer—whether they are self-assessments, peer assessments, or teacher assessments—should build and be usable in the summative assessment. As you can see, the same learning goals are assessed informally, formatively, and finally summatively. Lastly, note that even the summative assessment may have some elements of formative feedback; this is not uncommon in writing courses, since it can encourage students to continue to transfer feedback and gains to the next writing project.

Activity 14.4 Generating appropriate formative and summative assessments for a unit

Fill in the following chart, using the completed boxes as a possible model.

	Verbal or informal formative assessments:	Written formative assessments:	Summative assessments:
Example: What learning will you assess?	**Learning goal 1:** understanding of key terms (e.g., literacy) **Learning goal 2:** understanding of the purpose of a literacy narrative (narrate and reflect) **Learning goal 3:** understanding of key features of that genre (narrative action, sensory detail, reflection on significance)	Assess progress on learning goals 1–3	Final assessment of learning goals 1–3 Feedback on other writing features worked on thus far in term Progress thus far in term (or over multiple assignments)
What learning will you assess?			
Example: How will you assess (key evaluation criteria and method)?	**Goal 1:** Cold-call students for definitions to review; generate group definition. **Goals 2 and 3:** After discussing and reading models, have students map features from reading on board; debrief.	**Goal 1:** peer/group feedback on how key terms are used **Goal 2:** peer or teacher feedback on how the purpose is or is not achieved **Goal 3:** self-assessment, using the assignment or a rubric; teacher written feedback on where draft is succeeding and where it is not yet fulfilling expectations	Based on goals 1–3, strengths and weaknesses are identified and linked to specific examples in the text. A grade may or may not be assessed, depending on teacher's portfolio philosophy. Consistently provides students with information on their progress toward learning goals.
How will you assess (key evaluation criteria and method)?			
Why does this kind of assessment make sense?			

Now, bearing in mind your sense of when formative assessment might be more appropriate than summative assessment, take your thinking a step further. Since you know that your formative assessments will help students prepare for the eventual summative assessments, figuring out the summative assessment is crucial if you are to work backward.

Activity 14.5 Mapping assessments, learning outcomes, and your teaching philosophy

In the following chart, generate the summative assessments for at least two of your major writing assignments, including a portfolio if you plan on using one. Draw on assignments you created in Chapter 6 (Activity 6.8), any related plans you made in Chapter 8 and Chapter 9, and your ideas about useful feedback generated in Activity 13.4.

Key summative assessments in your course:	How each assessment fits with learning from the unit:	Key criteria used in each assessment:	How the criteria fit with both the assessment and your philosophy:

How will you use rubrics in assessing student writing?

Rubrics offer a systematic and often visual way to assess work. Usually taking the form of a graph or chart, a rubric organizes and places value on different components of a piece of writing.

Rubrics have several benefits for you as a teacher:

- The process of designing the rubric helps you clarify your objectives for a particular assignment.
- The rubric helps you during the grading process when you are not sure about a paper or when you feel you are "drifting" as you mark a large number of papers.
- The rubric "keeps you honest" with the paper. We have all been swayed by a particular aspect of a paper that impresses us or discourages us; the rubric helps us avoid the danger of bumping the grade too far up or too far down.
- The rubric "keeps you honest" with the student writer. Psychologists have noted that the human mind exhibits selection bias. If you are expecting something good from a particular student, you tend to see good things in his or her paper, and vice versa. Unfortunately, this can bias us when we are grading papers from students who we feel are "strong" or "weak."

Rubrics also have several benefits for your students:

- The rubric communicates to students what you value in writing and what you want them to practice and learn.
- The rubric gives you and your students a common language in which to talk about a particular piece of writing.
- The rubric can help during the peer-response and revision process because it shows students what to focus on.
- The rubric conveys a sense of fairness to students.
- Even a summative assessment (a "postmortem" on an assignment) can be formative if the rubric shows students how to improve.

Depending on your teaching context, you may find yourself designing assignment rubrics from scratch. If you have never done this before, it can be a daunting task. However, the more specific rubrics are to your students, course, and institution, the more potential they have to clarify learning goals and actually be useful to students. Later in this chapter, we will explore how to adapt or use a mandated rubric. But first we will look at some of the key dimensions of rubrics and how they can fit with and support your assignments and learning objectives.

General versus assignment-specific rubrics

The first issue to tackle in designing rubrics is to distinguish general rubrics (which can be used for multiple assignments) and assignment-specific rubrics. The following chart lists some of the distinguishing characteristics and benefits of both types.

General rubric	Assignment-specific rubric
The connections across assignments are clearer. Students can see that general writing skills underlie multiple assignments.	The particulars of a specific assignment are clearer. Students can see that different types of writing, different genres, and different rhetorical modes have different characteristics.
Students can more easily compare their growth across assignments.	Students can more easily compare their growth across a specific draft. Students can focus on different assignment-specific criteria with each draft.
It may help students focus on improving their overall writing abilities rather than simply completing a checklist of specific requirements on individual assignments.	It may help students develop flexibility in their writing practices because the audience, genre, and stylistic elements of each specific assignment can be spelled out in the rubric.
The general rubric may be used across course units or throughout a program to highlight central values or goals. However, it may be too general to give students much guidance or clarity.	The assignment-specific rubric gives teachers more flexibility to articulate specific criteria or characteristics. If an assignment is shared across a program, the rubric may also be shared.

Now take a look at the course arc that you designed in Chapter 5 and Chapter 6 as you begin to develop general and assignment-specific rubrics.

Activity 14.6   Designing a general rubric

In this activity, you will come up with a general rubric that would fit most of the assignments for your course. Using the following chart, define the characteristics of passing papers and non-passing papers, rather than define the characteristics for each particular grade. (As we proceed through the chapter, we will begin to flesh out descriptions for more specific grades.)

For all the assignments in your course . . .	
Characteristics of a passing paper:	**Characteristics of a non-passing paper:**

In completing Activity 14.6, you probably noticed at least two tensions:

- Your definition of a passing paper and a non-passing paper probably changes across the arc of the semester. Writing that you might have considered "passing" on the first assignment might be inadequate for an end-of-semester assignment.
- Your criteria probably change from assignment to assignment as well. For example, on a personal narrative you might want student writing to exhibit a strong, involved voice, while for a research paper you might want students to adopt a more dispassionate voice.

To resolve these tensions and distinguish between criteria for different assignments at different points in the semester, we can create assignment-specific rubrics.

 Activity 14.7   Designing an assignment-specific rubric

Choose one of the assignments that you designed in Chapter 6. Try to choose an assignment that stands out as a bit different from the other assignments in your course. Then, for that assignment, try to articulate specific characteristics that would make a paper passing or non-passing. Complete the following chart.

For this particular assignment . . .	
Characteristics of a passing paper:	**Characteristics of a non-passing paper:**

Now compare your general rubric and your assignment-specific rubric, and think about the following questions: What elements were you able to capture in the assignment-specific rubric that you were not able to capture in the general rubric? What elements were you able to capture in the general rubric that you were not able to capture in the assignment-specific rubric?

One possible way to reap the benefits of both general and assignment-specific rubrics is to create a general rubric that you will use throughout the semester, but tweak this rubric a bit for each assignment to make it more specific. This allows students to see both the consistency of writing goals across assignments and the particulars of each assignment.

Activity 14.8   Designing general and specific rubrics for each assignment

In the following chart, sketch out the general and specific criteria that you want to see in a passing paper for the major or more formal graded assignments in your course. Activity 6.8 may once again prove helpful.

General characteristics that you want to see in all formal assignments:	
Specific characteristics that you want to see in each formal assignment:	
Assignment:	**Characteristics:**
1	
2	
3	
4	
5	

Holistic versus analytic rubrics

Typically, when you grade, you must do more than just assign passing or non-passing grades; therefore, your rubrics will need more complexity. This raises the next question to tackle when designing a rubric: Should I use a holistic or analytic rubric?

A holistic rubric groups together a number of traits for each possible grade. This is the type often used in scoring placement and exit tests, where the goal is to come up with a single score for each paper rather than give a breakdown of specific strengths and weaknesses. The advantage of holistic rubrics is simplicity: You merely find the one category that best describes the paper:

A essay	Description of criteria
B essay	Description of criteria
C essay	Description of criteria
D essay	Description of criteria
F essay	Description of criteria

Activity 14.9 Designing a holistic rubric

Select one of the assignments that you worked on in Activity 14.8 and try to flesh out the details of each grade. You can use the A-B-C-D-F scale shown in the example, or you can use the required grading scale at your institution. For example, our undergraduate writing program grades on an A-B-C-NC (no credit) basis. Complete the following chart.

Grade	Criteria for a paper of this grade:
A	
B	
C	
D	
F	

You probably noticed a tension as you attempted to define the difference between the grades: What grade does a paper receive if it has some of the characteristics of an A paper but also some of the characteristics of B or C papers? One way that teachers tackle this issue is through an analytic rubric, which analyzes the characteristics of a paper separately. Analytic rubrics are typically set up with the vital traits, qualities, or dimensions on the left-hand side and the rating scale along the top. The rating scale is not usually expressed in letter grades because you will need to weight the various components before you translate them into a letter grade (which you will do in the next activity).

An analytic rubric allows you to "give credit" to a student for one characteristic (for example, having excellent ideas), while still holding the student accountable for weaker areas (for example, mechanics). For an analytic rubric to be fair, effective, and easy to use (particularly for you when you are grading), you must define each point of the scale. In other words, you must define "excellent content," "weak content," and so on. In the rubric shown in Activity 14.10, a teacher has sketched out possible definitions for each point on the scale for one of the traits, "content/ideas."

Activity 14.10   Designing an analytic rubric

Choose one of the assignments you designed for your course, and create an analytic rubric for it. Write the traits that you will evaluate in the column on the left. Then define "excellent," "good," "fair," and "weak" for each trait. You may want to do this on your computer, as it generally takes up a full page. One trait has been completed as an example.

Key trait:	Excellent:	Good:	Fair:	Weak:
Content/ideas	Original and insightful ideas; shows strong analysis and deep thought	Shows analysis; goes beyond reiterating the class discussion	Perfunctory presentation of ideas; does not go beyond reiterating the class discussion	Contradictory, incoherent, or incomplete ideas

In the prior activities, you decided what traits you want a writing assignment to exhibit, and you decided how to rate each of those traits. You still need to do one more step in designing a rubric: weighting the traits so that you can turn the traits into a grade.

We have seen a wide range of teacher practices regarding weighting. At one end of the continuum are teachers who use the analytic rubric as a feedback tool but do not assign hard-and-fast weights to each trait; they essentially give the paper a holistic assessment and use the rubric to help students self-assess and revise. This approach allows the teacher to individualize grading. For example, if a student has been struggling with one particular writing skill and has made dramatic improvement on a particular essay, the teacher might weight that trait more highly. This more open type of grading also fits with the psychological reality of grading that comes with experience: When reading a paper, teachers often have a gut-level sense of the appropriate grade and then use the analytic rubric to "flesh out" the grade.

At the other end of the continuum are teachers who give a specified number of points for each item or assign each item a specific percentage of the grade. For example, a teacher might weight various elements of an essay as follows:

	Excellent	Good	Fair	Weak
Content/ideas (50 possible points)	50 points	45 points	40 points	35 points
Organization/development (25 possible points)	25 points	20 points	15 points	10 points
Mechanics/grammar (25 possible points)	25 points	20 points	15 points	10 points

This type of rubric has two main advantages:

- For students, it conveys a sense of fairness in grading. Students generally see numerically calculated grades (on a multiple-choice test, for example) as somehow more objective than other grades.
- For teachers, it serves as a tool to maintain grading consistency. We may be "wowed" by the ideas in a paper and want to give it an A+, but this kind of rubric forces us to think about the actual traits that we have said we are grading.

The main disadvantage is complexity. If you are grading a huge stack of essays, you might find the specificity and the "fussiness" of adding up points to be a distraction from your primary role as a teacher: helping students with writing.

You will have to figure out for yourself what kind of rubric (if any) feels most comfortable and most effective for you. (See "Taking It Further" later in this chapter.) The next activity asks you to articulate your position on rubrics: Are you drawn more to general rubrics or to assignment-specific rubrics? Are you drawn to more open-ended rubrics that give you lots of freedom in grading or to more mathematical rubrics with exact points?

 Activity 14.11   Exploring your philosophy on rubrics

In your teaching journal, discuss the following questions. Be sure to note any questions or issues that you are still wrestling with.

- What kinds of rubrics appeal to you? Why?
- How does this fit with your beliefs about your authority role as a teacher and other elements of your philosophy?

We should add a couple of important caveats to our discussion about rubrics. First, we have found that, in a desire for "certainty" in grading, new teachers often overuse rubrics. Writing is a complex art, and it is exceedingly difficult to capture all the traits of good writing in a few simple categories. And even if one does use a rubric with many diverse writing traits, it is impossible to quantify those traits with absolute objectivity. Thus a rubric may give you a false sense of certainty.

Second, we have found that new teachers tend to adopt rubrics wholesale—from colleagues, textbooks, and online sites—without thinking about how a rubric fits with their philosophy, their course, and their assignment goals. For example, a rubric designed by a text-focused, convention-focused, grammar-focused teacher will be ill-fitting if your composition philosophy emphasizes creativity, expression, personal voice, and individuality. Similarly, a rubric designed for "postmortems" on final drafts will be ill-fitting if your course design emphasizes ongoing revision or portfolios.

How will you use portfolios in assessing student writing?

As composition scholar Brian Huot argues in his seminal article "Toward a New Discourse of Assessment for the College Writing Classroom" and in his longer works, "Portfolios undermine the current assumption that it is possible to ascertain a student's ability to write from one piece of writing, or that writing or a writer's development can be inferred incrementally through the evaluation of individual products or the aggregate of individual evaluations." Just as important, portfolios shift much of the assessment onto the student; students practice self-assessing through the process of creating their portfolio. It is for these reasons that scholars like Kathleen Blake Yancey have highlighted the three crucial principles of portfolios: selection, collection, and reflection. As students select the work that represents them, meaningfully arrange it in a portfolio, and reflect on their learning and how the portfolio demonstrates that learning, they go a long way toward assessing their own performance.

Portfolio grading can take many forms. In Chapter 8, you looked at a course design in which students assembled two portfolios: one midway through the course and one at the end of the course. Another option is to have students assemble a single portfolio at the end of the course. For the next activity, imagine that you will require students to assemble a portfolio at the end of the course. As you answer the questions, think about how your responses fit your teaching philosophy.

Activity 14.12 Exploring questions about portfolio grading

In your teaching journal, discuss the following questions. Be sure to note any questions or issues that you are still wrestling with.

- Will you allow students to put any pieces of writing they want in their portfolios, or will you require specific types of writing (e.g., at least one argumentative essay and one research paper)? Why?

- Will you give students an additional round of feedback on the essays that they plan to put in their portfolios, or will you expect them to revise the essays on their own? Why?

- How will you grade students who simply put their essays in the portfolio with little or no revision? Why?

- To what extent will you require students to reflect on their portfolios and self-assess? What types of reflection would you like to see? How will you grade students who simply put their essays in the portfolio with little or no significant reflection? Why?

- What kind of rubric will you use for the portfolio? Why?

Turning to the field:
Using assessments to strengthen your teaching

As research in the field of composition has grown more sophisticated, so too has our understanding of assessment. At the college level, our assessments can often be guided more by our local curricular decisions, faculty, and programs than in K–12 education. Despite less standardization in college-level writing assessments, the field of composition has nonetheless reached some consensus regarding *best practices* in assessment. For example, consider this statement from the Conference on College Composition and Communication (CCCC) regarding the goals of assessment:

> Assessments of written literacy should be designed and evaluated by well-informed current or future teachers of the students being assessed, for purposes clearly understood by all the participants; should elicit from student writers a variety of pieces, preferably over a substantial period of time; should encourage and reinforce good teaching practices; and should be solidly grounded in the latest research on language learning as well as accepted best assessment practices.

 Activity 14.13 Translating assessment principles into your practice

To consider how you might implement such recommendations, or what they would look like in practice, complete the following chart. The first column lists specific recommendations culled from the CCCC position statement. Use the chart to brainstorm how each recommendation may or may not be useful in your course.

CCCC-recommended assessment practice or principle	What will this mean in your course? What might you do to follow this recommendation?	What questions or tensions does this raise for you?
Writing assessment is useful primarily as a means of improving teaching and learning.		
Best assessment practice engages students in contextualized, meaningful writing. Assessment must be contextualized in terms of why, where, and for what purpose it is being undertaken.		
Best assessment practice supports and harmonizes with what practice and research have demonstrated to be effective ways of teaching writing. What is easiest to measure — often by means of a multiple choice test — may correspond least to good writing. . . . Essay tests that ask students to form and articulate opinions about some important issue, for instance, without time to reflect, talk to others, read on the subject, revise, and have a human audience promote distorted notions of what writing is.		

Best assessment practice uses multiple measures. Ideally, writing ability must be assessed by more than one piece of writing, in more than one genre, written on different occasions, for different audiences, and responded to and evaluated by multiple readers as part of a substantial and sustained writing process.		
Best assessment practice respects language variety and diversity and assesses writing on the basis of effectiveness for readers, acknowledging that as purposes vary, criteria will as well. Assessments that are keyed closely to an American cultural context may disadvantage second language writers. . . . [Students should not be] arbitrarily punished for linguistic differences that in some contexts make them more, not less, effective communicators.		
Best assessment practice includes assessment by peers, instructors, and the student writer himself or herself. Valid assessment requires combining multiple perspectives on a performance and generating an overall assessment out of the combined descriptions of those multiple perspectives.		

Source: CCCC Executive Committee, "Writing Assessment: A Position Statement." Copyright © 2009 by National Council of Teachers of English. www.ncte.org/cccc/resources/positions/writingassessment.

As we began to explore in Chapter 8, assessments are helpful not only for seeing where students are but also for reflecting on your teaching. In this way, assessments give us valuable information that can feed back into our pedagogies, or "close the loop" by using assessment to improve both teaching and learning. The next three activities include excerpts from some of the rubrics used to evaluate new teacher candidates and their teaching in California. As these rubrics are quite detailed and specify different levels of pedagogical development and sophistication, you can use them to identify any elements of assessment that you need to think more about as a teacher.

Activity 14.14 Assessing your teaching

For each rubric point in the charts that follow, brainstorm how you can strengthen your own assessment practices. It might help to have a particular assessment in front of you as you complete this activity, perhaps one you mapped out earlier in this chapter.

Analyzing Student Work from an Assessment

How does the candidate demonstrate an understanding of student performance with respect to standards/objectives?

Level 1	Level 2	Level 3	Level 4
• The criteria/rubric and analysis have little connection with the identified standards/objectives. OR • Student work samples do not support the conclusions in the analysis.	• The criteria/rubric and analysis focus on what students did right or wrong in relationship to identified standards/objectives. • The analysis of whole class performance describes some differences in levels of student learning for the content assessed.	• The criteria/rubric and analysis focus on patterns of student errors, skills, and understandings to analyze student learning in relation to standards/objectives. • Specific patterns are identified for individuals or subgroup(s) in addition to the whole class.	All components of Level 3 plus: • The criteria/rubric and analysis focus on partial understandings as well. • The analysis is clear and detailed.

Source: PACT, "Performance Assessments for California Teachers." Copyright © 2013 by PACT. Reprinted by permission. www.pacttpa.org.

1. What elements of assessing student performance do you do well? On which elements could you focus more attention?

2. What questions could you ask yourself as you create criteria/rubrics or as you read student work to help you perform a stronger assessment?

Using Assessment to Inform Teaching

How does the candidate use the analysis of student learning to propose next steps in instruction?

Level 1	Level 2	Level 3	Level 4
• Next steps are vaguely related to or not aligned with the identified student needs. OR • Next steps are not described in sufficient detail to understand them. OR • Next steps are based on inaccurate conclusions about student learning from the assessment analysis.	• Next steps focus on improving student performance through general support that addresses some identified student needs. • Next steps are based on accurate conclusions about student performance on the assessment and are described in sufficient detail to understand them.	• Next steps focus on improving student performance through targeted support to individuals and groups to address specific identified needs. • Next steps are based on whole class patterns of performance and some patterns for individuals and/or subgroups and are described in sufficient detail to understand them.	All components of Level 3 plus: • Next steps demonstrate a strong understanding of both the identified content and language standards/objectives and of individual students and/or subgroups.

Source: PACT, "Performance Assessments for California Teachers." Copyright © 2013 by PACT. Reprinted by permission. www.pacttpa.org.

1. What elements of using assessment to inform your teaching do you need to work on?

2. What questions can you ask yourself or what practices can you adopt to consistently use assessment data to inform your next steps for teaching?

Using Feedback to Promote Student Learning

What is the quality of feedback to students?

Level 1	Level 2	Level 3	Level 4
• Feedback is general and provides little guidance for improvement related to learning objectives. OR • The feedback contains significant inaccuracies.	• Timely feedback identifies what was done well and areas for improvement related to specific learning objectives.	• Specific and timely feedback helps the student understand what s/he has done well, and provides guidance for improvement.	• Specific and timely comments are supportive and prompt analysis by the student of his/her own performance. • The feedback shows strong understanding of students as individuals in reference to the content and language objectives they are trying to meet.

Source: PACT, "Performance Assessments for California Teachers." Copyright © 2013 by PACT. Reprinted by permission. www.pacttpa.org.

1. What aspects of offering feedback to promote student learning do you do well? On which elements could you focus more attention?

2. What goals can you set for yourself to ensure that your feedback promotes learning? Why are these goals integral to your philosophy of how assessment works in your writing class?

Taking it further:
Thinking outside the traditional rubric

In this era of high-stakes testing and mandated learning outcomes, it is often difficult to imagine allowing students simply to write—to explore ideas, to experience affective pleasure, to express themselves, or to experiment with textual forms or language. When teachers do encourage such writing, it is often in the form of ungraded, informal assignments.

However, there is an argument to be made for also forgoing rubrics on larger, more formal assignments. For example, one might ask students to create a draft of an assignment first, and then—during the process of class discussions, drafting, revising, teacher-student conferences, and peer response—you can figure out the full criteria for the assignment and gain an understanding of the options for successful writing (perhaps negotiating this in collaboration with students). Rubrics can run the risk of doing a disservice to this more process-based and learning-focused approach; similarly, they can prompt us to focus on responding to student work in ways that run counter to our teaching philosophy.

In the following situations, having more flexible criteria (or perhaps not using a rubric) might be helpful:

- When experimenting with a new type of writing assignment. For example, the first time one assigns a literacy narrative, it is hard to predict where students will go with their essays, let alone define the criteria for different grades.
- When we want students to brainstorm and come up with a class rubric, based on the work they have already done in researching and drafting and based on their reading of one another's in-progress drafts.
- When we want students to set their own writing goals, especially for highly individualized projects (e.g., a semester-long blogging assignment on a topic and for an audience that the student selects).
- When we simply want to talk to students about their writing, brainstorming together to see where a particular piece of writing could or should go during the revision process.

Now examine the course plan that you have been working on to determine where it might be beneficial to forgo using a rubric. (Look back at the unit and lesson plans in Chapter 8 and Chapter 9.)

 Activity 14.15   Working without rubrics

To help you think about when to use rubrics and when to use other forms of feedback, answer the following questions.

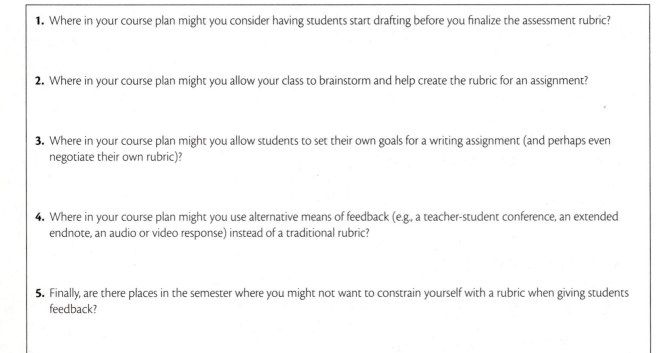

1. Where in your course plan might you consider having students start drafting before you finalize the assessment rubric?

2. Where in your course plan might you allow your class to brainstorm and help create the rubric for an assignment?

3. Where in your course plan might you allow students to set their own goals for a writing assignment (and perhaps even negotiate their own rubric)?

4. Where in your course plan might you use alternative means of feedback (e.g., a teacher-student conference, an extended endnote, an audio or video response) instead of a traditional rubric?

5. Finally, are there places in the semester where you might not want to constrain yourself with a rubric when giving students feedback?

Reflections from experienced teachers

In this chapter, you have thought more deeply about how assessment will help you ascertain what your students are learning and point them toward future learning. You have considered how best to communicate your assessments of their learning in terms of formative and summative comments, and you have explored the different tools that can assist you with assessment, such as rubrics and portfolios. At the end of the day, assessment happens with actual student work; however, it can be hard to think about how you will assess something if you have not yet seen responses to the given assignment. Bearing this in mind, it is helpful to know that you will need to revise, retool, and seek opportunities to discuss your assessment with colleagues; like writing, assessment is an ongoing practice and process. Until then, as you continue working with evaluation and assessment, the following ideas from experienced teachers might offer some starting principles:

- Assessment is always a balancing act. Experienced teachers juggle their institutional expectations; their philosophy of teaching, learning, and writing; the affective needs of their students; and the limits on their time and energy. In this way, this chapter and Chapter 4 overlap significantly.

- Assessment occurs throughout the course, not just when you are facing a stack of final drafts or their end-of-term grading rosters. Ongoing assessment—whether informal or formal, whether self-assessment, peer assessment, or teacher assessment—helps students know where they are and what they need to keep working on. It also helps minimize "surprises" that result in frustration, confusion, and even grade disputes.

- Even simple and informal assessments, such as checking for understanding or having students explain tasks or concepts to one another, are useful for thinking of assessment as a continuing process.

- Working with other faculty—sharing and discussing student writing—is a great way to sharpen assessment skills. However, we also know that even seasoned faculty often disagree on the grade a paper should receive. There is no such thing as an absolute, unequivocal, immutable definition of an A paper, a B paper, or a C paper—even when teachers are following a well-normed scoring rubric.

- Longtime teachers may still find it difficult to give negative feedback on a "weak" paper, regardless of their teaching philosophy or their teaching persona. To help with this challenge, veteran teachers often try to keep in mind the bigger picture of their students' overall growth as writers and thinkers. Honest feedback on an early paper may challenge a student to grow much more as a writer throughout a course, especially if that honest feedback is coupled with strategies for improvement and success.

- Different students want and expect different things from assessment. Some students (such as newly arrived international students) may want extensive feedback on every grammar and idiom error. Other students (such as those who excelled in high school English) may be expecting nothing but praise. While it is neither possible nor desirable to please every student, experienced teachers do strive to make the assessment process easier and more transparent by explaining how they are assessing papers and why they are giving feedback in a particular manner.

Putting it together:
Articulating your approach to assessment

Assessment is an essential part of the feedback loop in a writing class. If you continually assess student understanding and writing throughout the term, both you and your students will have a clearer sense of where you are headed and how you are performing (where students need to focus their energies and where you might need to reteach or add instruction to support them).

 Activity 14.16   Explaining your assessment views and practices

To crystallize the thinking you have done in this chapter, imagine that you are preparing for an interview for a teaching position. You know that you will be asked about your assessment beliefs and practices in the context of your teaching philosophy. In the space provided, describe one major summative assessment you plan to use, and explain how earlier informal and formative assessments will build toward it. You will then expand on this in your teaching journal when you articulate your assessment philosophy.

The final activity of this chapter asks you to describe how your assessment philosophy fits with your philosophy of teaching, learning, and writing. Be sure to discuss what things you value in student writing (Activity 1.4 and Activity 1.11), how you will teach those things, and how you will assess whether students have learned what you have taught (Activity 14.4 and Activity 14.5). Also discuss how your beliefs about assessment fit (or conflict) with the roles that you choose to take on as a teacher, as well as the institutional roles that are imposed on you, as you explored in Chapter 3 and Chapter 4.

Activity 14.17 Integrating your assessment philosophy
and your teaching philosophy

*In your teaching journal, discuss the following questions. Be sure to note any questions
or issues that you are still wrestling with.*

- What assessment principles are most important to you, and how do these principles help you teach students how to create "good writing"?

- How do these principles align with your personal and institutional roles as a teacher?

   As we do throughout this book, we advise you to make careful, informed choices about how and when you adopt teaching practices and teaching materials. This is even more important when it comes to assessment, since assessment decisions can often feel more fraught. Particularly for summative assessments (including end-of-term grades), these decisions also have a real-life impact on your students. The best we can do, then, is to encourage you to adapt practices and materials to fit your teaching philosophy (Chapter 1 and Chapter 2), your teaching persona (Chapter 3 and Chapter 4), and your particular instructional context (explored in Activities 5.5, 5.9, and 14.5). In this way, you will constantly move back and forth between trying out new ideas and practices in your classroom, and stepping back to observe, reflect, and revise those practices in line with your larger goals and philosophy. This process will likewise be helpful as we move to the final part of *Informed Choices*. Reflecting on the informed choices you make will help you create the best teaching and learning possible, whether you are exploring effective ways to teach diverse student populations, looking for ways to effectively integrate technology into your teaching, or exploring your own ongoing growth and development as a teacher.

Further Reading

- Bloom, Lynn Z. "Why I (Used to) Hate to Give Grades." *College Composition and Communication* 48.3 (1997): 360–71. Print.

- CCCC Executive Committee. *CCCC Position Statement on Writing Assessment.* National Council of Teachers of English. 2009. Web. 29 Sept. 2014. <http://www.ncte.org/cccc /resources/positions/writingassessment>.

- Huot, Brian. "Towards a New Discourse of Assessment for the College Writing Classroom." *College English* 65.2 (2002): 163–80. Print.

- Moore, Anna. "Where Does Spite Fit into the Rubric?" *The Quarterly* 24.4 (2002): 3–5. Print.

- *Resource Topics: Research-Assessment.* National Writing Project. Web. 29 Sept. 2014. <http://www.nwp.org/cs/public/print/resource_topic/research_assessment>.

- White, Edward. "The Scoring of Writing Portfolios: Phase 2." *College Composition and Communication* 56.4 (2005): 581–600. Print.

- Yancey, Kathleen Blake. "Looking Back as We Look Forward: Historicizing Writing Assessment." *College Composition and Communication* 50.3 (1999): 483–503. Print.

PART 4

Engaging Twenty-First-Century Composition

CHAPTER 15

Choices about Teaching Diverse Students

In prior chapters, you worked through many of the philosophical and pragmatic choices you face in designing a course: choosing your readings, creating writing assignments, structuring class activities, providing feedback, and assessing student writing. This final part of *Informed Choices* now asks you to revisit all those choices by considering your teaching in the twenty-first century. Specifically, we ask you to deepen the thinking you have already done by reconsidering your course and your teaching through three specific lenses: diversity, technology, and your own professional development.

In this chapter, you will reexamine the decisions you have made so far in light of a student population that is increasingly diverse in terms of language, culture, ethnicity, socioeconomic background, educational goals, academic preparation, and learning needs. Although we have asked you to think about diversity throughout the book, focusing more deeply on diversity in this chapter will give you new insights into the choices that you have made and will help you adjust some of those choices so that you can better meet the needs of all your students. As you work through this chapter, then, continue to cycle back to your writing and reading assignments (Chapter 6 and Chapter 7), your course planning (Chapter 8 and Chapter 9), and your assessment plans (Chapter 14). By the end of the chapter, you will be ready to test out the work you have done with your developing teaching philosophy and the course goals you have been shaping and reshaping throughout this book.

What characterizes your diverse student population?

The postsecondary student population has changed significantly over the past half century. A number of political, social, and economic factors have contributed to this change:

- Increased globalization
- The GI Bill, which financed college for returning veterans who might not have afforded college otherwise
- A dramatic increase in immigration after the 1964 Immigration Act and influxes of refugees since the 1970s

- The open admissions movements of the early 1970s, during which time colleges and universities loosened their restrictive "gatekeeping" admissions mechanisms
- The affirmative action policies of the 1970s and 1980s
- The progress of the civil rights movement in general, which has been bolstered at the university level by support programs for underrepresented student populations (e.g., equal opportunity programs, Upward Bound) and by the hiring of faculty who more accurately represent the ethnic, cultural, and linguistic landscape of U.S. society

The increase in social, cultural, ethnic, and linguistic diversity has enriched postsecondary education as students bring more diverse funds of knowledge, life experiences, and worldviews to the classroom. However, it has also made the task of teaching college writing more complex; as a teacher, you will probably find your writing classrooms populated by some or all of the following:

- Monolingual native speakers of English
- Bilingual or multilingual native speakers of English
- Speakers of more "dominant" varieties of English, as well as speakers of various community dialects (African American Vernacular English, Chicano English, Nuyorican English, regional dialects, and sociolects)
- Immigrant students, ranging from those who are newly arrived to those who arrived at a very young age (sometimes called Generation 1.5)
- American-born children of immigrant families, who speak English and may or may not be fluent or literate in a "home language" other than English
- International students who will only be in the United States for the duration of their education

Among these groups you will find some students who are well prepared to take on college-level academic reading and writing tasks, who are highly committed to the habits of mind required by postsecondary education (see the *Framework for Success in Postsecondary Writing*), and who are familiar with the teaching processes that you will use in your class, such as collaborative learning and peer response. However, among all these groups you will also find students who are underprepared and academically less experienced. This chapter will help you think through ways to meet the needs of the rich and diverse twenty-first-century student population.

We should also note that some of the "new" demographics that we see in our classrooms are, in fact, not new at all; as educators, we have simply become more cognizant of these demographics. For example, students' linguistic backgrounds have traditionally been occluded by the English-only ideologies of our school system. Bilingual students who developed strong academic English skills were typically treated as monolingual native English speakers, with little attention to the rich bicultural and biliterate resources that they could bring to the classroom. Bilingual students with weaker academic English skills were typically treated as "remedial students"—a conflation of language development needs and broader academic needs. Similarly, many students' learning difficulties (anything from dyslexia to affective challenges) were conflated with a lack of academic preparation; such students often found themselves in remedial classes.

> "The most important quote I remember from my grad school education is this one: "You have to meet your students where they are." It's futile to talk about where students "should be" in terms of skills. This diverse group of students is in my class already, and it's my goal to help them develop as writers. This fundamental orientation really helps me as a writing teacher of diverse students.
>
> —*Mark*

Furthermore, we have always had a rich variety of learning styles in our college classrooms—styles that went unrecognized in the traditional, one-size-fits-all, "chalk and talk" or "drill and skill" college classroom. Students with different learning styles or learning needs were forced to adapt as best they could to the mainstream mode of instruction. Moreover, educational systems such as tracking, special education programs, or gifted programs offer examples of the ways schools have homogenized classrooms and encouraged one-size-fits-all teaching. As we have learned more about the many different ways that individuals learn, we have become more aware of the range of differences that exist in our classrooms. Similarly, we have always had students who come from diverse socioeconomic backgrounds (e.g., students who are the first in their families to go to college, as well as nontraditional students who are working full-time while going to school). Fortunately, in the past few decades schools have come to recognize the rich variety of student populations and now provide support services, curricular options, and more varied teaching approaches to boost these students' chances of success.

Identifying the students at your institution

Educational discussions about diversity typically focus on ethnic diversity. We would like you to step back a bit and get an even broader view of the richness and complexity of your student population—both at your institution and in your classroom. We ask this not because ethnic diversity is unimportant, but rather because student populations vary in multiple, complex, overlapping, and ever-changing ways. In fact, as teachers, we need to continually ask ourselves, "Who are my students right now?" If you are new to your institution, you may only have a general sense of your student population. If you have been at your institution for a while, you probably have a clearer picture of the kinds of students you will see in your classes each semester. However, even experienced teachers can benefit from stepping back and learning more about the big-picture demographics at their institutions. In fact, if you are teaching at an institution where the demographics are changing rapidly, you may find that many of your English faculty colleagues are grappling with (or perhaps even resisting) new demographic realities. For example, we have more than thirty years of teaching experience combined, yet each semester we still discover new complexities and nuances in our student population, especially as our institution grows and changes. We begin by asking you to investigate key questions about the students at your institution.

Activity 15.1 Finding out who your students are

Answer the questions that follow about your student population. You can find this information through your institution's Web site, or you can ask your colleagues or supervisors. (If you do not have time to research the answers to these questions right now, we recommend that you go through the list to assess how much you already know and what you might want to inquire about in subsequent conversations with colleagues.)

1. What are the demographics of your institution's student population in terms of ethnicity?

2. What are the demographics in terms of socioeconomic background? How many students receive need-based financial aid? How many are working full-time? How many are the first in their families to go to college?

3. If you are teaching at a two-year school, how many students plan to go on to four-year institutions? If you are teaching at a four-year school, how many students come in as transfer students rather than as first-time freshmen?

4. What is the age range of the student population at your institution? Do you have many older returning students? Do you have many veterans? Do you have many students who are already embedded in career paths? Do you have many students who are working parents?

5. Does your school have a large number of multilingual students? Are they mainly international students who are here just for the duration of their studies, or are they immigrant students who reside permanently in the United States?

6. If your school has a placement test or some other assessment for determining "college readiness," what percentage of freshmen place directly into first-year composition classes, and what percentage must do preparatory work (e.g., developmental writing, basic skills, or remedial coursework)?

Bearing in mind the information you gathered in the previous activity, you will now brainstorm about the particular experiences, characteristics, and needs these various students might bring to your classroom. You will also brainstorm about the particular challenges you might face in meeting your students' needs.

Activity 15.2 Anticipating students' experiences, characteristics, and needs

Down the left side of the chart, list the learning needs of various student populations that you may work with at your institution (e.g., newly arrived international students, older students returning to school, students working full-time). Brainstorm a few of this population's possible unique needs. Down the right side of the chart, brainstorm challenges that you—as a teacher—might face in meeting the needs of each population.

Learning needs of various student populations:	Challenges you might face in meeting those needs:

The activities in this chapter may help you address some of the needs that you have identified. In addition, Chapter 17 will guide you in creating a career development plan that will help you meet current and future student needs.

Now that you have a bit more information about the diversity of your institution, you can begin to flesh out your beliefs about working with a diverse student population. We begin with tensions that we often hear colleagues express. As you work through the activity, you may feel torn between two conflicting beliefs. This response is fine; simply note that tension.

Activity 15.3 Balancing conflicting views about serving diverse writing students

Circle any ideas that resonate with you, and mark with an asterisk any ideas that cause tension. Unpack at least one of the tensions in your teaching journal.

When teaching a diverse population of student writers, I tend to believe . . .	
Good teaching is just good teaching. Effective teaching strategies benefit all students.	Different students have different needs. Teachers must have a broad repertoire of teaching strategies to meet those needs.
I have to be fair to everyone in the class, so I avoid making special accommodations for individual students.	A one-size-fits-all approach is unrealistic; I need to allow individual students leeway in completing assignments.
Catering to special needs would mean lowering my standards.	I can maintain high standards *and* allow for individual differences.
I need to maintain standards, even if it means that some students will fail.	I need to help all students succeed, even if it means I have to be flexible with standards.
We need to think of every student as a unique individual because thinking about students as cultural groups tends to lead to stereotyping.	We need to think about different groups of students because different groups bring different cultures, histories, and experiences to the classroom.

YOUR TEACHING JOURNAL: Engaging with tensions

Choose the pair of beliefs that caused the most tension for you, and brainstorm about it in your teaching journal. Consider the following questions:

- Why do you feel torn?
- Are the two poles really incompatible?
- Are there ways of teaching that might allow you to hold true to both beliefs?
- What would you need to learn in order to do this?
- How could you ask colleagues for help?

Thinking in terms of "special accommodation"

Another way to flesh out your philosophy about working with diverse students is to think about two undercurrents that often characterize discussions of diversity. Sometimes discussions about diverse student needs have an undercurrent of "student as problem." These discussions tend to frame diversity as a need for special accommodation. This line of thinking can be like quicksand; if you define every learning difference as a "problem" that must be "accommodated," you can become overwhelmed as you ask yourself a never-ending series of questions: How do I accommodate the ESL student? How do I accommodate the academically underprepared student? How do I accommodate the student with learning disabilities? How do I accommodate the student who has underdeveloped study skills? How do I accommodate the student who brings in different cultural repertoires? How do I accommodate the student who has had unconventional life experiences that do not match my expectations?

Thinking in terms of "universal design"

Sometimes discussions about diverse student needs take quite a different tack: Teachers talk about creating courses, learning activities, and assignments that are designed to be accessible to as many students as possible. The field of education now employs a term first used in architecture, *universal design*, which means designing things so that everyone is able to use them (including people with hearing, vision, or mobility impairments). The term has entered the field of education because it is a useful heuristic for thinking about teaching and learning.

How will you serve a diverse population of students?

Imagine a typical scenario: During the last five minutes of a class meeting, the teacher verbally announces a homework assignment. Which students might have trouble with this quite conventional practice?

- English learners who have difficulties with listening comprehension
- Academically inexperienced students who might not immediately grasp the form and purpose of the assignment

- Students who are juggling heavy responsibilities and who might remember the specifics of the assignment initially but then have trouble reconstructing it later—even if they took notes
- Students who need to ask questions to clarify the assignment

An alternative approach that could—by design—reach a broader range of students might look something like this:

- Write the homework assignment on the board at the beginning of class (so that students can see it and write it down).
- Announce the assignment well before the end of the class (so that students can ask questions).
- Post the assignment on a class Web site with further explanation (for students who need to see it and mull it over).
- Send the class an e-mail reminder before the next class meeting (including clarification about any questions that students have asked you in the interim).

As this comparison reveals, accessibility practices are often quite easy to implement. Writing assignments on the board at the beginning of the class, posting assignments on a class Web site, or sending students an e-mail reminder takes little additional time. Announcing assignments well before the end of class may take time because of student questions, but answering these questions will save you valuable time during the next class meeting because more students will be well prepared.

Unfortunately, we sometimes hear a classic objection from colleagues: "These are college students, so they should be able to do these things on their own." We try to counter this objection with a question: "Would you rather have students come to class well prepared so that your lesson goes smoothly, or would you rather be constantly 'putting out fires' because students have misunderstood assignments?" Our response comes from an overall teaching perspective that does not dwell on the question, "What should students be able to do already when they get to my class?" Asking the alternative question, "Where are my students now, and how do I help them learn what they need to learn?" is surely more productive.

As a teacher, you will develop many ways of understanding students' diverse learning needs and adapting your classes to those needs. As always, you can also profit from strategies that experienced teachers already use. Activity 15.4 below asks you to explore some of these strategies.

Activity 15.4   Adapting universal design strategies for your course

Fill in the following chart. Next to each strategy listed, note where or how you might apply the strategy in your course design. If you have conflicted or negative thoughts about a strategy, note how you might test it out in some small way to see if it might indeed have a place in your pedagogy.

Universal design strategy:	How to apply elements of this strategy:
Build in lots of different kinds of assignments that allow students to participate and interact with material in many ways: freewriting, reader-response journals, blogs, online class discussions, small-group discussions, whole-class discussions, individual presentations, group presentations, short formal papers, longer formal papers.	
Give students lead time so they can start preparing for assignments early. For example, announce a longer piece of reading well ahead of time so that students who need to can get a head start or budget their time if they are juggling multiple responsibilities.	
Scaffold the reading/writing process. Divide assignments into small chunks, and provide opportunities for support along the way. Not all students will need all the scaffolding that you provide, but many students will need individual parts of the scaffolding. For example, ESL students may need proofreading/editing time in class during which they can ask you or their classmates grammar questions.	
Give students opportunities for follow-up. Give students who receive a poor grade on a paper an opportunity to work with you or with a tutor to revise the paper.	
Be flexible in your requirements. Instead of singling out individual students for special treatment, be flexible with all your students. For example, some teachers give all students one "late essay coupon" that they can use for any reason. Some teachers allow all students to revise a paper if it earns less than a certain grade. Some teachers use a portfolio approach in which students can revise any essay that they choose to put in their portfolio.	
Be multimodal whenever possible. Say it, write it, show examples, and give opportunities to talk about it so you reach students with a wide variety of learning styles (and so you avoid burnout from having to respond repeatedly to things students have misunderstood).	

Of course, for all of these strategies, you will need to develop a sense of how much is too much. Too many assignment types—particularly informal assignments—can confuse students about what is important in terms of the course goals. Too much lead time can encourage students to procrastinate.

Students may take advantage of overly flexible assignment requirements, and they may become irritated or bored with too much redundancy.

Finally, universal design does not circumvent the need for accommodations for specific individual needs (for example, accommodations to help a mobility-impaired student write). Throughout your teaching career, you will have students who need unique accommodations that cannot be addressed by universal design principles. However, we believe that if you have created a course that incorporates lots of universal design flexibility—a course that does not presuppose that all students participate, read, write, think, and study in exactly the same way—it will be far easier for you to offer accommodations for specific individual needs and to create bridges that will allow all students to participate and learn. And perhaps most important, if you offer flexibility and individualization for everyone, then the students who do receive individual accommodations will not feel quite so singled out.

In Activity 15.1, you mapped the terrain of diversity within your institution. We now offer you strategies for mapping the diversity within your classroom. We have seen at least four main ways that teachers gain richer insights into their students' experiences and needs:

- Beginning-of-semester surveys
- One-on-one conferences with students
- In-class community-building activities
- Writing activities that allow students to incorporate personal experiences

Beginning-of-semester surveys

Many teachers ask students to fill out a beginning-of-semester survey or information sheet. Over the years, we have seen many variations of these surveys and have noticed that the questions sometimes focus too heavily on demographic details (e.g., "Are you a U.S. citizen or an international student?"). Students may perceive such questions as "prying" or as an attempt to single them out as having special needs.

Instead, we recommend asking questions that allow all students to talk about their reading and writing experiences, which will yield much more useful information than mere census-like queries. Here are some possible questions:

- Do you enjoy reading for pleasure? If so, what kinds of things do you like to read?
- When reading for school, what do you find enjoyable, and what challenges or difficulties do you experience?
- What did you enjoy about prior English classes? What did you find challenging?
- Do you regularly use any languages other than English? Can you read and write in those languages?
- Do you think you might want tutoring or any extra assistance this semester? If so, what would you like to work on? Who would you feel most comfortable working with (the professor, a student tutor, someone from the academic support center)?

> "The professional development workshops and graduate training I received early on did a good job emphasizing the importance of student diversity on the abstract level. But they didn't really address how to work with diverse student writing. I've had to figure a lot of that out myself, mostly by trying different strategies and gauging the results, talking to my colleagues, and even asking my students what helps them learn best.
>
> —*Tara*

Activity 15.5 Coming up with inviting survey questions

In the space provided, brainstorm some questions that you might ask your students in a beginning-of-semester survey.

One-on-one conferences with students

Most teachers conduct individual student conferences at some time during the semester, most often to discuss an intermediate or final draft of an essay. However, most teachers we work with have found that conferences at the beginning of the semester (even before students have written a first draft) can have a profoundly positive effect on student performance.

Even a five- or ten-minute "getting to know you" conference can reframe an incoming student's perception of a college writing class. For academically inexperienced students, this conference also serves as a valuable opportunity to locate your office and get a feel for attending office hours. You can use your student survey as a springboard for the conversation, or you can ask students to bring in their own questions. If your course allows students choices in reading/writing topics, you can also use the time to find out what your students are interested in. We recommend that you try these beginning-of-semester conferences with at least one class and see what effect they have on the students and on your teaching; you may well find that you want to meet with the students in all your classes. (Of course, you may also find that these conferences do not fit well with your teaching persona or your workload; you will have to experiment to find what is right for you.)

Activity 15.6 Brainstorming key questions for your beginning-of-semester conferences

Complete the following chart to brainstorm the questions that you will ask to help you in conferences.

Questions to ask in conference:	What this question could help me ascertain about student needs:

In-class community-building activities

When planning the first week or two of the semester, teachers often focus on the logistics of course content (e.g., "How will I introduce my students to the material that I am going to be teaching this semester?") and the rules and regulations of the course (e.g., "How will I make my grading policy clear?"). However, this kind of planning neglects the equally important affective aspects of a course: how the class will function as a learning community in which students feel invested. It is important to think through these affective aspects ahead of time because even the first few minutes of the very first class meeting can set the emotional tone for the semester.

Many teachers thus think of their opening class meetings as opportunities to start building community and relationships. The goals of community-building activities are generally to:

- Get students talking in class so that they feel comfortable participating and sharing their views and experiences
- Get students talking to one another so that they see classmates as a resource and a support
- Get students invested in the course and in their success in the course

A Web search of the term "community-building activities" will give you endless variations of activities. Students respond best to activities that serve both to build community and to introduce the content and process of the class. Compare, for example, the following two community-building activities:

Option 1	Option 2
Interview several classmates about their hobbies and interests. Then report to the class on what you have discovered.	Interview several classmates about their language and literacy backgrounds and the reading and writing they do during an average week. Then report to the class on what you have discovered.
Students might see this activity as "busy work."	Students could see this activity as integral to a reading/writing class that will explore literacy as a topic through frequent group discussions and peer review, and they will get to know one another in the process.

Another way to build community while at the same time introducing students to the content and process of the course is to do a literacy activity. You may want to structure the first class meeting so that students meet in small groups to read and react to very short texts that elicit personal experiences and set up the content of the first teaching unit. For example, if your first reading/writing unit is on the topic of education, you could give each group a short quote from an educational theorist (e.g., Paulo Freire, John Dewey), and have the students discuss the quote in terms of their own experiences. If you want to increase the community-building aspect of this activity, during the first two or three class meetings you could have students rotate through as many groups as possible so that every student has a chance to work with every other student.

Writing activities that incorporate personal experiences

Another way to gain deeper insights into your students' experiences and needs is to include various forms of personal writing in your course design. As you explored in earlier chapters of this book, some teachers firmly believe that personal narrative essays can play an important role in helping students develop writing skills; they feel that personal narratives build students' sense of efficacy and ownership over their texts. Other teachers firmly believe that students should spend their time writing purely academic essays because this prepares them more directly for the type of writing they will encounter in other classes across the curriculum. The next activity asks you to explore these ideas in relation to your classroom and students.

 Activity 15.7 Integrating personal writing into your course

Complete the following chart. To help determine the role that personal writing will play in your class, engage with some common assumptions and think about assignments that you could use in your class to test out these assumptions.

Assumption about personal writing:	Assignment to test out this assumption in your class:
Writing improves when students have a personal stake in an assignment — whether overt (as in an autobiographical piece) or subtle (as in a pro/con research paper about a topic that is important to the student).	
Writing improves when students have opportunities to do different kinds of informal, more personal writing tasks to support learning: reader-response journals, personal reflections, blog posts, freewriting.	
More informal, personal writing tasks offer students "spaces" to reveal and explore their identities to the extent they feel comfortable. They also offer opportunities for the teacher and other students to get to know one another more individually.	

Earlier in this book, we asked you to design elements of your course, including the big-picture semester plan (Chapter 8), individual writing and reading assignments (Chapter 6 and Chapter 7), and classroom activities

(Chapters 9, 11, and 12). In the next activity, we ask you to look back at those elements and think about ways to make them more open and accessible for diverse students.

✎ Activity 15.8   Brainstorming ways to tweak your course design

In your teaching journal, discuss the following questions. Be sure to note any questions or issues that you are still wrestling with.

- Where can you provide a greater variety of writing assignments?
- Where can you add more multimodality to the way you convey information to students?
- How can you provide more lead time?
- Where can you provide more scaffolding?
- How can you provide more opportunities for follow-up?
- How, or in what situations, can you be more flexible?

Choosing readings for a diverse class

When we ask teachers-in-training to design a composition course for a diverse student population, they often try to shoehorn readings written by racially or ethnically diverse authors into their existing course design. Though well intentioned, this approach treats both course readings and diversity as a superficial "overlay" rather than as an integral part of the intellectual work of the course. This approach can also lead to stereotyping and tokenism. For example, we have often heard teachers ask, "Does anyone know a good reading by an Asian American author that I can assign in my first unit?"

We find that experienced teachers tend to think of course readings and diversity in a much deeper way: Rather than selecting "token representatives" of individual racial or ethnic groups, these teachers choose reading/writing topics that get students intellectually (and personally) engaged with the diversity of society, the diversity of the classroom, and the aspects of their individual identities that are continually constructed by diversity.

The best way to illustrate this is to compare assignments that reflect a shallow tokenism with assignments that ask students to engage with diversity at a deeper level.

Shallower approach to diversity	Deeper approach to diversity
Task: a personal narrative about how you have experienced prejudice Readings: narratives of racially or ethnically diverse authors	Task: a personal narrative about how you negotiate your identity in different social contexts, going with and against the grain of social expectations Readings: narratives by and about people who actively and consciously negotiate their racial, ethnic, or cultural identity positions
Task: an analysis of characters who are outsiders in fiction writing Readings: multicultural short stories	Task: an analysis of how and why characters move between insider and outsider positions through their language choices, including their use of various "Englishes" Readings: short stories that show characters moving between outsider and insider positions and reflecting on this experience
Task: a pro/con paper on gay marriage Readings: articles by proponents and opponents of gay marriage	Task: an analysis of how the notion of "family" is culturally constructed Readings: articles by authors from diverse social, cultural, and ethnic groups reflecting on what "family" means to them

To concretize this approach, take a moment to look back at the course design choices you made about writing and reading assignments in Chapter 6 and Chapter 7. Brainstorm ways that you might tweak the readings to push students to engage with diversity in a deeper way. Activities 6.8, 7.2, and 7.3 might be particularly useful to revisit.

 Activity 15.9 Approaching diversity more deeply with reading assignments

Complete the following chart with any needed revisions to your reading assignments.

Original reading assignment:	Revised reading assignment:

Creating writing tasks for a diverse class

In the preceding section, you started thinking about ways to tweak your reading list. The following chart draws on the wisdom of experienced teachers to offer suggestions on tweaking writing tasks to do justice to the complexity of diversity.

Instead of assigning tasks that . . .	You might try assigning tasks that . . .
Pressure particular students to be spokespeople for the racial, cultural, or social groups they represent	Invite all students to share their identity positions and the nuances of those identity positions
Ask students to speak as members of a fixed racial, ethnic, or cultural category	Ask students to talk about how they continually negotiate their identity
Ask students to argue for simplistic pro/con positions that are linked to the interests of specific groups (e.g., affirmative action, Mexican immigration, gay marriage)	Ask students to examine a pro/con debate itself (e.g., What is really at stake underneath all the hyperbole and arguments? Who is defining the terms of the debate? How does each side of the debate use language?)
Encourage students to write a self-evident thesis statement (e.g., "Discrimination is bad.")	Encourage students to write a more nuanced thesis statement (e.g., "Contrary to general beliefs, discrimination is sometimes perpetuated by . . .")

Again, take a moment to look back at the course design choices you made about writing and reading assignments in Chapter 6 and Chapter 7. Brainstorm ways that you might tweak the writing in your course to avoid some of the pitfalls listed in the preceding chart.

Activity 15.10 Approaching diversity more deeply with writing assignments

Complete the following chart with any needed revisions to your writing assignments.

Original writing assignment:	Revised writing assignment:

Turning to the field:
Working specifically with linguistic diversity

Because you are a writing teacher, your class's diversity will probably be most salient in the language, style, and rhetorical forms that students use in their essays. In fact, new teachers often feel overwhelmed when they receive their first batch of student essays—essays that they see as "stylistically inappropriate" and "riddled with errors."

However, it is not just new teachers who react to student essays in this way. Some longtime teachers are still surprised by (and grumble about) the language issues in each batch of student essays. In contrast, other seasoned teachers might look at the same batch of student essays and see some level of writing competence—and the potential for even greater writing competence.

Why would two groups of experienced teachers react so differently to the same batch of essays? Teachers who are continually "surprised" by students' "lack of proficiency" often define themselves as error-hunters and gatekeepers. They have an internalized standard of what student writing should look like, and they see their job as finding and cataloging student deficiencies. Other teachers take a more open and inquisitive approach to student error: They seek to understand how and why students write the way that they do. Many compositionists find this second, more inquisitive approach to be much more conducive to long-term development and the avoidance of teacher burnout. Some of our colleagues have been teaching for decades and yet still find things in student writing that are puzzling or even perplexing. They see these perplexing aspects of writing as an invitation for dialogue with students rather than as an alarm signal.

In his article "The Myth of Linguistic Homogeneity in U.S. College Composition," Paul Kei Matsuda explores another reason why experienced teachers might differ in their response to the same essays: our larger cultural view of linguistic difference and diversity. Matsuda explores the history of writing instruction in the United States in terms of how the U.S. has imagined English as the primary language of its citizens and sought to contain other language practices. In this way, the United States has created and perpetuated the "myth" that students are linguistically homogeneous, which is problematic for our understanding of both language use and our students, as well as problematic for our practice.

Instead, Matsuda insists that to "work effectively with the student population in the twenty-first century, all composition teachers need to reimagine the composition classroom as the multilingual space that it is, where the presence of language differences is the default." One way to do this is to start with the student essays themselves, instead of with an absolute standard for performance. Teachers can then ask themselves:

- What are students doing well already?
- What are students doing that differs from my expectations?
- Why might students do these things?
- Do students have a different understanding of the task that I assigned? What could account for this?
- Do students have different expectations and beliefs about academic writing?
- Are students making "errors" because they are not trying hard enough? Or are they making errors because they are trying hard to take on a new academic voice that is quite unfamiliar to them?

This internal dialogue can be revealing, especially when it comes to grammatical, rhetorical, or stylistic conventions.

 Activity 15.11   Thinking about sources of error

Consider the many reasons why a puzzling error might occur, and jot down some notes about how you would respond. We have included two possible responses for the first example to encourage you to think of multiple ways you might respond.

Possible source of the error or problem:	Ways to respond:
A student is wholly unaware that a convention or practice exists (as sometimes is the case with plagiarism).	**1.** Craft a teaching activity that shows this convention in action, in both student writing and professional writing. **2.** Have students brainstorm possible reasons for the convention or practice: Why do academic writers follow it? What purpose does it serve?
A student intends to follow a convention but inadvertently slips (e.g., by not revising or proofreading).	
A student is aware of a convention but does not understand its internal logic and thus cannot implement it effectively (e.g., incorporating partial quotes into sentences).	
A student is aware of a convention but does not have specific strategies for applying it (e.g., the student knows that sentence boundaries are somehow important, but she does not know how to find fragments and run-on sentences in her own writing).	

A student is deliberately flouting a convention for rhetorical effect. (Skilled writers flout conventions all the time, but they do so in strategic ways.)	
A student has a set of "rules" for writing, picked up in various English classes, but these rules do not accurately reflect college writing conventions or come from a classroom operating under a pedagogical perspective that differs from your own (e.g., "Never use *I* in an essay").	
A student brings different discourse patterns to academic writing. (English speakers will sometimes bring "oral" conventions, and learners of English will sometimes bring rhetorical and grammatical conventions from their own language.)	

How will you deal with "error" in diverse students' writing?

Writing teachers are charged with helping students achieve a certain level of grammatical proficiency (see our earlier discussion on institutional expectations and Activities 3.3, 4.4, and 5.4), and we do not want to dismiss teachers' concerns about this. Instead, we would like you to think about how experienced teachers sometimes deal with error and see how you might combine these ideas with your teaching philosophy.

📁 **Activity 15.12** Experimenting with approaches to error

Complete the following chart by jotting down ideas about how you might draw on the approaches to error listed in the left column, keeping in mind your teaching philosophy, your views of error, and any institutional constraints, such as program-wide requirements.

Effective approaches to error:	Ways to test out each approach:
Take more of an inquiry approach to error by realizing that one's understanding of how English grammar functions (and changes) is a long-term developmental process. Even teachers with strong linguistic backgrounds are constantly discovering new things about how language functions.	
Focus on content, organization, and development in student essays before dealing with grammar. Some "grammar problems" fix themselves as students clarify their ideas and get a better understanding of what they want to say in their essays.	
Build proofreading and editing time into classroom instruction. Sending students to a tutor in hopes of a "quick grammar fix" might improve one essay, but the skills probably will not transfer to subsequent writing assignments.	

Teach editing practices rather than give abstract grammar lectures. Having students practice proofreading strategies in class will pay higher dividends than a thirty-minute lecture on coordinate versus subordinate conjunctions.	
Approach errors realistically. Marking every imaginable type of error in a student essay will overwhelm both the student and the teacher — and will lead to teacher burnout. Instead, focus on patterns of error, marking only the errors that occur frequently or that interfere with meaning.	
Give students opportunities to revise grammatically problematic essays, either to improve the grade or to put the essay in a portfolio to be reevaluated at the end of the course.	

Taking it further:
Mapping the terrain of diversity terminology

Throughout this chapter, we have encouraged you to think about meeting the needs of diverse student populations. In this section, we will complicate your thinking by asking you to unpack the assumptions, ideologies, and rhetoric behind diversity discussions at your institution.

In discussions about teaching diverse students, terminology abounds. This dense thicket of terminology may both aid and hinder your thinking about diverse students:

> "When I first started teaching, I thought of students in very broad categories: Latinos, ESL students, strong/weak students, and so on. But over the years, I've become more aware of nuances, contradictions, and unexpected surprises. Many of my Latino students don't speak Spanish. Some of my ESL students are my strongest writers. Some of my "weak writers" are actually my most insightful and motivated students.
>
> —Tara

- Some terms focus primarily on students' "deficits" and thus have pejorative connotations, while other terms may be seen as neutral or even positive.
- Some terms have clear definitions and thus can be quite useful in pedagogical discussion, while others are ambiguous and only add confusion to discussions.
- Some terms tend to be used by teachers, others by administrators, others by academics, and yet others by students themselves.
- Some terms are used throughout the field of postsecondary education, while others might be used just within a particular institution or even a particular program.

As a first step in cutting through this cloud of terminology, we ask you to look at the word cluster in Activity 15.13.

Activity 15.13 Examining diversity terminology at your institution

Circle any ideas that resonate with you, and mark with an asterisk any ideas that cause tension. Unpack at least one of the tensions in your teaching journal.

Terms used to describe students at your school . . .

basic writer   special admit   immigrant   first-generation college student

remedial   learning disability   Generation 1.5   basic skills

students of color   underprepared   unmotivated   nontraditional student

ESL   special needs   nonnative speaker   reentry student

international student   at-risk   gifted   economically disadvantaged

nonstandard dialect speaker

Additional terms that come to mind. . .

YOUR TEACHING JOURNAL: Engaging with tensions

In your teaching journal, brainstorm the following questions:

- What do you notice about this terminology?
- Does the terminology tend to frame diversity as a strength or as a liability?
- In what ways might you want to change the terminology that you use?

Now you will take a step toward critically analyzing some of the terminology about diverse students that you hear at your institution. While some terminology that we have heard from teachers and administrators is unequivocally pejorative (e.g., "slow students"), most terminology is more ambivalent. Labels may be used to marginalize students, but they also may be used to highlight needed changes in teaching, administration, and resource allocation.

Activity 15.14 Examining the pros and cons of specific terminology

Select several terms that you often hear used at your school, and analyze them in the following chart. The first row has been completed for you as a possible model.

Terms used at your school:	Why this term is particularly prominent in discussions at your school:	How this term is helpful in your discussions about students:	How this term is negative or unhelpful:
Generation 1.5 student	We have a lot of students who are not native speakers of English but have lived here so long that they do not really fit into ESL courses. In fact, they may or may not still speak their "home language." We do not know where to place them or what to call them.	It gives us a shorthand way of talking about students who used to slip through the cracks and were ignored. It encourages us to develop new teaching strategies for students who have very strong oral skills but weaker academic writing skills.	The term can sometimes be a code word for *deficit*. Some teachers see these students as "problem" students. The term is very fuzzy. Many teachers seems to mean something different.

Reflections from experienced teachers

As teachers, it is our job to help all students learn, but this can be challenging when we have highly diverse classes filled with students who have unique skills and needs. Teachers must walk a tightrope, then, between expectations, support, flexibility, and accommodation. As teachers become more experienced working with diverse populations, this tightrope walk becomes less scary. Experienced teachers know that each semester they will face a new group of students, most with familiar skills and needs and some with quite unfamiliar skills and needs. Experienced teachers also know that each semester they must learn about their students and learn from them. And experienced teachers know that they must be both patient and creative to expand their repertoire of teaching practices as they develop as teachers.

We have found that teachers who are experienced in working with a diverse student population benefit most from the following practices and orientations:

- Experienced teachers accept that all people—and thus all learners—are different; there is no one "best way" to be a student. Using a questionnaire or a self-reflective writing assignment can help you get more information about your students' language and literacy histories and their prior reading and writing experiences. It is useful to ask students what has worked for them and helped them succeed in the past.

- Scaffolding reading, writing, and discussion activities—especially at the beginning of the semester—gives all students a chance to acclimate to the class and learn what is expected. Veteran teachers look for ways that pedagogical changes can support not only students with particular pedagogical needs but all students in the class (that is, universal design).

- Consider finding ways to hold your standards high but allow students multiple ways to reach that bar. For example, some students will need to write more drafts and get more teacher or tutor feedback to reach the bar. Developing benchmarks suited to different levels or types of learners can help all students achieve success.
- Successful teachers of diverse students cultivate a fundamental orientation: that diversity offers rich learning opportunities for all students. Find ways to draw on the wealth of different experiences and perspectives that diverse students bring to the classroom.

Putting it together: Articulating your philosophy about working with diverse students

The activities in this chapter have helped you flesh out and articulate your philosophy for teaching socially, culturally, ethnically, and linguistically diverse student populations. You have pondered ways of thinking about and meeting student needs, you have analyzed the terminology used to describe student needs, and you have considered perspectives that experienced teachers bring to the classroom, such as universal design (Activity 15.4). Now use the two activities that follow to concretize your philosophy on diversity in the classroom.

Activity 15.15 Explaining how you view and serve a diverse student population

Many interview committees ask some version of the following questions, either in an interview or as a requested "diversity statement" to be submitted with teaching materials: How do you teach diverse students? How do you make your teaching accessible to diverse populations of students in terms of readings, assignments, assessments, and classroom interaction? In the space provided, brainstorm, cluster, or chart specific answers and examples to help you answer these questions.

Now take the plunge and add a section on diversity to your teaching philosophy. Although you may also try to weave your beliefs about diversity and teaching into your philosophy, we ask you to compose a separate section for several reasons. First, you will find it useful in your professional development: Because many job applications and interview questions focus specifically on diversity, it is important to have thought through these issues in depth. Second, having a clearly articulated philosophy on student diversity will help you become a stronger advocate for students at your institution. Third, your statement on working with diverse students can act as a lens through which you can reexamine other aspects of your teaching philosophy. (For example, you will be able to ask yourself critically whether your views on reading assignments and writing assessment work in harmony with your views on the diverse funds of knowledge and repertoires of skills that your students bring to your class.)

In writing this draft, pay particular attention to the terminology that you use to describe diversity. Remember that terminology is often ideologically charged; a term that is widely used in one institutional context (e.g., policy makers' discussion of "the remediation problem") may be considered a red flag in another context (such as a job interview for a position teaching developmental writing). Look back at your work in Activity 15.13 and Activity 15.14 for help.

Activity 15.16   Articulating the philosophical rationale for your approach to diversity

In your teaching journal, discuss the following questions. Be sure to note any questions or issues that you are still wrestling with.

- How do you perceive the mission of your institution — and your class — in terms of serving a diverse student population?

- How exactly do you conceptualize diversity? What richness does the diversity bring to your class? What challenges does it bring to your teaching?

- How will you meet the challenges of helping a diverse population of students succeed in your class and in your school as a whole?

As in prior chapters, we ask you to note questions and tensions in your teaching journal after composing your developing rationale. We have said before that the art of reflective teaching involves a great balancing act: At each moment you must make conscious, informed choices about what and how you are teaching, but you must also hold on to questions and uncertainties. Working with a diverse student population is perhaps the most challenging part of the balancing act, as you are continually called on to foster the success of new students whose needs and experiences you might not yet fully grasp. Keeping your tensions and questions in mind as you move forward to consider other elements of twenty-first-century teaching that also offer both challenges and opportunities — discussed in the next two chapters — will ensure that you continue to grow as a reflective practitioner.

Further Reading

- Canagarajah, A. Suresh. "TESOL at 40: What Are the Issues?" *TESOL Quarterly* 40.1 (2006): 9–34. Print.

- Cleary, Michelle Navarre. "Anxiety and the Newly Returned Adult Student." *Teaching English in the Two-Year College* 39.4 (2012): 364–76. Print.

- Fraiberg, Steven. "Composition 2.0: Toward a Multilingual and Multimodal Framework." *College Composition and Communication* 62.1 (2010): 100–126. Print.

- Horner, Bruce, Samantha NeCamp, and Christine Donahue. "Toward a Multilingual Composition Scholarship: From English Only to a Translingual Norm." *College Composition and Communication* 63.2 (2011): 269–300. Print.

- Horner, Bruce, and John Trimbur. "English Only and U.S. College Composition." *College Composition and Communication* 53.4 (2002): 594–630. Print.

- Matsuda, Paul Kei. "The Myth of Linguistic Homogeneity in U.S. College Composition." *College English* 68.6 (2006): 637–51. Print.

- Miller-Cochran, Susan. "Beyond 'ESL Writing': Teaching Cross-cultural Composition at a Community College." *Teaching English in the Two-Year College* 40.1 (2012): 20–30. Print.

- Perin, Dolores. "Literacy Skills among Academically Underprepared Students." *Community College Review* 41.2 (2013): 118–36. Print.

- Silva, Tony. "On the Ethical Treatment of ESL Writers." *TESOL Quarterly* 31.2 (1997): 359–63. Print.

CHAPTER 16

Choices about Writing in a Digital Age

Over the past several decades, we have seen technology permeate almost every area of our lives. So it is important to spend some time thinking about the extent to which technology will influence teaching and learning in the college composition classroom. Those who philosophize about technology and writing offer conflicting views. Some argue that the "digital age" has radically transformed the very foundations of thinking, communicating, reading, and writing. Others argue that writing itself has always been an evolving "technology"—from the earliest grapheme systems to the printing press, the typewriter, the word processor, and now social media; therefore, reading and writing are in many ways constant (but always in evolution). Our own philosophy lies somewhere between these two extremes. We believe that the digital age offers new opportunities to think, communicate, read, and write. It also offers new opportunities to teach and learn. And of course, we believe that teachers should make thoughtful, well-informed decisions about these opportunities. This chapter will help you enlarge and deepen your pedagogy through an examination of all that the digital age has to offer.

What role will technology play in your teaching?

At every level of education (and in daily life), technology influences our choices and ways of learning from and interacting with the world. At the simplest level, teachers bring technology-focused reading and writing topics into their classes, just as they would bring in any topic of current interest. This includes everything from dystopian fiction, to texting and driving, to genuine inquiry about how technology is changing our lives and relationships.

Many teachers go beyond "technology as topic," however, and directly address the proficiencies in reading, writing, communicating, and thinking that are necessary for academic success in the digital age. For example, it is common to teach students to critically evaluate Web-based sources. Some teachers also use computer-equipped classrooms to introduce students to various forms of electronic writing.

At the deepest level, teachers can use technology to enhance or expand the reading and writing experiences of students—offering new audiences, new writing processes, new genres, and new forms of feedback. By talking to your

> "In the last few years, I've heard my colleagues rant more and more about how technology has "ruined" students' ability to read full books and write coherent, grammatically correct prose. But we've always had students who've struggled with reading and writing; that's nothing new. What does seem new to me is the challenge of how to link students' social media and other literacy practices to the writing they do in the classroom.
>
> —Mark

students about how they already use technology to read and write, you can help them find connections and ways to build on the reading and writing they do both inside and outside of school. In addition, you can find ways to use students' comfort with technology to enhance learning. For example, most writing teachers at our institution now use online discussion boards as a complement to class discussions. Many assign student blogs in addition to more formal writing assignments. Some conduct peer response electronically (either in real time in a computer classroom or asynchronously), and some ask students to create electronic portfolios of their work at the end of the term. Finally, some teachers are experimenting with student-authored multimedia presentations, such as digital storytelling, class wikis, and the like.

In these ways, teachers have moved from thinking about technology merely as a tool (or what scholars like Stuart Selber would term "functional computer literacy"), to thinking about the critical and rhetorical literacies that our emerging technologies demand. Selber describes this shift as one that moves from students as users of technology, to students as "informed questioners" of technology, to the most rhetorical and creative use of all: students as "reflective producers" of technology. This understanding highlights our lived reality of digital culture and can help us think about how we can harness technology, media, and online connection and community to enhance teaching and learning.

As in previous chapters, rather than giving you a list of best practices, we ask you to stake out your own philosophical position and embed this position into your overall teaching philosophy.

📁 Activity 16.1   Examining technology at your institution

To begin exploring your philosophy of technology and writing, list all the ways that you, your colleagues, and your students have incorporated technology in classes — as either a topic, an instructional medium, or a learning process. Then note your observations in the following chart.

Ways you use technology in your teaching:	Additional ways your colleagues use technology in their teaching:	Additional ways students use technology to learn at your institution:
What do you notice about the lists above?		

To expand your thinking, look at Activity 16.2, which lists many terms that show up in discussions of technology and teaching.

 Activity 16.2 Looking at technology opportunities in your class

Circle any ideas that resonate with you, and mark with an asterisk any ideas that cause tension. Unpack at least one of the tensions in your teaching journal.

Terms related to technology and the teaching of writing . . .			
distance learning	Wikipedia	Facebook	plagiarism checker
new media	cut and paste	automated essay scoring	editing
online grade book	online plagiarism	online discussion	multimedia
webinar	critical thinking	computer classroom	connection
class wiki	evaluating sources	fast response time	digital divide
spell-checker	blogging	enhancing access	instant messaging
online drill	multiliteracies	gaming	patchwriting
hypertext	jobs for the future	texting in class	"digital native"
	e-book		real-world audience

Additional terms that come to mind . . .

YOUR TEACHING JOURNAL: Engaging with tensions

Choose the term that you feel most uncomfortable with, and brainstorm about it in your teaching journal. Consider the following questions:

- In what ways does the term clash with your experience or teaching philosophy?
- Is there anything about the term that is positive?
- How could you integrate the term into your teaching or your teaching philosophy if pressed to do so (by department mandates, for example)?

What role will electronic literacies play in your teaching?

Just as the debate around the value and effects of technology continues to rage on in schools and in the popular media, so too do the more specific debates about the changing nature (and demands) of literacy in the digital age. For example, some surveys, like those conducted by the National Endowment for the Arts ("To Read or Not to Read" 2007), suggest that people are reading fewer books today than in the past. However, other studies suggest somewhat contrary results—that college students, especially, are reading and writing more, are writing for more varied audiences, and are often writing outside of school ("Stanford Study of Writing"). As technology proliferates, we are still working to figure out the dimensions and implications of electronic literacies—those reading, writing, and understanding processes that happen via technology or online environments.

As a starting point, the next cluster of activities asks you first to examine the role of technology in your teaching and learning life. Then you will return to the *Framework for Success in Postsecondary Writing* to put your experiences in dialogue with the *Framework for Success's* recommendations for composing in multiple writing environments.

Activity 16.3 Brainstorming about your experiences with electronic literacies

Brainstorm about your experiences with electronic literacies and ponder the use of a new technology. Answer the following questions.

1. What has technology allowed you to learn or do?

2. Have there been any downsides to developing or engaging electronic literacies?

3. Thinking of your writing life both on and off the page, do you think technology is making you read and write less, or is technology helping you read and write more (albeit differently)? Explain.

YOUR TEACHING JOURNAL: Engaging with tensions

Think of one specific technology, type of digital media, or platform that has, in some significant way, shaped your literacy. In your teaching journal, brainstorm the following questions:

- How has this technology enabled or constrained new pursuits or dimensions for you as a reader or writer?

- What principles or questions can you abstract from these experiences that might inform your teaching — especially your use of technology?

The prior activity asked you to think specifically about the types of electronic literacies you have developed. Just as *literacy narratives* ask us to reflect on how our past literacy experiences have shaped who we are as readers and writers, *technology/electronic literacy narratives* ask us to think specifically about how new technology is affecting us. This type of reflection can help us as teachers, but it can also help our students become more self-aware: As you design your writing courses, you might consider including an assignment that asks students to reflect on both their literacy practices and their technology/electronic literacy practices.

Now, to put your experiences in dialogue with recommendations from the field of composition, think about the goals listed in the following excerpt. The recommendations suggest how teachers can help students strengthen the eight critical habits of mind (Activity 5.7) by composing effectively in different "environments" — from pen-and-paper writing to electronic environments.

Teachers can help writers develop as thoughtful, effective users of electronic technologies by providing opportunities and guidance for students to

- use a variety of electronic technologies intentionally to compose;
- analyze print and electronic texts to determine how technologies affect reading and writing processes;
- select, evaluate, and use information and ideas from electronic sources responsibly in their own documents (whether by citation, hotlink, commentary, or other means);
- use technology strategically and with a clear purpose that enhances the writing for the audience;
- analyze situations where print and electronic texts are used, examining why and how people have chosen to compose using different technologies; and
- analyze electronic texts (their own and others') to explore and develop criteria for assessing the texts.

Source: Council of Writing Program Administrators, "WPA Outcomes Statement for First-Year Composition." Copyright © 2014 by the Council of Writing Program Administrators. Reprinted by permission. http://wpacouncil.org /positions/outcomes.html.

 Activity 16.4   Translating goals into practices

In the following chart, translate at least two of the goals or recommendations from the Framework for Success *into a specific practice that fits with your philosophy of teaching.*

Goal or recommendation from the *Framework for Success*:	Specific activity or practice to achieve that goal in your class:

To think more deeply about attending to a range of texts and composing environments, we will investigate a particular kind of literacy that many teachers hope their students will develop: visual literacy. Visual literacy requires that we pay attention to images, videos, advertisements, and even design elements in the environments with which we interact, reading them critically as texts. Since images, ads, and even our built surroundings encircle us daily, many teachers hope to encourage students to be more critically attentive to these texts.

As you read the excerpt in Activity 16.5 from the *Visual Literacy Competency Standards for Higher Education*, consider how becoming visually literate might be important for your students. If the concept of visual literacy is new to you, then much of what you read here may cause tension or generate questions.

Activity 16.5   Examining visual literacy

Circle any ideas that resonate with you, and mark with an asterisk any ideas that cause tension. Unpack at least one of the tensions in your teaching journal.

The importance of images and visual media in contemporary culture is changing what it means to be literate in the 21st century. Today's society is highly visual, and visual imagery is no longer supplemental to other forms of information. New digital technologies have made it possible for almost anyone to create and share visual media. Yet the pervasiveness of images and visual media does not necessarily mean that individuals are able to critically view, use, and produce visual content. Individuals must develop these essential skills in order to engage capably in a visually oriented society. Visual literacy empowers individuals to participate fully in a visual culture.

Visual literacy defined
Visual literacy is a set of abilities that enables an individual to effectively find, interpret, evaluate, use, and create images and visual media. Visual literacy skills equip a learner to understand and analyze the contextual, cultural, ethical, aesthetic, intellectual, and technical components involved in the production and use of visual materials. A visually literate individual is both a critical consumer of visual media and a competent contributor to a body of shared knowledge and culture.

In an interdisciplinary, higher education environment, a visually literate individual is able to:

- Determine the nature and extent of the visual materials needed
- Find and access needed images and visual media effectively and efficiently
- Interpret and analyze the meanings of images and visual media
- Evaluate images and their sources
- Use images and visual media effectively
- Design and create meaningful images and visual media
- Understand many of the ethical, legal, social, and economic issues surrounding the creation and use of images and visual media, and access and use visual materials ethically

---

Source: Association of College and Research Libraries, "ACRL Visual Literacy Competency Standards for Higher Education." Copyright © 2011 by Association of College Research Libraries, a division of the American Library Association. Reprinted with permission. www.ala.org/acrl/standards/visualliteracy.

YOUR TEACHING JOURNAL: Engaging with tensions
Choose one of the practices you feel most uncomfortable with, and brainstorm about it in your teaching journal. Consider the following questions:

- Why might this idea cause tension with your beliefs about teaching?
- What would happen if you implemented this idea?

In the next two activities, you will explore literacy beyond the printed page in two ways: first, by thinking more concretely about visual literacy, and second, by pinpointing and analyzing another key literacy that you might need to factor into your teaching.

Activity 16.6 Exploring the importance of visual literacy

To deepen your thoughts on visual literacy, answer the following questions.

1. Is visual literacy important for your students? Explain.

2. How might practicing increased visual literacy help your students improve their writing?

3. Looking back at the plans you made in Chapter 8 and Chapter 9, which particular units, lessons, activities, or interactions with texts could benefit from some focus on visual literacy?

Since we are constantly bombarded by images in our daily lives, visual literacy is an apt literacy practice to consider, as well as one that many teachers try to cultivate or attend to in some way. However, many other literacies shape our ability to make and communicate meaning in the world. The next activity asks you to extend your thinking to another digital or electronic literacy that might impact your students' abilities to learn, make meaning, or communicate with others.

 Activity 16.7 Articulating the importance of key literacies

Using the visual literacy statement excerpted in Activity 16.5 as a model, define another digital or electronic literacy, and articulate its importance. Possibilities include design literacy, social media literacy, "remix" literacy, coding literacy, and aesthetic literacy. Fill in the following chart.

Literacy defined:
Why literacy is important:
A literate individual should be able to . . .

What role will course-management systems play in your teaching?

One of the most popular ways that technology has filtered into the classroom is via course-management systems like Blackboard and iLearn, which allow teachers to share information with their students. Course-management systems typically offer ways to house and share content (like assignments, readings, and other media), as well as opportunities for students to interact, via discussion boards, virtual class meetings, chat, and so on. Teachers often use the logistical features of a course-management system—e-mail, an online grade book, "news" updates—to keep in touch with students and communicate key information about the course.

As a teacher, you might have a wide array of course-management and support systems available to you. Beyond a central course-management system, you might also have access to any of the following: an online writing lab (e.g., the Purdue OWL), an e-portfolio system, a digital archive system, electronic resources through your school's library, and publishers' resources (e.g., Macmillan Education's LaunchPad).

Activity 16.8 Evaluating platforms and systems for your course

In the following chart, map the resources available to you through your institution or the Web.

Course-management systems or technologies:	Whom can you contact for support (name, e-mail, Web site, phone)?	Possible benefits or uses:	Possible limitations or challenges:

What role will blogs, wikis, and other new media play in your teaching?

Many teachers are excited by the reading and writing opportunities that new technologies offer. As our world becomes more globally connected and interconnected, we might ask our students to extend their writing beyond the classroom, writing for audiences besides the teacher and their classmates. However, when we think about how writing connects affinity groups (those who share common interests), communities, or populations, we usually do not imagine a student posting a four- or five-page essay or term paper on the Web. What other genres might exist to connect student writers with new audiences?

One set of genres might include those that ask students to write, post, and connect continually. Blogs are perhaps the most popular genre for teaching in this regard. (WordPress and Blogger are popular platform choices.) Teachers often turn to blogs because they are fairly easy for students to set up and because they encourage writing practices that many teachers value: ongoing, regular writing; maintaining and deepening inquiry into a topic; and writing with a particular audience in mind. Blogs are also a useful teaching tool since they rely on connective writing. Digital media theorist Will Richardson defines connective writing as writing that responds to, synthesizes, or remixes other ideas (other writing) in order to continue or extend a conversation. Connective writing is meant to be shared. It is not writing in a vacuum, but writing that engages and enters into dialogue with other reading and writing.

Wikis (like Wikipedia) have a related goal of sharing information, although they often seem to lack the "personal twist" or passion for a particular topic that is readily apparent in blogs. Nonetheless, wikis—online resources that amass, curate, and refine information and knowledge from multiple users—can also be a valuable teaching tool, particularly for ongoing writing projects. Teachers might also consider showing their students how to use online tools and platforms such as RSS feed readers, social media (like Facebook, LinkedIn, Tumblr, and Twitter), or photography-oriented social media (like Instagram). Thinking about what different types of media and technology can help your students explore and achieve will obviously guide your choices, as will talking to your students about their technological practices and interests.

 Activity 16.9   Assessing the "new" in new media

Complete the following chart to explore opportunities to use new media.

Type of media or technology:	What's "new" in this new media? What connections does it promote?	What opportunities might it provide for teaching or learning?
Blogs		
Wikis		
Other new media		

Our students today are sometimes called "digital natives": They have grown up surrounded by technology, often learning and using technology naturally as part of their everyday lives. But just because they know how to use technology—how to make it function—does not mean they know how to use it critically. For example, many students use Wikipedia regularly; it provides quick access to lots of information (and the overall quality of this information is improving). But many students do not view wikis critically, understand how they can be part of the knowledge-creation process, or know how to use wikis strategically to find and pursue additional sources. This is where we come in.

As writing teachers, many of us have rhetorical goals for our students: We want them to become more adept at recognizing and navigating rhetorical constraints and seizing rhetorical opportunities. We also have critical goals for our students: We want them to think critically, analyze deeply, and question the world around them. As we work to capitalize on the teaching and learning benefits that technologies offer, we can find ways in which our critical and rhetorical goals can come into play with technological experiences.

Activity 16.10   Mapping learning goals

The following chart provides a model of how to map a learning goal onto the use of technology. Fill in the chart to map out some of your own learning goals the same way.

Learning goal:	Use of technology to achieve the learning goal:	Critical and rhetorical components:	Desired result from heightened critical or rhetorical engagement:
Share reading strategies with the whole class to develop and capitalize on expertise.	Students make a class wiki of reading strategies they are developing; this activity builds community around reading and lets students share their expertise and learn additional strategies.	Critical: Students first have to research wikis (like Wikipedia) and figure out how they work: Who can add information? How is this information vetted, and how can it be traced in the wiki history? Rhetorical: Will the wiki be only for our class, or will other students find it useful? If we have a larger audience, how will that shape our writing choices?	Students gain a much deeper understanding of where "information" comes from by engaging in the process of making their own reliable wiki. Students consider how they can productively share their expertise, learning, and experience through a potentially global platform.

Turning to the field:
Turnitin and anti-plagiarism technology

Just as we might begin to ask students to view technology with a critical eye, so, too, we as teachers must view our own classroom practices with technology through a critical lens. We must ask important questions about how and why we are using technology in our classes, as well as to what degree our use of technology fits with our larger beliefs about students, writing, and learning.

One particular technology that often causes tension for teachers is anti-plagiarism technology, such as Turnitin. On the one hand, most writing teachers believe it is important for students to learn how to include other voices and texts in their writing and how to give due credit to others' ideas. Many teachers find plagiarism to be a real problem in classes, since students often struggle with knowing when and how to cite ideas and how to integrate their ideas and words with those of others. Turnitin and other anti-plagiarism technology thus promise a "fix" that many teachers find appealing. On the other hand, some teachers realize that the solution that Turnitin offers may not be enough to effectively teach students what they need to learn: the complexity of balancing their ideas and words with others' ideas and words. Some teachers may feel that the view of plagiarism offered by anti-plagiarism software upholds a particular cultural view, one that privileges individual intellectual property.

Recent research, such as that emerging from the Citation Project (citationproject.net), complicates how we think about student research practices and plagiarism. This research finds that students often plagiarize because they are engaging "too shallowly" with sources. Students also often rely on "patchwriting," in which they restate part of a piece of source text but do not paraphrase fully or quote correctly. Both practices often result in unintentional plagiarism.

Thus, having a rich understanding of plagiarism, its causes, and how we can help students avoid it is important for many teachers. In the next activity, you will read and reflect on the best-practices statement on plagiarism from the Council of Writing Program Administrators (WPA). Since the statement is a valuable resource, you may want to print it out and annotate it as you read.

 Activity 16.11 Responding to the WPA's plagiarism statement

Go to http://wpacouncil.org/files/wpa-plagiarism-statement.pdf, and read the WPA's statement on plagiarism. Then answer the following questions.

1. What points in the document resonate with your beliefs and practices?

2. What points in the document are new to you or do you have questions about?

3. How could you try out a key idea from this document in your teaching? Be specific.

With an enriched understanding of plagiarism in mind, now think about how anti-plagiarism technology could help you achieve particular objectives. Activity 16.12 asks you to explore the effects of Turnitin or other anti-plagiarism technology.

 Activity 16.12 Using anti-plagiarism technology for different goals

Complete the following chart.

Using anti-plagiarism technology mainly for surveillance or to correct student citation errors might look like this:	Using anti-plagiarism technology mainly as a teaching tool might look like this:

Like all the other decisions that you make as you plan your course, your decisions about technology should be in harmony with your teaching philosophy. Now that we have explored some dimensions of teaching writing in the digital age, we will revisit our four hypothetical teachers, each of whom focuses on a particular dimension of the writing situation.

Activity 16.13 Examining teachers' uses of technology

Circle any ideas that resonate with you, and mark with an asterisk any ideas that cause tension. Unpack at least one of the tensions in your teaching journal.

A text-focused teacher might say:	A context/culture-focused teacher might say:
I use technology in many ways. PowerPoint is great for presenting mini-lectures on essay structure, style issues, and grammar points. I also post the presentations and additional handouts online to help students with particular difficulties. Technology really helps me individualize my instruction; in fact, I have individualized grammar units online too, with self-tests, so that students can focus on their individual needs. I also teach students how to use spell-checker and grammar-checker — in intelligent ways — because you can't rely on them to be accurate. I also use technology for interactive things; when we're in a smart (technology-enabled) classroom, I can put paragraphs up on the screen, and students can work in pairs identifying things like topic sentences and supporting evidence.	I certainly use technology in my teaching. But I don't use it for "transmission teaching." In other words, I don't give PowerPoint lectures — the kind that students are used to from high school. Instead, I mostly use technology to look at technology itself. We do online discussions, and then we critically analyze the discourse moves we make; this helps us think critically about the identities we construct online. We keep blogs so that we can examine how power and identity function with our own "affinity communities," like gardening or sports enthusiasts. And of course, the online world offers infinite ways to examine culture, class, power, identity, and ideology. We analyze news Web sites from different political perspectives. We look at gendered online magazines. We compare online advertising targeted toward different ethnic communities. It's all rich stuff for critical analysis.

A writer-focused teacher might say:	A reader-focused teacher might say:
My students use lots of technology. They come into class fully "literate" in terms of using technology to express themselves. They text. They read and write on Facebook. Some of them blog, or at least read blogs. Many subscribe to e-lists. So they've already got a good foundation in digital literacy. So I just build on that foundation. I assign blogs; each student has a space online to be an "author" and develop confidence as a writer. We also do a lot of real-time freewriting in class, and I encourage students to compose wherever they're comfortable (on paper or on their laptops). We experiment with quick-writes, looping, listing, and brainstorming. It's great because we can write and share, write and share, write and share. It has a sense of immediacy. It also shows students that writing and thinking are processes and that students have the ability to generate and explore their own ideas. I also like to include an electronic portfolio in the class. It's pretty much like a normal portfolio, but it's online and it's public so it has a sense of audience. In the portfolio, I let students include additional creative projects — digital storytelling, self-designed wikis, or whatever genres they want to use to express their ideas.	Reading and writing are communicative acts. And the digital age broadens our possibilities of communication: new audiences, new ways of addressing audiences, new discourse communities with new rhetorical and linguistic conventions. I have students study discourse communities online. They do mini-ethnographies. And then they experiment with communicating within those communities. For example, they might start by following blogs about a social or political issue, and then they analyze the kinds of communication this community uses, the kinds of positions people "stake out" in their blogs, and they think about what counts as a "meaningful" blog post. Then I ask them to participate in that community by commenting online and writing their own blogs. As a class, we compare and contrast communicative strategies among these discourse communities. Students also do a unit in which they analyze professional electronic communication in their chosen discipline. Again, my goal is to help them see how communication works and how discourse "gets things done" in the real world.

YOUR TEACHING JOURNAL: Engaging with tensions

Choose the approach that you feel most uncomfortable with, and brainstorm about it in your teaching journal. Consider the following questions:

- How does this approach clash with your experience or philosophy about technology?
- How might this approach fit with other teaching contexts, classes, levels, or with certain student populations?
- Can you think of ways to bridge all four views of technology, particularly the approach you are most uncomfortable with?

It might be helpful to take a moment to note where you stand now in terms of using technology in your writing class.

 Activity 16.14 Exploring your ideas about technology

Answer the following questions.

1. What ideas or practices related to technology are you comfortable with or excited to try out? Why?

2. What ideas or practices do you have questions about or are you hesitant about? Why? Formulate any questions that you have.

Taking it further:
Students as media consumers; students as media creators

A central tension teachers need to engage is the use and consumption of technology in the classroom. As we discussed earlier, many teachers hope to help their students become more critical users of technology; they want students to use technology actively and mindfully and to be able to analyze technologies for both their benefits and their shortcomings (similar to the work you did in Activity 16.10). In this pursuit, we can see parallels to teachers who hope students will use writing to critically analyze texts (including media texts and advertisements) and to understand more deeply how texts work rhetorically.

The second tension inherent in technology consumption is whether we should encourage students to become more than consumers of technology — becoming, instead, active creators. Teachers committed to this perspective might begin by asking students to reflect on these two questions:

- Are you simply *using* a given technology?
- Or is that technology *also using you*, by molding and shaping your behavior, for example as consumers or citizens?

Activity 16.15 will help you test these ideas and consider to what extent each of these goals is important to you and necessary for your students.

 Activity 16.15   Considering new media activities, practices, and pedagogies

In the following chart, brainstorm activities or practices that position students as primarily consumers or primarily creators. Then consider what pedagogical supports would be necessary to foster creative production.

New media:	Students are consumers when . . .	Students are creators when . . .	Necessary context or pedagogy to foster creative production:
Community-oriented social media (e.g., Facebook)			
News- or interest-oriented social media (e.g., Twitter, Tumblr) or photography-oriented social media (e.g., Instagram)			
Search engines (e.g., Google, Siri, Yahoo)			

Web sites			
Blogs			
Wikis			

Reflections from experienced teachers

One of the tensions that can plague teachers is an all-or-nothing approach to technology. Between the gadget lover, who longs to have the latest software and hardware with all the bells and whistles, and the Luddite, who forswears any technology and despairs that no one reads books anymore, there is a fruitful middle ground where technology and digital media support learning and writing.

Many teachers worry that their students might know more than they do, or that they will have to become "experts" in things they know little about. If this describes you, do not worry. Your campus has resources to help acquaint you with available technologies and how to use them in the classroom; share your goals and concerns with your school's academic technology division. Remember also the resources that are close by: your colleagues, your students, and perhaps your family members. Think about which aspects of your classroom could productively use some of the advantages technology offers, and try to introduce one or two new approaches a semester. Be patient with yourself as you are learning. Ask students what they think: Did the technology help or hinder? As you experiment with different modes and different levels of technology to achieve different purposes, you will eventually find the practices that best support your teaching and your students' learning.

In the meantime, we offer these principles from experienced teachers:

- Teachers often have the most success in introducing new technology when they have a clear purpose for what they hope technology will help them (and their students) achieve. This means being wary of introducing the new for the sake of the new; instead, ask yourself, what can this technology contribute or achieve that is not happening already (or well enough) in my class?

- More and more teachers are tapping into the powerful ways that technology can bridge the writing that students do in class with the other types of writing they do in the world, perhaps closing the distance between the two somewhat. Closing this gap can help students recognize and deploy the writing knowledge or audience awareness that they cultivate every day in their lives.

- Many teachers find that using digital resources can enhance certain features of their classes that promote and sustain learning, including faster or real-time feedback, real-world applications, and wide distribution of ideas, including beyond the walls of the classroom.

- Teachers who are experienced in using technology in their classes often find that student knowledge about technology can cut both ways. It is often helpful to ask students about their experiences, and it is sometimes appropriate to ask for help using a particular application. But it is important not to assume that all students know everything about technology just because some have grown up in a digital world. Students need guidance in the critical literacy they bring to technology, and they need opportunities to practice not just consuming technological content but producing it as well.

Putting it together:
Articulating your approach to technology

Now that you have explored your course design and pedagogy through the lens of technology, we ask you to synthesize the thinking and writing you have done in this chapter. Look back at the activities you have completed, and think specifically about technologies that could benefit students as they write.

Activity 16.16   Experimenting with technology in your classroom

Imagine that an interview committee will ask you the following questions: What technologies have you incorporated into your classroom, and why? What technologies are you interested in experimenting with, and what might they contribute to your students' learning? In the space provided, brainstorm, map, or cluster notes that would help you answer these questions. Be sure to jot down the benefits and challenges that each technology might present.

> "In my composition grad seminar, I often ask my students to write weekly blogs about their learning. At first, some students hate it — fussing with the technology, sharing their ideas publicly, being accountable to the class. But by the end of the semester, I always have many converts who comment that blogging really helped them develop an academic voice, helped them dig more deeply into a topic or question, or helped them connect with a real audience. Many of those graduate students who initially resisted blogging now use blogging as a key part of their own pedagogy.
>
> —*Mark*

Now consider how to explain your rationale regarding how and why you employ technology in your class. Be sure to directly connect your reasons and examples to your larger views of writing, your course goals, and your teaching philosophy.

Activity 16.17   Articulating the philosophical rationale for your use of technology

In your teaching journal, discuss the following questions. Be sure to note any questions or issues that you are still wrestling with.

- Is technology integral to the teaching and learning in your writing classes? Why or why not?
- Describe a specific way you use technology in your class, as well as your rationale for this use. What effect does it have on learning?

In this chapter, you have explored ways that technology has affected the teaching of writing, adding complexity to the choices that you must make as teachers. You have also pondered the ways that you may want to incorporate technology into your own teaching, particularly through new types of activities and assignments. With this chapter, we conclude our discussion of teaching *practices*. In the next and final chapter, you will step back and take a "big picture" look at your future growth as a teacher and your role in the teaching profession.

Further Reading

Blogs
- Andrea Abernathy Lunsford: http://andrealunsford.com/blog
- Bits: Ideas for Teaching Composition (Bedford): http://macmillanhighered.com/bits
- Digital Digs: An Archeology of the Future (Alex Reid): http://www.alex-reid.net
- Lawrence Lessig (Creative Commons): http://www.lessig.org/topics/creative-commons
- Mike Rose: http://mikerosebooks.blogspot.com
- Stump the Teacher (Josh Stumpenhorst): http://stumpteacher.blogspot.com (K–12 teaching with a Twitter focus)

Online Journals and Research
- Citation Project: http://site.citationproject.net
- *Composition Forum*: http://www.compositionforum.com
- *Composition Studies*: http://www.compositionstudies.uwinnipeg.ca
- Comppile (online composition database/search engine): http://www.comppile.org
- *Computers and Composition*: http://www.bgsu.edu/departments/english/cconline
- *Enculturation* (special issue on computers and writing): http://www.enculturation.net/14
- TED Talk from Joyce Valenza (Changing Student Research Practices): https://www.youtube.com/watch?v=VmLwl7ybDFw&feature=player_embedded#t=0s.

CHAPTER 17

Choices about Your Future Growth in the Profession

You have done an incredible amount of work to arrive at this last chapter. You have articulated and revised your philosophy of good writing and good teaching; designed a full course of engaging writing, reading, and activities; and inspected your pedagogy through the vital lenses of diversity and technological change. In many ways, this chapter points you forward beyond the pages of the book, as it asks you to explore and plan how you can continue to grow as a teacher. Teaching, like writing, is a process of revision. Reflecting regularly on your practice and making connections with other writing teachers can help you stay engaged, find the resources you need, avoid burnout, and experience meaningful, rewarding professional growth as a teacher. It is our hope that you will return to this chapter—and others—whenever you need to refresh your practice, work through pressing problems, or set your goals for the next steps of your teaching career.

How will you stay engaged as a member of the profession?

It can be easy to get caught up in the day-to-day challenges of teaching multiple classes and responding to countless essays, thus losing sight of the big picture and your overall professional goals and commitments. One of the most important ways to stay engaged, energized, and committed to the work you do as a writing teacher is to pause to remember why you became a teacher to begin with.

 Activity 17.1   Thinking about your engagement with teaching

Answer the following questions.

---

1. Why did you begin teaching?

2. What excited or motivated you as a student?

3. What do you love about your students? What do you love about teaching writing?

4. How can your reflections above inform your classroom practice?

Having a clear sense of why your work is valuable and what excites you about this profession can sustain you through the challenging moments you will inevitably encounter as a teacher. You may find it helpful to return to the notes you jotted down in Activity 17.1 throughout your career.

Another route to staying engaged is to build flexibility into your classroom. Just as some elements of structured choice can encourage your students to stay engaged, student choice can also keep you, as a teacher, on your toes as you experience the new texts, projects, or materials that students bring into the classroom. Throughout this book, we encouraged you to build your course and your writing and reading assignments around genuine inquiry questions—intellectual questions that have no right or wrong answers and that model the academic exploration you expect of your students. Exploring such "live" questions in your class can help keep your teaching fresh and relevant, and it can balance out the more routinized teaching.

 Activity 17.2   Keeping your teaching fresh

Complete the following chart with three genuine inquiry questions you might explore with your students, as well as some possibilities for building flexibility and choice into your courses.

Genuine inquiry questions to discuss and explore with students:	Ways to offer flexibility and choice to keep things fresh for you and your students:

How will you be a reflective practitioner?

People often draw a sharp line between the learning they do in grad school and the teaching they do after grad school. But the reality is much more fluid. Learning and teaching are intertwined processes that continue throughout your entire career. Some teachers continue their education in formalized ways, such as by earning additional certificates, degrees, or professional qualifications, by attending regional conferences, or by joining a writing or grading group. But most of us continue to learn by reading about teaching, reflecting on our practice, and sharing ideas with colleagues, both in our own department and in professional association meetings such as the Conference on College Composition and Communication (CCCC). You might take advantage of all of these ways of learning at different times during your career, depending on your needs and interests.

A productive way to think about your evolving teaching is through the concept of reflective practice, a term coined by George Hillocks Jr. but used by many experienced and successful teachers (see Chapter 2). Reflective practice is just what it sounds like: reflecting on why you made the choices you have, observing the results of those choices, and revising your teaching and pedagogy in an ongoing, thoughtful manner. Cultivating your ability to reflect about what works, what does not, and other options available to you as a teacher is, of course, a key way of staying engaged and improving your teaching over time. You will want to act as a reflective practitioner in two major spheres of your teaching: your individual classrooms and your overall pedagogy or teaching career.

Continuing to revise course documents, materials, and activities

As you try out assignments, encounter different students and their writing, and finish teaching a given course for the first time, you will be making lots of revisions, both large and small. This is particularly the case when you prepare to teach a course again or in a different context. Approach this task, when you can, with a "let's try it and see" attitude. As you observe the results of your decisions, you can make short-term revisions—things you will change for the next class or the next unit—as well as make notes for longer-term revisions ("I need to remember to change X next time around!"). As you gain experience, you might need to attend to the following elements of your class:

- *The rationale for policies and the structure of the class.* As you see which policies best fit your teaching persona, your philosophy, and your students, you will want to make necessary adjustments. Remember that you should have—and explicitly provide—intellectual reasons for all course policies. This helps students see how the rules or boundaries are set up to assist their learning, which can improve their buy-in and help you create productive boundaries and flexibility when needed.

- *The timing between assignments.* As you gain experience, you will get faster, more efficient, and more focused about the kinds of feedback you want to give, and you will also learn what works for you in terms of balancing the paper load and timing your assignments.

Continuing to revise pedagogy

You will continue to revise your pedagogy as your career progresses. As you adapt to new courses, new students, new program requirements, and new situations, you will inevitably need to reflect on your pedagogy and revise it accordingly. The following pedagogical dimensions will likely be key areas to focus on as you grow as a teacher:

- *Bridges between levels of your teaching.* This is an element of your pedagogy that will grow over time. As you gain experience with students and with teaching writing, you will better be able to both anticipate issues and tailor your teaching to avoid them. One way to strengthen your practice is to work hard to develop connections between all levels of your teaching. Your feedback on student work should connect to and refer back to previous lessons, your class discussions might build on student writing with an eye toward the next assignment, and so on. Ideally, every element of your class should interact with every other element in a consistent, dialogic way.

- *Use of teaching time*. Everything you do precludes something else. Remember that every moment you spend on X in your class means one less moment spent on Y. Awareness of this trade-off can be a useful check on how you are spending your time, especially in terms of how much time you are giving students to write or discuss writing during class.

- *Real questions*. Discovery is just as important for you as a teacher as it is for your students. Continue working on balancing information-giving techniques with inductive, inquiry techniques to create a balanced teaching style. If you can enjoy what your students can teach you, you are more likely to enjoy the time you spend with them and the time you spend reading and responding to their work.

How will you represent your achievements as a professional?

One of the ways that you will likely be asked to represent yourself as a writing instructor—at some point in your career—is through a teaching portfolio. Teaching portfolios collect examples of your work as a teacher into a coherent "picture" of your pedagogy. Portfolios often contain some combination of the following:

- A statement of your teaching philosophy
- Your CV (curriculum vitae) or résumé, clearly listing the courses you have taught and other literacy-based instruction (e.g., tutoring)
- Sample syllabi for a range of courses you have taught, highlighting those you designed yourself
- Sample assignments that give a sense of what your classes focus on
- Examples of student writing with your feedback
- Evaluations of your teaching (from students and from colleagues who have observed your class)

Elements of a Successful Statement of Teaching Philosophy

- Use something concrete and specific to illustrate your philosophy and pedagogy writ large. A small anecdote or an exemplary assignment or action in your class will give readers a clear example that embodies your larger goals and commitments.

- In your description, foreground students at work, and describe how you facilitate and assist their learning. Make students the actors (and subjects) of your sentences.

- Consider using present tense to engage your audience.

- Be sure to define any "shorthand" language or descriptors.

- Limit references to other theorists; instead, focus on your methods and pedagogy.

- Try to avoid broad statements; stay specific.

- Remember that there are no magic bullets. Committing to a "student-centered classroom," a "student autonomy," or a particular kind of assignment does not magically make learning successful. Highlight the specific ways you will make something work for your students.

Your portfolio should begin with a statement of your teaching philosophy. In about a page (single-spaced), this document should highlight your strengths, use concrete examples to explain your approach, and paint a picture of a typical class (or a typical assignment). The most effective teaching philosophies typically show all of this by employing an example that represents your larger philosophy. Since your readers may be looking at a stack of teaching portfolios—especially if you are applying for a job—you will want to use specific, concrete examples so that readers can discern exactly who you are as a teacher (even if they just skim your statement).

Activity 17.3 Finding concrete examples to anchor your teaching philosophy

A small, illustrative detail that stands in for your larger beliefs will give readers something specific to remember about you. Use the following chart to brainstorm possible examples.

Illustrative assignments, strategies, or practices that exemplify your teaching:	Illustrative anecdotes, exchanges, or student comments that exemplify your teaching:

Once you have some options, choose the example you would like to develop in your teaching philosophy. This document will likely take several drafts and will benefit from having several readers. Once you have a solid draft of your document, find some colleagues who can give you feedback to guide your revision. You might ask them, "If you had to read fifty documents like this, what would you remember about me as a teacher?" Use their feedback to make sure you are conveying a clear, memorable representation of yourself that fits who you are as a teacher. As you write and revise, remember to look back and draw on the earlier chapters of this book where you identified your central values and beliefs about teaching writing.

Activity 17.4 Analyzing the working draft of your teaching philosophy

Once you have a solid working draft of your teaching philosophy, answer the following questions.

1. Who are you in this document? Where in the document do you see those representations of yourself?

2. Which words and phrases match your image of who you would like to be as a teacher? Which words or phrases present an image that does not match or that you might want to revise?

3. When people read your statement, what will they think you value as a teacher?

4. Have you shown how students learn X (argument, self-awareness, confidence, and so on) and how you structure or contribute to that learning?

5. Is the view you present in your teaching philosophy demonstrated consistently across all the other aspects of your teaching portfolio? Note any discrepancies that need to be revised or tweaked.

As you are assembling these documents, you will want to keep in mind the image of yourself that you want to portray. The teaching portfolio thus becomes both a representation of you as a teacher and a way to contextualize your pedagogy and approach. After perusing your collected materials, readers should have a clear sense of what you would bring to their faculty and their students.

Turning to the field:
Habits of mind for teachers

In this, our last "Turning to the Field" section, we ask you to return to the list of habits of mind that we introduced earlier and have been exploring throughout *Informed Choices* (refer particularly to Activities 2.6, 5.7, 7.7, 11.7, and 12.9). This time around, you will consider how the academic habits of mind that the *Framework for Success in Postsecondary Writing* presents as being vital to student success might also be integral to your success as a teacher.

Activity 17.5   Considering habits of mind

Brainstorm how each of the habits of mind listed in the following chart might influence your teaching. Also devise strategies you can use to develop these habits and sustain your teaching practice.

Habits of mind:	How will you work to cultivate these habits of mind in your teaching?
• **Curiosity** — the desire to know more about the world. • **Openness** — the willingness to consider new ways of being and thinking in the world. • **Engagement** — a sense of investment and involvement in learning. • **Creativity** — the ability to use novel approaches for generating, investigating, and representing ideas. • **Persistence** — the ability to sustain interest in and attention to short- and long-term projects. • **Responsibility** — the ability to take ownership of one's actions and understand the consequences of those actions for oneself and others. • **Flexibility** — the ability to adapt to situations, expectations, or demands. • **Metacognition** — the ability to reflect on one's own thinking as well as on the individual and cultural processes used to structure knowledge.	

Source: Council of Writing Program Administrators, "WPA Outcomes Statement for First-Year Composition." Copyright © 2014 by the Council of Writing Program Administrators. Reprinted by permission. http://wpacouncil.org/positions/outcomes.html.

Taking it further:
Teacher self-efficacy

Now that you have explored strategies for promoting your own positive habits of mind, we can get even more specific about what influences teacher self-efficacy. Although much of Susan McLeod's book *Notes on the Heart* explores student engagement, she also spends some time discussing teacher self-efficacy. Teachers with positive self-efficacy are confident, assured, and feel able to tackle challenges to promote their own success. But having a high sense of self-efficacy is not solely an individual choice; our self-efficacy is affected by the situations in which we find ourselves. To get a sense of how context may contribute to your self-efficacy, consider the environments and social factors that McLeod describes.

Microsystem: the teacher's immediate setting (classroom)	**Mesosystem:** relationships among the teacher's major settings (e.g., classroom, school, home)
• Students and their abilities • The teacher's level of expertise • The teacher's view of his or her role	• Climate of the department or school • Relationships with colleagues • Relationships with administrators • Home/work balance

Exosystem: forces and structures that influence the teacher's settings (e.g., mass media, legislation that impacts teaching) • Assessment/evaluation structures • Legislation or policies (e.g., No Child Left Behind, Common Core accreditation) • Budgets or budget cuts • Morale, including the public's view of and confidence in education	**Macrosystem:** cultural beliefs that impact teachers • Cultural beliefs about education • Cultural beliefs about "the learner," "the teacher," and "writing" • Cultural values (e.g., meritocracy, American dream)

Source: Susan McLeod, from *Notes on the Heart: Affective Issues in the Writing Classroom*. Copyright © 1996 by Southern Illinois University Press. Reprinted by permission.

Now consider the larger contexts that shape your views of yourself and your attitudes about how effective you can be in the classroom.

 Activity 17.6 Finding goals and strategies to maintain positive self-efficacy

In the following chart, note goals and strategies to help you maintain your self-efficacy at each of the levels that McLeod describes.

Microsystem:	**Mesosystem:**
Exosystem:	**Macrosystem:**

Reflections from experienced teachers

Perhaps the most important way to stay engaged and energized by your teaching and your students is to find and build relationships that you feel support you in your professional life. Whether this means making a regular date to meet with colleagues or following blogs about teaching and writing instruction that feel relevant, finding ways to stay connected can make the difference between feeling burnt out and feeling purposeful and excited by your teaching. Finding ways to learn about new ideas, share experiences, and stay up to date on research can help you feel connected to the larger profession and can infuse your pedagogy with new approaches and insights.

Consider the range of ways that experienced teachers "connect" to stay engaged:

- *Connecting with colleagues.* Whether you are a new or veteran teacher, one of your most valuable support systems is your colleagues—other teachers who may be experiencing similar challenges as you are. Reach out to the person in the office next to yours or the person who teaches in the classroom after you. The strongest teachers are most often those who take advantage of faculty development opportunities—informal brown-bag lunches, lectures, working groups, committees, or specialized training sessions—to stay current, meet other teachers, and continue to grow.

- *Connect with organizations or groups.* Your colleagues extend beyond your own hallway and institution. What local organizations might you consider joining? Is there a local consortium, conference, or network that could be a support system for you? You might consider signing up for an e-mail distribution list (such as the Writing Program Administrators' list or a list that represents local or similar institutions) to get a sense of what your colleagues are talking about. At the national level, consider joining the Conference on College Composition and Communication (CCCC), the National Council of Teachers of English (NCTE), the National Writing Project (NWP), or other major organizations that promote effective teaching and writing instruction. Also explore the rich library of resources and conversations available online. Where are people talking about the issues that most affect you as a teacher, and how can you join those conversations?

- *Connecting your students to future college work.* Having a sense of where your students go after your class—and what they will be asked to do—can help you stay connected to other courses in your writing program, as well as to the larger university community. As you settle into your teaching, explore current research on learning transfer and consider how you can help students connect the practices and strategies they learn in your class to other contexts (including both their other classes and their out-of-school lives). Thinking about transfer and making connections between your class and other classes can help you avoid viewing your course as isolated, and it will of course help your students see how relevant the practices from your course are (and how they might apply them in other spheres). It can also help you build bridges with colleagues and feel connected to the larger mission of your department or school.

- *Connecting with curricula.* After teaching for a while, many teachers want to get involved on a scale beyond their classroom. Pursue your own research, or partner with other teachers to build a new course or program. Look for opportunities to partner with your colleagues on curriculum design, Writing across the Curriculum/Writing in the Disciplines programs, or student learning initiatives to build connections between different levels of your writing program.

- *Connecting with research.* Whenever they can, experienced teachers seize opportunities to learn about current research and to recharge their practice. The easiest way to do this is of course to read the new literature in the field (available through electronic journals or databases via your university library). But you might also consider applying for a grant to attend a conference, or asking your institution for support or sponsorship. And you might contribute your own knowledge, as well, by submitting a proposal to a conference or to a journal you read and enjoy. Finding ways to challenge yourself and to continue learning will keep your teaching fresh and alive for years to come.

Putting it together: Articulating a professional development plan

You have now arrived at the final section of the final chapter. Throughout the book, you deeply explored your philosophies of teaching and writing, planned a course, and wrestled with the complex choices that teaching writing always demands. Earlier in this chapter, and as a result of Activity 17.3 and Activity 17.4, you penned a final working version of your teaching philosophy. Unlike earlier chapters, where we concluded by asking you to articulate your rationale for both yourself and possible outside audiences, we now ask you to complete two final activities primarily for yourself. We hope these activities will help you crystallize the significant work you have done and map out a plan to continue carrying this work, and your growth, forward.

 Activity 17.7   Crystallizing the work you have done

Use the following chart to map out tensions and questions that remain after working through Informed Choices, *as well as resources to help you find answers.*

Most pressing tensions or questions you want to answer:	Resources (people, places, texts) that might provide answers:
Tensions between your philosophy and your institution or department:	**Resources (people, places, texts) or strategies that might help you resolve or negotiate these tensions:**
Day-to-day challenges you anticipate facing:	**Resources or strategies that might help with these challenges:**
Longer-term challenges you anticipate facing:	**Resources or strategies that might help with these challenges:**

Activity 17.8 Creating a professional development plan

Use the following chart to map your goals and to create a professional development plan to help you continue to grow as a teacher.

	Goals:	Ways to achieve those goals:
Goals to complete before the semester begins:		
Goals and strategies to pursue during the semester to stay engaged:		
Goals and strategies for after the semester to reflect and recharge:		
Goals and strategies to connect over the next year:		
Goals and strategies to connect over the next three to five years:		

With the plan you have now crafted, the vast collection of notes in your teaching journal, and the extensive materials you designed for your writing course, you are now ready to take a leap into teaching, whether it is for the first time, for a new course, or with renewed energy and focus about your goals and beliefs. As you move forward, we hope this book has given you the space to reflect, the encouragement to experiment and change, and the confidence in your capabilities both to make informed choices and to question and revise your choices when needed. When new teaching challenges arise—as they always do!—we hope you will return to this book as a history of your committed thinking and planning, as a compendium of best practices and new ideas, and as a methodological resource that helps you use writing to think through your pedagogy. As the National Writing Project maintains, "The best writing teachers are those who write." We hope this book has given you an opportunity to do just that.

Further Reading

Print Resources

- Gee, Michael A. "On Keeping an Academic Journal." *Teaching English in the Two-Year College* 32.1 (2004): 26–29. Print.

- Hillocks, George, Jr. *Teaching Writing as Reflective Practice*. New York: Teachers College P, 1995.

- Schön, Donald A. *The Reflective Practitioner: How Professionals Think in Action*. New York: Basic, 1983.

Web Resources

- Council of Writing Program Administrators: http://wpacouncil.org (sign up to be part of the group's listserv)

- National Council of Teachers of English: http://www.ncte.org (includes links to the Conference on College Composition and Communication)

- National Writing Project: http://www.nwp.org

Suggested Reading

Anthologies

Cushman, Ellen, et al., eds. *Literacy: A Critical Sourcebook*. Boston: Bedford/ St. Martin's, 2001.

Miller, Susan, ed. *The Norton Book of Composition Studies*. New York: Norton, 2009.

Villanueva, Victor, and Kristin L. Arola, eds. *Cross-Talk in Comp Theory: A Reader*. 3rd ed. Urbana: NCTE, 2011.

Histories of Composition

Berlin, James. *Rhetoric and Reality: Writing Instruction in American Colleges, 1900–1985*. Carbondale: Southern Illinois UP, 1987.

Connors, Robert J. *Composition-Rhetoric: Backgrounds, Theory, and Pedagogy*. Pittsburgh: U of Pittsburgh P, 1997.

Teaching Guidebooks

Barkley, Elizabeth F., et al. *Collaborative Learning Techniques: A Handbook for College Faculty*. Hoboken: Wiley, 2004.

Dethier, Brock. *First Time Up: An Insider's Guide for New Composition Teachers*. Logan: Utah State UP, 2005.

Glenn, Cheryl, and Melissa A. Goldthwaite. *The St. Martin's Guide to Teaching Writing*. New York: Bedford/St. Martin's, 2007.

Goldschmidt, Myra M., and Deb Ousey. *Teaching Developmental Immigrant Students in Undergraduate Programs: A Practical Guide*. Ann Arbor: U of Michigan P, 2011.

Jago, Carol. *Papers, Papers, Papers: An English Teacher's Survival Guide*. Portsmouth: Heinemann, 2005.

Lindemann, Erika, and Daniel Anderson. *A Rhetoric for Writing Teachers*. Oxford: Oxford UP, 2001.

McGlynn, Angela Provitera. *Successful Beginnings for College Teaching*. Madison: Atwood, 2001.

Newkirk, Thomas. *Nuts and Bolts: A Practical Guide to Teaching College Composition*. Portsmouth: Heinemann, 1993.

Tate, Gary, Amy Rupiper, and Kurt Schick. *A Guide to Composition Pedagogies*. Oxford: Oxford UP, 2001.

White, Edward M., and Cassie Wright. *Assigning, Responding, Evaluating: A Writing Teacher's Guide*. 5th ed. Boston: Bedford/St. Martin's, 2016.

Composition Theory and Practice

Bartholomae, David. *Writing on the Margins*. Boston: Bedford/St. Martin's, 2005.

Bartholomae, David, and Anthony Petrosky. *Facts, Artifacts, and Counterfacts*. Portsmouth: Heinemann, 1986.

---. *Ways of Reading*. 9th ed. Boston: Bedford/St. Martin's, 2010.

Bawarshi, Anis S., and Mary Jo Reiff. *Genre: An Introduction to History, Theory, Research, and Pedagogy*. Anderson: Parlor, 2010.

Bean, John C. *Engaging Ideas*. San Francisco: Jossey-Bass, 2011.

Bean, John C., et al. *Reading Rhetorically*. 3rd ed. New York: Longman, 2010.

Clark, Irene L. *Concepts in Composition: Theory and Practice in the Teaching of Writing*. New York: Routledge, 2011.

Coles, Bill. *The Plural I*. Portsmouth: Heinemann, 1988.

Corbett, Edward, and Robert Connors. *Classical Rhetoric for the Modern Student*. Oxford: Oxford UP, 1998.

Dobrin, Sidney I. *Constructing Knowledges: The Politics of Theory-Building and Pedagogy in Composition*. Albany: State U of New York P, 1997.

Elbow, Peter. *Writing without Teachers*. 25th anniversary ed. Oxford: Oxford UP, 1998.

Ferris, Dana. *Response to Student Writing: Implications for Second Language Students*. New York: Routledge, 2003.

---. *Teaching College Writing to Diverse Student Populations*. Ann Arbor: U of Michigan P, 2009.

Fitts, Karen. *Left Margins: Cultural Studies and Composition Pedagogy*. Albany: State U of New York P, 1995.

Goldberg, Naomi. *Writing Down the Bones*. Boston: Shambhala, 2010.

Graff, Gerald, and Cathy Birkenstein. *They Say, I Say*. New York: Norton, 2009.

Groden, Suzy, Eleanor Kutz, and Vivian Zamel. *The Discovery of Competence: Teaching and Learning with Diverse Student Writers*. Portsmouth: Heinemann, 1993.

Hardin, Joe Marshall. *Opening Spaces: Critical Pedagogy and Resistance Theory in Composition*. Albany: State U of New York P, 2001.

Haswell, Richard H., and Min-Zhan Lu. *Comp Tales: An Introduction to College Composition through Its Stories*. New York: Longman, 1999.

Huot, Brian. *(Re-)Articulating Writing Assessment*. Logan: Utah State UP, 2002.

Huot, Brian, and Peggy O'Neil, eds. *Assessing Writing: A Critical Sourcebook*. Boston: Bedford/St. Martin's, 2008.

Kameen, Paul. *Writing/Teaching*. Pittsburgh: U of Pittsburgh P, 2000.

Lamott, Anne. *Bird by Bird*. Norwell: Anchor, 1995.

McLeod, Susan. *Notes on the Heart*. Carbondale: Southern Illinois UP, 1997.

Nagin, Carl, and the National Writing Project. *Because Writing Matters: Improving Student Writing in Our Schools*. San Francisco: Jossey-Bass, 2003.

Nowacek, Rebecca. *Agents of Integration: Understanding Transfer as a Rhetorical Act*. Carbondale: Southern Illinois UP, 2011.

Ritter, Kelly, and Paul Kei Matsuda. *Exploring Composition Studies: Sites, Issues, Perspectives*. Logan: Utah State UP, 2012.

Roberge, Mark, Meryl Siegal, and Linda Harklau. *Generation 1.5 in College Composition: Teaching Academic Writing to U.S.-Educated Learners of ESL*. New York: Routledge, 2009.

Schön, Donald A. *The Reflective Practitioner: How Professionals Think in Action*. New York: Basic, 1983.

Selber, Stuart. *Multiliteracies for a Digital Age*. Carbondale: Southern Illinois UP, 2004.

Selfe, Cynthia. *Multimodal Composition: Resources for Teachers*. New York: Hampton, 2007.

Sidler, Michelle, et al., eds. *Computers in the Composition Classroom*. Boston: Bedford/St. Martin's, 2007.

Soliday, Mary. *Everyday Genres: Writing Assignments across the Disciplines*. Carbondale: Southern Illinois UP, 2011.

Sommers, Nancy. *Responding to Student Writers*. Boston: Bedford/St. Martin's, 2012.

Straub, Richard, ed. *A Sourcebook for Responding to Student Writing*. New York: Hampton, 1999.

Sullivan, Patrick, and Howard Tinberg. *What Is "College-Level" Writing?* Urbana: NCTE, 2006.

Sullivan, Patrick, Howard Tinberg, and Sheridan Blau. *What Is "College-Level" Writing?* Vol. 2: *Assignments, Readings, and Student Writing Samples*. Urbana: NCTE, 2010.

Wiggins, Grant P., and Jay McTighe. *Understanding by Design*. 2nd ed. Boston: Pearson, 2005.

Wysocki, Anne Frances, et al. *Writing New Media: Theory and Applications for Expanding the Teaching of Composition*. Logan: Utah State UP, 2004.

For more critical sourcebooks, teaching guides, background readings, and bibliographies from Bedford/St. Martin's, visit macmillanhighered.com /teachingcentral.

For a more exhaustive and annotated list of resources in rhetoric and composition, consult *The Bedford Bibliography for Teachers of Writing*, 7th ed. (Boston: Bedford/St. Martin's, 2012), or visit macmillanhighered.com/bb.

Index

day-to-day planning (*continued*)
  explaining goals and activities and, 128–29
  newer teachers' use of detailed plans for, 127, 129
  outlining an individual class period in, 127
  patterns of class-period elements in, 127
  planning for multimodal learning in, 131
  planning for multiple class formats in, 132–34
  practicing board work for a lesson in, 128–29
  reflections from experienced teachers on, 135
  scripting rationale for activities in, 129–30
  structuring individual class periods using, 125–27
  teacher's planning style and, 126, 136
  visual reference of daily activities and homework in, 128
  zooming in and out in, 106
demand verbs
  clear statement of writing task using, 75, 81
  troubleshooting, 83
departments
  complexities of course design and, 105, 106
  course goal requirements of, 55, 56–57, 59, 66
  exploring possible course designs incorporating requirements of, 109
  genres in writing assignments and, 70, 72
  textbooks mandated by, 138, 146–47
designing courses. *See* course design
development plan for teachers, 272–73
dialogue
  brainstorming dialogic connections for an assignment, 159–60
  examples of, 159
  writing opportunities for, 158–59
digital age. *See* technology
digital natives, 255
discussions. *See* class discussions
distance learning, 131
diverse student population, 223–45
  adapting universal design strategies for courses for, 230–31
  anticipating students' experiences, characteristics, and needs in, 227
  articulating philosophical rationale for an approach to, 244
  balancing conflicting views about serving, 228–29
  beginning-of-semester surveys for, 231–33
  brainstorming ways to tweak course design for, 235
  characteristics of, 223–25
  choices about teaching, 223–45
  choosing readings for, 235–36
  diversity terminology and, 240–41
  examining the pros and cons of specific terminology used with, 241–42
  experimenting with approaches to error in writing of, 239–40
  finding students in, 225–26
  going deeper with readings for, 236
  how to serve, 228–29
  in-class community-building activities with, 233–34
  integrating personal writing into courses for, 234
  inviting survey questions for, 232
  language issues with essays from, 237–38
  learning styles of, 225
  linguistic backgrounds of, 224
  one-on-one conferences with, 232
  range of students in, 224
  reflections from experienced teachers on, 242–43

  special accommodation for, 228
  thinking about sources of error or problems in, 238–39
  tweaking writing tasks for, 236–37
  universal design and, 228
  writing activities incorporating personal experiences of, 234–35
diversity-based writing groups, 170
"Diving In: An Introduction to Basic Writing" (Shaughnessy), 45
Diving In stage of teacher development, 45, 47
Downs, Douglas, 15
drafting process, feedback during, 187
drafts
  of professional development plan, 273
  of teaching philosophy, 268

editing, and grammar feedback, 195
effective teaching. *See* good teaching
Elbow, Peter, 7
electronic literacies
  articulating importance of, 252
  teachers' experiences with, 249–50
electronic literacy narratives, 249
emotion. *See* affective dimensions of teaching
"endnote mush," in feedback, 187–88
engagement, practicing in teaching, 26
environment. *See* learning environment
ethnic diversity. *See* diverse student population
ethnographic projects, as writing assignments, 76
ethnolinguistic minority students, 5–6
evaluation, self-assessment for, 158
exit tests, rubrics for, 207
expectations of students, about assessment, 217
expectations of teachers
  about grammatical proficiency in diverse student population, 239
  writing assignments and, 74, 83
experience of students
  in diverse student population, 227
  as media users and media creators, 259–60, 261
experience of teachers as students
  with assessment, 199–200
  describing effectiveness in teaching based on, 20–21
  with electronic literacies, 249–50
  with reading, 90–91
  reflecting on teachers based on, 31–32
experimentation in writing, 166
expert role of teachers, 33, 35
expressivism, 5, 6, 8

face-to-face responses, online responses compared with, 178
facilitator role of teachers, 33, 35
feedback, 183–98
  anchoring in a teaching philosophy, 198
  articulating an approach to, 197–98
  assessing quality of, 215
  assessment using, 201
  avoiding burnout in, 193
  balancing paper load in, 193
  choices about, 183–98
  creating a definition of, 186
  creating a plan for, 186
  earlier stages of drafting process and, 187
  "endnote mush" in, 187–88

evaluating students at different proficiency levels during, 195
examining notions of, 185
examining terminology of, 184
on grammar, 194–96
knowledge of conventions and, 190–91
navigating conflicting grammar demands in, 196
reflecting on feedback received, 183–84
reflections from experienced teachers on, 196–97
self-assessment and, 197
students' applying and capitalizing on, 197
T-chart approach to, 188
teaching philosophy reflecting strategies for, 185–86
timing of peer review with, 180–81, 196
when and how to give, 186–87
feminism, 6
first-year composition courses
average length of writing assignments in, 78
course goals and, 67
number of writing assignments per semester in, 78
flexible writing processes, 162, 163–64
formative assessment
description of, 118
generating for a unit, 203
summative assessments differentiated from, 202
testing separated from, 200
foundation for teaching
authority as a, 42–49
philosophy of teaching and, 20–30
philosophy of writing and, 3–19
teaching persona and, 31–41
Framework for Success in Postsecondary Writing
    (Council of Writing Program Administrators,
    National Council of Teachers of English, and the
    National Writing Project)
composing in electronic environments learning
    objective from, 106–7
course goals and, 59, 61
critical thinking excerpt from, 94
developing flexible writing processes and, 163–64
diverse student population and, 224
habits of mind of. *See* habits of mind
knowledge of conventions and, 190, 191
metacognition in, 162, 163
technology use and, 250
working with, in writing assignments, 70–71
freewriting, 117, 130, 153, 187
Fulkerson, Richard, 4, 20
functional computer literacy, 247

gatekeeper role of teachers, 34
general education writing requirement, 57–58
general rubrics, 205, 206, 208
Generation 1.5 students, 224, 241
genres
determining types, 69–70
expectations of readers for, 72
matching purpose and, 71–72
using topical readings and model readings with, 93
written textual conventions in, 5
goals
class, 128–29
course. *See* course goals
of teachers, 270, 273
goal setting by students, using writing opportunities,
    158, 166

good teaching
course goals and beliefs about, 67
drawing on experience as a student to describe,
    20–21
examining conflicting ideas about, 23–24
examining notions of, 22–23, 27
firming up a definition of, 29–30
homing in on definition of, 21–22
ideas about learned from great teachers, 20
planning practice and, 106
popular conceptions about, 27–28
reflections from experienced teachers on, 28
good writing
brainstorming to begin defining, 8
course goals and beliefs about, 67
creating an evolving definition of, 10
examining diverse views of, 8–9
examining seemingly contradictory notions about,
    9–10
how to create. *See* writing process
key terms and phrases describing, 17
reflections from experienced teachers on, 16–17
grading, 200. *See also* assessment; rubrics
grammar, 194–96
diverse student population and errors in, 239–40
embedding feedback on into larger framework of
    editing, 195
evaluating students at different proficiency levels
    in, 195
explaining views on, 197
general principles feedback on, 194–95
navigating conflicting demands in, 196
group work
accountability and responsibility in, 180
articulating response to, 181–82
best practices for, 176–77
reflections from experienced teachers on, 180
See also collaboration; peer review; writing groups
Guarding the Tower stage of teacher development,
    45, 46

habits of mind, *Framework for Success in Postsecondary
    Writing*, 26
affective component of teaching, 39
developing through reading multimodal texts, 97
diverse student population and, 224
examining, 60, 61
metacognition as, 162, 163
practicing in teaching, 26
practicing through writing assignments, 78
for teachers, 258–59
handbooks, textbooks as, 138, 148
"Helping Peer Writing Groups Succeed" (Bishop),
    176–77
heuristics
creating personalized, 80–81
Lindemann's heuristic for the writer of writing
    assignments, 79–80
Hewett, Beth, 178
Hillocks, George, Jr., 25, 264–65
holistic rubrics, 207, 208
homework
diverse student population and, 228–29
visual reference of daily activities and, 128
Hull, Glynda, 96
Huot, Brian, 211

identifying key intellectual issues to be explored in, 91

putting in conversation with one another, 100–101

sources for finding, 98–99

strategies for selecting, 91, 97–99, 102–3

textbooks with wide range of, 140

timeframe within course for selecting, 97

using to teach writing, 101–2

reflections from experienced teachers

on assessment, 217

on authority, 47–48

on big-picture planning, 122–23

on course goals, 65–66

on day-to-day planning, 135

on diverse student population, 242–43

on feedback, 196–97

on good teaching and philosophy of teaching, 28

on good writing and philosophy of writing, 16–17

on opportunities for writing and writing instruction, 166

on peer review, 179–81

on professional growth, 270–72

on reading assignments, 102–3

on teaching persona, 39–40

on technology, 260–61

on textbooks, 147–48

on writing assignments, 87

reflective practice, 25–26, 264–65

reflective writing, 156–58, 166

relationships with students, and authority as a teacher, 44–45

required courses, and writing course goals, 58

research

Framework for Success excerpt on critical thinking through writing, reading, and, 94

professional growth using, 271–72

researched problem/solution essay, as writing assignments, 76

responsibility, in revision, 192

revision, 188–92, 197

anchoring in teaching philosophy, 198

encouraging persistence and responsibility in, 192

encouraging students to practice significant revision, 190

integrating teaching philosophy with, 188

knowledge of conventions in, 189–92

writing classes using, 188

"Revision Strategies of Student Writers and Experienced Adult Writers" (Sommers), 189

rhetorical knowledge

Framework for Success on, 70–71

gaining through reading, 96

matching genre and purpose with, 71–72

rhetorics, textbooks as, 138

Richardson, Will, 254

roles of teachers

affective responses to students and, 38

authority as a teacher and, 42, 44, 48–49

course goals and, 54, 61

examining difficult teaching situations and, 36

examining those chosen by, 32–34

examining those imposed on, 34–35

reflections from experienced teachers on, 39

See also teaching persona

rubrics, 204–11

assessing teaching using, 214–15

benefits for students of, 205

benefits for teachers of, 204

designing, for each assignment, 208

designing, for passing papers and non-passing papers, 205, 206, 207–8

exploring a philosophy on, 210–11

general versus assignment-specific, 205

holistic versus analytic, 207

new teachers' adoption of, 211

overuse of, 210

researching assessment using, 201

thinking outside traditional, 215–16

weighting traits in, 209–10

when to work without, 216

rules, in teaching approaches, 4–5

scaffolding, 230, 235, 242

Schön, Donald, 25

scripting rationale for activities, 129–30, 135

Selber, Stuart, 247

self-assessment

feedback and, 197

writing opportunities for, 158

Selfe, Richard and Cynthia, 96

self-efficacy

of students, 5

of teachers, 37, 40, 45, 269–70

sequence of writing assignments

building bridges between and across writing assignments and, 85

explaining, 87–88

logical order in, 84–85

mapping (fitting major assignments together) and, 78–79

using "backward design" for, 85–86

Shaughnessy, Mina, 45–46

short essays, as writing assignments, 76

social diversity. *See* diverse student population

social media, 254

sociocultural theory, 6, 7

Sommers, Nancy, 189

Sounding the Depths stage of teacher development, 45, 47

speaking, planning for multimodal learning using, 131

special accommodation, 228, 231

standards, in teaching approaches, 5

Standard Written English, 5

statement of teaching philosophy, 266

strategizing, writing opportunities for, 158

student-centered classroom, 169. *See also* collaboration; peer review

student conferences, feedback on peer review in, 180

student-created writing groups, 171

student learning outcomes (SLOs)

course goals compared with, 62

course goals and learning objectives related to, 63

reflections from experienced teachers on, 65

translating course goals into learning objectives and, 63–64

student population

course goals and, 66–67

diversity in. *See* diverse student population

genres in writing assignments and, 72

matching writing assignments with, 72–73

textbook fit with, 144, 149